Music, Words
and Voice

A Reader

Music, Words and Voice

A Reader

Edited by
MARTIN CLAYTON

Manchester University Press
Manchester and New York

distributed exclusively in the USA by Palgrave

Published in association with

The Open
University

Published by Manchester University Press
Oxford Road, Manchester M13 9NR, UK
and Room 400, 175 Fifth Avenue, New York, NY 10010, USA
www.manchesteruniversitypress.co.uk

in association with The Open University

First published 2008

Distributed exclusively in the USA by
Palgrave, 175 Fifth Avenue, New York, NY 10010, USA

Distributed exclusively in Canada by
UBC Press, University of British Columbia, 2029 West Mall, Vancouver, BC,
Canada V6T 1Z2

British Library Cataloguing-in-Publication Data
A catalogue record for this book is available from the British Library

Library of Congress Cataloging-in-Publication Data applied for

Typeset by SNP Best-set Typesetter Ltd., Hong Kong
Printed and bound in the United Kingdom by Antony Rowe Ltd, Chippenham, Wiltshire

This book forms part of an Open University course AA317 *Words and Music*. Details of this and
other Open University courses can be obtained from the Student Registration and Enquiry Service,
The Open University, PO Box 197, Milton Keynes, MK7 6BJ, United Kingdom:
tel. +44 (0)845 300 60 90, email general-enquiries@open.ac.uk
http://www.open.ac.uk

ISBN 978 0 7190 7787 6 hardback

ISBN 978 0 7190 7788 3 paperback

17 16 15 14 13 12 11 10 09 08   10 9 8 7 6 5 4 3 2 1

Contents

List of figures

Acknowledgements

The editor and publisher would like to thank the following for permission to publish the enclosed extracts:

Jean-Jaques Rousseau, from *Essay on the Origin of Languages and Writings Related to Music* (translated and edited by John T. Scott) © 1998 by the Trustees of Dartmouth College. Reprinted by permission of University Press of New England, Hanover, NH. Charles S. Myers, from 'The beginnings of music', in *A Psychologist's Point of View*, Heinemann, 1933. Reprinted by permission of Elsevier. George List, from 'The boundaries of speech and song', *Ethnomusicology* 7/1 © 1963 Society for Ethnomusicology. Reprinted by permission of the Society for Ethnomusicology. Jacques Derrida, from *Of Grammatology* (corrected edition, translated by Gayatri Chakravorty Spivak) © 1998 The Johns Hopkins University Press. Reprinted by permission of The Johns Hopkins University Press. David Hughes, from 'No nonsense: the logic and power of acoustic-iconic mnemonic systems', *British Journal of Ethnomusicology* 9/2 © British Journal of Ethnomusicology 2000. Reprinted by permission of the author and the British Journal of Ethnomusicology. George Herzog, from 'Drum-signaling in a West African tribe', in Thomas A. Seboek and Donna Jean Umiker-Seboek (eds), *Speech Surrogates: Drum and Whistle Signals* © 1976, Mouton & Co., B. V., Publishers, The Hague. Reprinted by permission of Mouton de Gruyter, a division of Walter de Gruyter GmbH & Co. Simon Frith, from 'The voice', in *Performing Rites* (Oxford University Press, 1996) © Simon Frith 1996. Reprinted by permission of Oxford University Press. S. Feld, A. A. Fox, T. Porcello and D. Samuels, from 'Vocal anthropology', in Alessandro Duranti (ed.), *A Companion to Linguistic Anthropology* © 2004 Blackwell Publishing Ltd. Reprinted by permission of Blackwell Publishing. Roland Barthes, from 'Music, voice, language', in *The Responsibility of Forms: Critical Essays on Music* (translated by Richard Howard). Translation © 1985 by Farrar, Straus & Giroux, Inc. Reprinted for outside of the UK by permission of Hill and Wang, a division of Farrar, Straus & Giroux, LLC. Reprinted for the UK by permission of Blackwell Publishing. Tim Riley, from *Tell Me Why: A Beatles Commentary* (The Bodley Head, 1998) © Tim Riley 1988. Reprinted by kind permission of the author. Virginia Danielson, from *The Voice of Egypt: Umm Kulthūm, Arabic Song, and Egyptian Society in the Twentieth Century* © 1997 by The University of Chicago. Reprinted by permission of The University of Chicago Press and the author. Sheila Dhar, from *'Here's Someone I'd Like You to Meet': Tales of Innocents, Musicians and Bureaucrats* (Oxford University Press) © Sheila Dhar 1995. Reproduced by the kind permission of Professor P. N. Dhar. Peter Manuel, from *Thumri in Historical and Stylistic Perpectives* © Motilal Banarsidass 1989. Reprinted by permission of Motilal Banarsidass Publishers (P) Ltd. Victor Zuckerlandl, from 'The meaning of song', in *Sound and Symbol: Volume*

2 © 1973 Princeton University Press, 2001 renewed PUP. Reprinted by permission of Princeton University Press. Hiromi Lorraine Sakata, from 'Hazara women in Afghanistan: innovators and preservers of a musical tradition', in Ellen Koskoff (ed.), *Women and Music in Cross-Cultural Perspective* © 1987 by Ellen Koskoff. Reproduced by permission of Greenwood Publishing Group, Inc., Westport, CT. Susan McClary, from *Georges Bizet, Carmen* © Cambridge University Press 1992, reproduced by permission of Cambridge University Press and the author. Richard Middleton, from *Voicing the Popular: On the Subjects of Popular Music* (Routledge, 2006) © 2006 by Richard Middleton. Reproduced with permission of the author via Copyright Clearance Center. Christopher Alan Waterman, from *Jùjú: A Social History and Ethnography of an African Popular Music* (The University of Chicago Press, 1990) © 1990 by The University of Chicago. Reprinted by the permission of the publisher and author. Robert Walser, from 'Rhythm, rhyme and rhetoric in the music of Public Enemy', *Ethnomusicology* 39/2 © 1995 by the Board of Trustees of the University of Illinois. Reprinted by permission of the Society for Ethnomusicology. J. Bolwell and K. Kaa, from 'Maori dance: an indigenous view', in *Garland Encyclopedia of World Music, Volume 9* © 1998 Adrienne L. Kaeppler and J. W. Love. All rights reserved. Reproduced by permission of Routledge, a division of Taylor & Francis Group. K. Palmer and R. W. Patten, from 'Some notes on wassailing and ashen faggots in south and west Somerset', *Folklore* 82/4 (Winter 1971). Reprinted by permission of The Folklore Society. Frank Howes, from *The English Musical Renaissance* (Secker and Warburg, 1966). Reprinted by permission of David Higham Associates Ltd. Marina Roseman, from *Healing Sounds From the Malaysian Rainforest: Temiar Music and Medicine* (The University of California Press, 1991) © 1991 by The Regents of the University of California. Reprinted by permission of The Regents of the University of California via Copyright Clearance Center. Elizabeth Tolbert, from 'Women cry with words: symbolization of affect in the Karelian lament', in *Yearbook of Traditional Music* 22 (1990). Reproduced with the permission of the International Council for Traditional Music. Richard Taruskin, from *Stravinsky and the Russian traditions: A Biography of the Works Through Mavra*, two-volume set (The University of California Press, 1996). Reprinted by permission of the author and the publisher via Copyright Clearance Center. Pieter C. Van den Toorn, from 'Stravinsky, Les noces (Svadebka), and the prohibition against expressive timing', in *The Journal of Musicology* 20/2 (2003). Reproduced by permission of The University of California Press and the author via Copyright Clearance Center. Edward T. Cone, from *The Composer's Voice* © 1974 by The regents of the University of California. Reprinted by permission of The University of California Press and George Pitcher via Copyright Clearance Center. Carolyn Abbate, from *Unsung Voices: Opera Music and Narrative in the Nineteenth Century* © 1991 by Princeton University Press, 1996 paperback edition. Reprinted by permission of Princeton University Press. Stephen Sondheim interviewed by Trevor Herbert, from 'Sondheim's technique', *Contemporary Music Review* 5 (1989) © Stephen Sondheim and The Open University in Wales. Reprinted by permission of Stephen Sondheim and The Open University. Music and lyrics for 'Send in the clowns' (from *A Little Night Music*) by Stephen Sondheim © 1973 (renewed) Rilting Music, Inc. All rights administered by WB Music Corp. All rights reserved. Used by permission

of Alfred Publishing Co., Inc. Amit Chaudhuri, from *Afternoon Raag* © Amit Chaudhuri 1993, reprinted by permission of Macmillan Publishers Ltd. and of the author care of Rogers, Coleridge and White, 20 Powis Mews, London W11 1JN. First published by William Heinemann 1993. Marcel Proust, from *Swann's Way*, translated by C. K. Scott-Moncrieff, in *Remembrance of Things Past: Volume 1* by Marcel Proust, translated by C. K. Scott-Moncrieff and Terence Kilmartin, published by Chatto & Windus © 1981 by Random House Inc. and Chatto & Windus. Reprinted by permission of The Random House Group Ltd. Reprinted for the USA by permission of Random House, Inc.

Every effort has been made to obtain permission to reproduce copyright material in this book. If any proper acknowledgement has not been made, copyright holders are invited to contact the publisher.

1

Introduction

Martin Clayton

'There is no science which exhausts the voice', claimed the ever-quotable French philosopher Roland Barthes: no matter how intensely, and from how many perspectives we study the human voice and its relation to music, there always seems to be more to say. While we cannot claim to have covered every possible angle in this collection, we have tried to put together a varied and stimulating collection of texts, all of which shed light on a common list of topics and key questions.

This book was developed as a set text for the Open University course AA317, Words and Music. The focus of both the OU course and this book is on why people sing, the differences between verbal and musical meaning and the ways in which the two combine and relate to one another. Its organisation differs slightly from that of the *Words and Music* course itself, with the thirty-six items being organised for convenience into five parts. We start in Part I with basic questions about the differences between speech and song, moving on in Part II to consider the relationship between text and voice in song. Part III is concerned with singing (and other vocal forms) as performances taking place in, and influencing, specific social situations, while Part IV looks at instances of song in the context of ritual performance, as well as the adaptation or representation of ritual in staged musical performances. Finally, Part V considers the relationships between words and music in the construction of narrative, ranging from literary evocations of musical performance to Broadway shows.

The texts collected here are deliberately diverse. In subject matter they cover pop songs and operas, lullabies and laments, rap and talking drums, and many points in between. The approaches of the various authors range from high theory to down-to-earth, practical advice. Although the focus is on music, the authors represent a wide range of academic fields – not only musicology, ethnomusicology and popular music studies, but also philosophy, literary theory, folklore, history, social history and anthropology – and these academic writings are complemented by several first-hand accounts from performers and composers.

The rest of this introduction sketches one possible route through the thirty-six items that follow. I have picked out some of the main themes as

I see them, added some quotes from other interviews we carried out for *Words and Music,* and suggested some of the many possible links between items. Anyone who familiarises themselves with the contents of this book will surely see many more themes and cross-references than I could draw attention to here, find different routes through the material and perhaps come to different conclusions. That is as it should be: such rich and varied material will always resist easy summary.

Part I Words and music

We begin with some of the oldest and most enduring questions about music: where does it come from, and how does it relate to language? We begin also with the oldest item in the volume, which is taken from Jean-Jacques Rousseau's famous 'Essay on the origin of languages' (written around 1760). In the space of a few short pages on music, Rousseau sets out some points that are key to his whole philosophy, and which have kept several later philosophers busy: speech and music, he argues, emerged together with the birth of human society, only later separating out into musical and verbal modes of communication. The effect of music is due to melody, since melody can imitate emotional inflections of the voice such as cries: music's effects are not due to 'the work of sounds' per se, since whatever sounds we produce have to be organised, and neither are they due to harmony, which separates song from speech. Rousseau's writing is immensely rich, both for the acuity of his ideas and – at a somewhat less elevated level – for the wit with which he expresses his prejudices (princi-pally against French music) and pursues a feud with his rival Jean-Philippe Rameau, who had made the contrary case for harmony.

The next four items relate to Rousseau's concerns in quite different ways. Charles Myers revisits 'The beginnings of music', more than a century and a half after Rousseau, in the light of evolutionary theory (Charles Darwin and Herbert Spencer had both written on the origin of music in the intervening period) and a couple of decades of ethnographic and psychological study on 'primitive' music. Myers comes to much the same conclusion as Rousseau, however: music and speech developed from a common precursor, speech dealing with knowledge and music with feeling, and musical meaning cannot be rendered in words. George List's 1963 article 'The boundaries of speech and song' (Item 4) broadens out this simple dichotomy, attempting to describe a framework within which a much wider variety of vocal forms (so-called 'heightened speech' forms, which exist in great diversity around the world) could be categorised. Jacques Derrida (Item 5) took Rousseau's *Essay* on in an extended critique which he used to develop his own philosophy: a brief extract of this is included here. Derrida comments on the difficulty of specifying Rousseau's distinction between the voice of words and the voice of song, which were one in the beginning but have since separated. A key contradiction he finds is Rousseau's contention that in order to elevate music to the status of a fine art it is necessary to employ melody in imitation of the inflections of the voice: in other words, in distinguishing itself from speech, music must imitate speech. By pointing out such logical contradictions in Rousseau's argument, Derrida suggests that in fact speech and song have 'always already begun to separate themselves' – they can never have formed a stable whole, but must always have been in the process of distinction.

Next, our item from Richard Wagner's theoretical work *Opera and Drama* considers the relationship between poetry and music. For Wagner – whose intellectual landmarks, like those of Rousseau, include the ancient Greeks and his French contemporaries – music is to words as feeling is to intellect: poetry is a form of heightened speech which draws on musicality, but paradoxically, great poetry is so perfect that it is impossible to set musically. 'We are completely unable to imagine an authentic relationship between verse and melody', he claims, a situation he aimed to change. Later in the volume more reflections are to be found on this paradox: Peter Manuel writes that simple texts are the best for singing in the Indian song genre *thumri* (Item 15), while Gordon Kalton Williams insists that a good libretto is not dependent on the beauty of the words (Item 33).

Concluding this first part are two pieces which look at the relationship between words and music at a more practical level: David Hughes describes the use of oral mnemonics in teaching the Japanese *noh* flute (that is, using spoken or sung syllables to render certain aspects of the instrumental music), while George Herzog elaborates on the use of drums to imitate speech among the Jabo people of eastern Liberia. As these items make clear, words – or at least spoken syllables – can imitate musical instruments and instruments can imitate speech, so however far the 'separation' discussed by Rousseau, Derrida and others progresses, words and music remain for ever in dialogue with each other: born together, always separating and yet also always recombining and imitating each other.

Part II Song, text and voice

Song is not always about words, as Inuit throat singer Tanya Tagaq reminded us in an interview carried out for *Words and Music*: 'There's songs about rivers and songs about mosquitoes and then some that are just there for the sounds, so they're all different. It's not words, it's the sound', she explained. Her description of these songs and their sounds, the way they imitate natural phenomena – and even more so her reflections on her own improvisation – speak of an intention beyond both text and rationality, in which she focuses instead on the bodily experience of singing. In opera, the listener's experience is sometimes similar; the words and their meaning may be subsumed to the beauty of the voice – the 'bel canto'. Words are, nonetheless, a part of most song repertoires, and in order to understand song we need to grasp the interplay between text and voice, between the meanings of the words and other aspects of singing, including the physicality to which Tagaq draws our attention. The items in Part II all shed light on the relationship between song as text and song performed: that is, on the complementarity of words and voice.

Simon Frith (Item 9) asks what voice we hear when we listen to a song, and having done so, carefully unpicks many different strands of meaning. For a start, he points out, we hear different voices in a single performance – those of singer, protagonist, lyricist and composer – and we can identify with one or more of these voices. Voices are never neutral, always identifiable, and this identity is normally gendered (among other things). Listening to singing voices implies relationships between self and other, with the microphone and recording technology making possible a particularly intimate, if disembodied, relationship.

In their different ways, each of the six items that comprise the remainder of Part II discuss this intimacy that can be engendered between a singer and her audience. Item 10 draws on Aaron Fox's writing on Texas country music, discussing the interplay of textual meaning and vocal effects (including distinctive and identifying timbres) in George Jones' 'He stopped loving her today'. A key feature of this vocal style is – and here we return to Rousseau territory – the imitation of particular inflections of the (non-singing) voice, for instance in so-called 'cry breaks'. Roland Barthes (Item 11) meditates on the voice of his former singing teacher Charles Panzéra, and the role of pronunciation and articulation in singing. Whereas for Wagner poetry resists setting to music, for Barthes when a text is set, 'music enters the language and rediscovers there what is musical': music is 'a quality of language' which can be awakened when the two modes are brought together. We return to anglophone pop with Tim Riley's dissection of The Beatles' 'Hey Jude' – which, as he points out, although it is based on the presentation of a (mostly) intelligible text, reaches its climax only once the words have been dispensed with. Perhaps we are returning here to the dichotomies of Part I, with an outburst of emotion and feeling necessitating the erasure of linguistic meaning.

Item 13 is an extract from Virginia Danielson's book on the Egyptian singer Umm Kulthūm, demonstrating that although Islamic culture brings new factors into the equation – the Qur'ān is *recited* not sung, since music would demean the religious message – many of the same issues apply here as they do with George Jones, Paul McCartney and Charles Panzéra. A key issue again is the balance in performance between text and vocal quality: Umm Kulthūm's rendition of the words was considered by many to be paramount, and yet her use of particular timbres was crucial in allowing people to identify with her voice and experience a powerful emotional affect.

Barthes's item was the first in this volume to explicitly raise the themes of desire and the erotic, which inescapably arise from the embodiment of the voice. The theme returns in the following two texts, which deal with the romantic *thumri*. The theme of desire is only briefly alluded to in Sheila Dhar's evocation of the famous singer Siddheshwari Devi's performance at a Delhi wedding in the 1930s (Item 14), since the tale is told as the recollection of her experience as a young girl, but this piece firmly places performance in a wider social context – the female singer, performing romantic songs in an intimate setting, enhances her singing and dancing with dramatic gestures and dancing for her admirers – within which the erotic dimension finds a natural place. Peter Manuel, in the following item, discusses the subject matter of these songs, and the relationship between the meaning of the text and the way it is presented, in much more detail. *Thumri* is a text-oriented singing, but nonetheless the best text for this type of performance is *incomplete:* somewhat along the same lines as Wagner had argued, for Manuel the finest poetry is not suitable for singing in *thumri* style since it leaves too little room for melodic invention.

Part III Song performance and society

Several of the preceding texts have started to draw us, inevitably, towards the topic of performance and the social location of singing. The items in Part III now consider some of the issues that emerge from this orientation. Viktor Zuckerkandl's observations (Item 16) on the meaning of song place social relationships right at the heart of singing, and in so doing evoke a somewhat different distinction to those raised by Rousseau and others whose writing has been presented thus far. The fundamental difference between linguistic and musical meaning, he argues, is that each presupposes a different kind of relationship between individuals: using words we communicate a message from one person to another, but in song subject and object come together and the individual self is subsumed within a greater whole. Thus in folk song, the 'voice' is the voice of the group rather than that of an individual.

Such a contention would seem to be supported by the English folk singer Norma Waterson, albeit given a more political dimension. Waterson suggested in an interview for *Words and Music* that 'the peasant class of these islands had no voice . . . The only voice that they had was their music.' One way to look at this is to claim that a group of people can express their communal voice through song. Conversely, a vocal or musical style can be taken to stand for the identity of a group, whether that group is defined geographically, in terms of gender, race or ethnicity, or in other ways. The notion that groups of people express themselves through their music is a powerful one that has often been exploited for political ends, whether in order to strengthen a particular group or to stereotype or undermine others: this is reflected in several of the items in this part.

One particular aspect of social identity that has great relevance to musical performance is gender: of the musicians we interviewed for *Words and Music* the one who addressed this most directly was Tanya Tagaq, whose Inuit throat singing is almost exclusively a female genre. 'We used to joke around and call it "uterus singing" because only women do it!' she told us, going on to explain that the sounds of throat singing, which to many can sound harsh and even ugly, can be read as a sign of femininity in a culture where, due to the extreme cold, 'you need a strong partner, you don't need some little thing that goes shopping and has long nails'.

The next item also considers a genre frequently associated with women, the lullaby. As Hiromi Lorraine Sakata shows in her writing about the Hazara people in Afghanistan (Item 17), the study of lullabies – an unassuming musical genre, perhaps – can shed light on several fundamental aspects of song. One such is the distinction between public and private spaces – the former generally male-dominated, the latter the preserve of women. Lullabies, in most contexts, seem naturally to fall into the latter category, but the situation may not be that simple. Sakata distinguishes between functional lullabies – sung by women with the intention of soothing children to sleep – and 'stylised' lullabies, performed in public by male singers. Looking at the relationship between the two allows her not only to highlight the private–public divide, but also to argue that the private, predominantly female genres actually form the basis of the entire music culture.

Gender is at issue once again in Susan McClary's study of the representation of cultural 'others' in *Carmen* (a major case study in *Words and Music*). One of the social roles of song performance in many contexts – nineteenth-century opera stands out in some respects, but is far from unique – is the presentation of others. The oriental, Jewish and gypsy characters with whom a predominantly white, gentile bourgeoisie entertained itself at the opera might have frequently been objects of desire – as in Carmen's case – but they were *different*, and their otherness is the point: the operas undoubtedly have a social and a political dimension.

The representation of otherness and the voice as a site of desire are themes which continue in the next item, in which Richard Middleton discusses the blues (Item 19). Blues, of course, is associated with the voice of African Americans, but Middleton points out that the reality is far more complex: themes of race and nostalgia were present in the music from the beginning, when it originated as a pop-music form, mediated by recordings and produced by both whites and blacks, but always referring back to a semi-mythical black folk culture. Given the complexities of the history, we might ask: whose voice do we hear when we listen to the blues?

The Nigerian pop form *jùjú* is also disseminated through recordings, but Christopher Waterman's description of a *jùjú* performance in Nigeria (Item 20) stresses the social functions of this music when performed live for a specific patron. In this case the singer and bandleader's main role is to serve his patron's ends: he does so already by providing music for dancing, demonstrating the host's wealth and generosity, and also by honouring and flattering through words – but at the same time he is enhancing his own status and negotiating relationships between band members.

The last two items in Part III focus on vocal genres intended to convey a message to, and about, their society as a whole: the first concerns the political rap of Public Enemy in the USA, the second the *haka* dance-song in New Zealand. Robert Walser (Item 21) considers not only the message that Public Enemy put into words, but also the significance of their music – in particular, the use of rhythm and the way different voices interact – in complementing that message. Jan Bolwell' s interview with Maori artist Keri Kaa focuses more on the relationship between language and gesture, and the way both combine, revealing but also concealing the messages of the songs.

Part IV Song and ritual

A particular way in which song can have a social significance is when it forms part of the enactment of ritual. Rituals, whether secular or sacred, are used to mark points of transition such as those between the seasons, or an individual's move from child to adult, unmarried to married, or living to dead. Music, of course, plays a crucial role in countless ritual practices, and the seven items in Part IV consider a range of calendrical and life-cycle rituals, as well as musical performances which represent or incorporate elements of ritual song. We begin with a couple of song genres from the British Isles that relate to calendrical rites, namely wassails and carols. Wassails form part of two related winter rituals, one involving the blessing of trees to ensure a good harvest of fruit the following summer, the other a procession from house to house. Palmer and Patten's article (Item 23) describes these rituals as they survived in Somerset in the second half of the twentieth century, placing the songs in their ritual context. Carols share some features with wassails, although as Frank Howes points out, their verbal content betrays input from various sources, with references to the Christian gospels often found alongside traces of the earlier beliefs expressed in the apple-tree wassails. (Traditional rituals don't have to be po-faced, of course, as Norma Waterson reminded us: '[wassailing] has a long tradition of people going out at probably the coldest and darkest time of the year and bringing a little cheer into a house . . . The farmers let you in, and you have groaning boards of food, absolutely wonderful. They usually make a hot mulled wine and so by the time we get home we're . . . We have to have a driver, who stays on the orange juice.')

Carols can incorporate both Christian and pre-Christian elements, and also combine Latin and vernacular texts. This combination of languages had troubled the Church back in the fourteenth century, as Robert Hayburn describes (Item 25), when increasing use of vernacular texts, as well as developments in polyphonic techniques, led to anxiety that newer styles of musical composition would inhibit devotion. Many sacred rituals involve the combination of words, melody, gesture and staging, and in view of the discussions earlier in this book on the relationship between words and music, it is interesting how for some religious traditions this combination is a source of anxiety, suggesting an awareness that while a musical setting can enhance the expression of a text, it can also become an end in itself and obscure the message the words are expressing.

Marina Roseman (Item 26) introduces a somewhat different function of song, this time in healing rituals. For the Temiar of the Malaysian rainforest, songs are paths that link people with the spirits of other creatures, plants or topographical features. Since illness is characterised as a spiritual disorder, these 'spiritguides' play a crucial role in healing, and their power is harnessed by mediums who take on 'the voice, vision and knowledge of the spiritguide'. Although this is a very different example to the previous three, again the voice is seen to have a crucial function in dealing with the point of crisis or transition marked by the ritual. The same can be said for traditional lamenting, which as Elizabeth Tolbert points out, is linked to ancient traditions of ancestor worship and shamanism. Laments, which are traditionally performed – if that is the right word – at weddings as well as funerals, link the 'spontaneous expression of emotion' with a 'symbol of affect': they clearly relate to 'real', spontaneous crying, but they are also stylised, performed by ritual specialists who turn that crying into something with a wider social and ritual meaning. Laments such as those of the Karelian refugees in eastern Finland considered here are also a form of communication with the dead, and as such involve the use of special words and linguistic features that make the words hard to understand for the living. The dead understand fully, but the living only grasp the 'emotional tone' of a lament.

Tolbert has gone as far as anyone in understanding the form and function of traditional laments, but the topic received considerable attention in Russia from the nineteenth century onwards. Stravinsky drew on ethnographic reports of traditional Russian wedding rites in the preparation of his concert and ballet piece *Les Noces* or *Svadebka*, which is the topic of the last two items in this part of the book (and of another *Words and Music* case study). Richard Taruskin (Item 28) describes the traditional wedding rites and the use Stravinsky made of them, while Pieter van den Toorn considers the extent to which the feeling expressed by the lamenting bride survives the rigid, formal construction of Stravinsky's piece. As in Tolbert's piece on the Karelian lament, the relationship between real, individual emotion and the ritual context is key – and it brings us back to the relationship between nature and imitation. Here, however, we have an extra layer – Stravinsky's wedding is not a real wedding but a staged representation of a wedding. Can a real human emotion survive this double transformation, into ritual practice and thence into staged performance?

Part V Words, music and narrative

Norma Waterson put it very concisely: 'To make a good singer you need to be able to tell a story.' But the significance of narrative in relation to song goes far beyond the matter of certain genres (for Barthes, folk song in general) focusing on storytelling. The final part of this collection considers musical narratives of three kinds: solo storytellers who convey narratives through song with musical accompaniment; staged narrative genres such as opera and musical theatre; and descriptions of musical performance from novels. The first of these is addressed by storyteller and anthropologist Mauro Geraci in his description of the Sicilian storyteller's art (Item 30). Geraci uses song and speech to tell stories on historical and contemporary themes, presenting a version of history for his audience's consideration and debate. He describes the performance as alternately 'presentation' and 'representation', depending on whether he is narrating or acting the part of a character in the story: his music (the guitar accompaniment) is there to serve the story, although he also describes his guitar as a kind of 'second voice'.

The description of the guitar as a voice brings to mind the ideas of Edward Cone, already referred to by Frith (Item 9) but now presented in their own right in Item 31. Cone's book *The Composer's Voice* elaborates an account of Western art music in terms of the voices – literal and metaphorical – that we hear: the voice of the protagonist of a drama, that of the singer herself, those of the instrumental lines, and – behind all of these – that of the composer. He discusses the relationship between musical and vocal 'personas' and – among much else – discusses the application of his theory to ritual performance. If there is one feature of his writing that is culturally specific, it is his anxiety over the possibility of listeners focusing on the 'performance itself' rather than on the complete musical persona created by the composer. Otherwise his ideas can be broadly applied, and explain a good deal about the ways in which we can experience music as a combination and layering of voices. Along the way Cone also grapples with the voice of the protagonist in opera (or other forms of musical narrative), who is frequently assumed to be unconscious of singing, such as when a character in a musical or Bollywood film bursts into song. Abbate refers back to this in her description (Item 32) of Delibes's Bell Song, and also takes us back once again to the respective roles of words and music, since an important feature of this song is the heroine's *wordless* singing – which, for Abbate, plays a crucial role in the story of the opera *Lakmé* by drawing our attention to the singing body, to desire, and to a form of vocal performance that overpowers the ostensible narrative.

From the role of voice in narrative we return to the role of words, with librettist Gordon Kalton Williams' essay on the art of libretto writing, which focuses on another *Words and Music* case study, his and Andrew Schultz's cantata *Journey to Horseshoe Bend*. His account describes the process of composition and the way librettist and composer work together, passing ideas back and forth. He also makes a plea for libretti to be judged in the context of their own specific function: a good libretto is one that helps to shape a piece and inspire the composer's imagination, and shouldn't be judged on its independent literary merit ('the beauty is not in the words'). There is an analogy here with Wagner's argument on the relationship between music and poetry, and with Manuel's comments on *thumri* singing: just as the best song texts don't necessarily read as great poetry, so the best libretti may not stand as great writing when viewed outside their musical context.

The next two items also draw on the reflections of well-known practitioners, in the form of two of the greats of the Broadway musical. First, composer and lyricist Stephen Sondheim addresses practical issues such as the way composers can write, or amend, songs in order to suit specific voices (his song 'Send in the Clowns' is a good example of this). In discussing the distinction between opera and musical, he makes the claim that a Broadway musical is primarily about telling the story, while opera is about watching singers perform (at which point the arguments of Cone and Abbate earlier in this section take on a different light). One of Sondheim's predecessors, the lyricist Oscar Hammerstein, also focuses on practical issues – rhyme, rhythm, phonetics and an awareness of voice production – in his entertaining and revealing essay on the art of lyric writing.

To this point in the collection fine literature has been discussed mainly as a lack, but the final two items redress this somewhat, and allow us to test Barthes's contention that 'No writer has spoken well about music, not even Proust.' Before getting on to Proust himself, Item 36 comprises two short chapters from Amit Chaudhuri's novel *Afternoon Raag*. Chaudhuri is a talented musician as well as a novelist, and his evocations of music sessions in India are written very much from an insider's perspective. He writes of singing with his teacher, using the metaphor of voice carrying voice 'as a boat carries a bewildered passenger', describing the occasion as a time when 'I would forget my voice was my own.' In these lines he recalls many of the themes addressed in earlier items: Roseman' s description of the Temiar metaphor of song as path (Item 26) and Zuckerkandl's claim that when we sing, self and other blend into one (Item 16), to cite but two.

Given Barthes's comment on writing about music, it is appropriate that we give Marcel Proust the final chance to prove him wrong. The extract here is one of the key passages in *Swann's Way*, describing his protagonist Charles Swann listening to the Vinteuil Sonata. This item could stand as easily as a contribution to Part II, for comparison with Dhar's and Waterman's descriptions of performances perhaps, given the detailed description of the bourgeois salon. Among many observations that one could pick out of this passage, I was struck by Swann's musing that 'A work of pure music contains none of the logical sequences whose deformation, in spoken language, is a proof of insanity' (he has been discussing the mental health of the fictional composer Vinteuil). Any composer might baulk at the suggestion that music contains no 'logical sequences', but nonetheless there is an interesting point here about the relationship between the kinds of structures that characterise music and language, respectively, one which could take us deeper into a debate as to whether music can be said to have a 'grammar', a topic that is beyond the scope of this volume.

And so we reach the end of this collection with – inevitably – more questions and more issues to explore. To do so one could do worse than to go to some of the works extracted here and read more – just so long as we do not expect to prove Barthes wrong and exhaust the subject.

A note on the editorial selection

Items have been edited to make them suitable for this volume – as far as possible long footnotes have been removed, as have sections rendered irrelevant by their extraction (such as references to other chapters of the original work): these cuts are indicated with square brackets and/or ellipses. The titles I have given to the items are intended to reflect the content of the items rather than the whole works from which they are taken, thus in some cases they differ significantly from any title in the original work. I have added short headnotes only where I felt it necessary to contextualise items, or to gloss specialist or foreign-language terms.

Part I

Words and music

2

The first voices

Jean-Jacques Rousseau

Jean-Jacques Rousseau, 'Essay on the origin of languages', trans. J. T. Scott, *The Collected Writings of Rousseau* (vol. 7, Dartmouth, NH: University Press of New England, 1998), Chs XII–XIV, pp. 317–23.

This item comprises chapters XII–XIV of Rousseau's *Essay*, the first three to focus explicitly on music. Rousseau (1712–78) is typically outspoken regarding his older contemporaries, naming here the composer and theorist Jean-Philippe Rameau (1683–1764), with whom he had a long and complicated relationship, as well as the musician Pierre-Jean Burette (1665–1747), who had published on the subject of ancient Greek music. The allusion to 'fountains' is a reference to Rousseau's theory that the first human societies emerged – and with them, the first language and the first music – as people began to settle around shared water sources such as wells (before that, he believed, gesture had sufficed as a means of communication).

Origin of music

Along with the first voices were formed the first articulations or the first sounds, depending on the kind of passion that dictated the one or the other. Anger wrests menacing cries which the tongue and the palate articulate; but the voice of tenderness is gentler, it is the glottis that modifies it, and this voice becomes a sound. Only its accents are more or less frequent, its inflections more or less acute depending on the feeling that is joined to them. Thus cadence and sounds arise along with syllables, passion makes all the vocal organs speak, and adorns the voice with all their brilliance; thus verses, songs, and speech have a common origin. Around the fountains of which I have spoken, the first discourses were the first songs; the periodic and measured recurrences of rhythm, the melodious inflections of accents caused poetry and music to be born along with language; or rather, all this was nothing but language itself in those happy climates and those

happy times when the only pressing needs that required another's help
were those to which the heart gave rise.

Relationships

The first stories, the first harangues, and the first laws were in verse; poetry
was discovered before prose; this had to be so, since the passions spoke
before reason. The same was so for music: at first there was no music at
all other than melody, nor any other melody than the varied sound of
speech, the accents formed the song, the quantities formed the meter, and
one spoke as much by sounds and rhythm as by articulations and voices.
In olden days to speak and to sing were the same thing, says Strabo; which
shows, he adds, that poetry is the source of eloquence. He ought to have
said that they both had the same source and at first were merely the same
thing. Considering the way in which the first societies were bound together,
was it surprising that the first stories were set to verse and that the first
laws were sung? Was it surprising that the first Grammarians subordi-
nated their art to music and were at the same time teachers of them
both?

A language that has only articulations and voices therefore has only
half its riches; it conveys ideas, it is true, but in order to convey feelings,
images, it still needs a rhythm and sounds, that is, a melody; that is what
the Greek language had, and what our lacks.

We are always astonished by the prodigious effects of eloquence, poetry,
and music among the Greeks; these effects cannot be sorted out at all in
our heads because we no longer experience similar ones, and all that we
can manage for ourselves, seeing them so well attested, is to pretend to
believe them out of indulgence for our Scholars. Burrette, having transcribed as best he could some pieces of Greek music into our musical notation, was simple enough to have these pieces performed at the Academy
of Belles-Lettres, and the Academicians had the patience to listen to them.
I admire this experiment in a country whose music is indecipherable for
every other nation. Give any foreign Musicians you please a monologue
from a French opera to perform: I defy you to recognize any of it. These are
nonetheless the same Frenchmen who presume to judge the melody of an
Ode of Pindar set to Music two thousand years ago!

I have read that the Indians in America, seeing the astonishing effect of
firearms, used to pick up the musket balls from the ground, then, throwing
them with their hands while emitting a loud noise from their mouths, were
quite surprised that they had not killed anyone. Our orators, our musicians, and our Scholars resemble these Indians. The wonder is not that we

no longer accomplish with our music what the Greeks did with theirs, on the contrary, it would be that the same effects should be produced with such different instruments.

On melody

Man is modified by his senses, no one doubts it; but because we fail to distinguish their modifications, we confound their causes; we attribute both too much and too little dominion to sensations; we do not see that often they affect us not only as sensations but as signs or images, and that their moral effects also have moral causes. Just as the feelings that painting arouses in us are not at all due to colors, so the dominion music has over our souls is not at all the work of sounds. Beautiful colors, finely shaded, please the sight, but that pleasure is purely one of sensation. It is the design, it is the imitation, that endows these colors with life and soul, it is the passions which they express that succeed in moving our own, it is the objects which they represent that succeed in affecting us. Interest and feeling do not depend on colors; the contours of a touching painting touch us in an engraving as well; remove those contours from the Painting, the colors will no longer do anything.

Melody does in music precisely what design does in painting; it is melody that indicates the contours and figures, of which the accords and sounds are but the colors. But will it not be said that melody is merely a succession of sounds? Doubtless; but design is also merely an arrangement of colors. An orator makes use of ink to pen his writings; does that mean that ink is a most eloquent liquid?

Imagine a country where no one had any idea of design, but where many people who spend their lives combining, mixing, and blending colors believed themselves to excel in painting; those people would reason about our painting precisely as we reason about the music of the Greeks. Even if they were told about the emotion that beautiful paintings cause in us and about the charm of being touched by a pathetic subject, would their scholars not straightaway probe the material, compare their colors with ours, examine whether our green is more delicate or our red more brilliant; would they not try to find out which accords of colors could cause weeping, which others could arouse anger? The Burettes of that country would put together a few disfigured fragments of our paintings on rags; then it would be asked with surprise what was so marvelous about such coloration.

And if, in a neighboring nation, someone began to form some sort of contour, a sketch, a still imperfect figure, it would all pass for scribbling, for a capricious and baroque painting, and, in order to preserve taste, they would hold onto this simple beauty, which in truth expresses nothing, but which makes fine shadings, large well-colored slabs, extended progressions of hues without any contour.

Finally, they might perhaps by dint of progress arrive at the experiment with the prism. Straightaway, some celebrated artist would establish a beautiful system on the basis of it. Gentlemen, he would say to them, in order to philosophize properly, one has to go back to the physical causes. Here you have the decomposition of light, here you have all the primary colors, here you have their ratios, their proportions, here you have the true principles of the pleasure that painting causes for you. All this mysterious talk of design, representation, figure is a pure chicanery on the part of French painters, who think that by their imitations they produce I know not what movements in the soul, while it is known that there is nothing in it but sensations. You are told of the marvels of their paintings, but look at my hues.

French Painters, he would continue, may perhaps have observed the rainbow; they may have received from nature some taste for shading and some instinct for coloration. But I, I have shown you the great, the true principles of the art. What am I saying, of the art? Of all the arts, Gentlemen, of all the sciences. The analysis of colors, the calculation of the refractions of the prism, gives you the sole exact relationships found in nature, the rule of all relationships. Now, everything in the universe is merely relationship. One therefore knows everything once one knows how to paint, one knows everything once one knows how to match colors.

What would we say about a painter so lacking in feeling and taste as to reason in this way, and stupidly to limit the pleasure that painting causes in us to the physics of his art? What would we say of the musician who, filled with similar prejudices, believed he saw in harmony alone the source of the great effects of music? We would send the first off to paint woodwork, and would condemn the other to compose French opera.

As painting is, therefore, not the art of combining colors in a way pleasing to the sight, no more is music the art of combining sounds in a way pleasing to the ear. If there were nothing but this in them, they would both be counted among the ranks of the natural sciences, and not the fine arts. It is imitation alone that elevates them to that rank. Now, what makes painting an imitative art? It is design. What makes music another? It is melody.

On harmony

The beauty of sounds is from nature; their effect is purely physical, it results from the interaction of the various particles of air set in motion by the sounding body, and by all its aliquots, perhaps to infinity. All of this together produces a pleasant sensation: every man in the universe will take pleasure in listening to beautiful sounds; but unless this pleasure is animated by melodious inflections that are familiar to them, it will not be delightful, it will not pass into voluptuous pleasure. The most beautiful songs, to our taste, will always only indifferently touch an ear that is not at all accustomed to them; it is a language for which one has to have the Dictionary.

Harmony, properly so called, is in a still less favorable situation. Having only conventional beauties, it in no way appeals to ears that are not trained in it; one has to have been long habituated to it in order to feel and savor it. Rustic ears hear only noise in our consonances. When the natural proportions are distorted, it is not surprising that the natural pleasure no longer exists.

A sound carries with it all of its concomitant harmonies, in the relations of strength and interval that they must have among themselves in order to produce the most perfect harmony of this same sound. Add to this the third or fifth or some other consonance, you do not add to it, but redouble it; you leave the relation of interval unchanged, but you alter that of the strength; by reinforcing one consonance and not the others, you disrupt the proportion. Wanting to do better than nature, you do worse. Your ears and your taste are spoiled by a misunderstood art. By nature there is no other harmony than unison.

M. Rameau claims that treble parts of a comparative simplicity naturally suggest their basses, and that a man who has a true but unpracticed ear will naturally intone this bass. That is a musician's prejudice, belied by all experience. Not only will a person who has never heard either a bass or harmony not find either this harmony or bass on his own, but they will even displease him if he is made to hear them, and he will like simple unison much better.

Even if one were to calculate the ratios of sounds and the laws of harmony for a thousand years, how will this art ever be made an imitative art? Where is the principle of this supposed imitation, of what is harmony the sign, and what do these chords have in common with our passions?

Were the same question put about melody, the answer would come of itself: it is in the readers' minds beforehand. Melody, by imitating the inflections of the voice, expresses complaints, cries of sadness or of joy, threats, and moans; all the vocal signs of the passions are within its scope. It imitates the accents of languages, and the turns of phrase appropriate in each idiom to certain movements of the soul; it not only imitates, it speaks, and its language, inarticulate but lively, ardent, passionate, has a hundred times more energy than speech itself. Here is from whence the strength of musical imitations arises; here is from whence the dominion of song over sensitive hearts arises. Harmony may, in certain systems, cooperate with this by linking the succession of sounds through certain laws of modulations, by making the intonations more exact, by providing the ear with reliable evidence of this exactness, by bringing together and determining imperceptible inflections into consonant and linked intervals. But by thus shackling the melody, it deprives it of energy and expression, it eliminates passionate accent in order to substitute the harmonic interval for it, it subjects to two modes alone songs which should have as many modes as they have oratorical tones, it effaces and destroys multitudes of sounds or intervals that do not enter into its system; in a word, it separates song from speech so much that these two languages combat one another, contradict one another, deprive each other of every characteristic of truth and cannot be united in a pathetic subject without being absurd. That is how it happens that the people always find it ridiculous for strong and serious passions to be expressed in song; for it knows that in our languages these passions have no musical inflections, and that the men of the north no more die singing than swans do.

By itself harmony is even inadequate for the expressions that appear to depend uniquely upon it. Thunder, the murmuring of waters, winds, and storms are poorly rendered by simple chords. Whatever one may do, noise alone says nothing to the mind, objects have to speak in order to make themselves heard, in every imitation a type of discourse always has to supplement the voice of nature. The musician who wants to render noise with noise is mistaken; he knows neither the weakness nor the strength of his art; he judges it without taste, without enlightenment; teach him that he should render noise with song, that if he would make frogs croak, he has to make them sing. For it is not enough for him to imitate, he has to touch and to please, otherwise his glum imitation is nothing, and, not interesting anyone, it makes no impression.

3

The beginnings of music

Charles S. Myers

Charles S. Myers, 'The beginnings of music', in *A Psychologist's Point of View* (London: Heinemann, 1933), pp. 200–3.

Better known in later life as a psychologist, in his early years Myers was an important pioneer of comparative musicology who published analyses of his own and others' field recordings of 'primitive' music. This short extract sees him reflecting on that earlier work, and what light the evidence he had seen shed on debates about the origin of music.

A general study of the cases in which, owing to cerebral lesion, musical appreciation is lost shows that such disturbances rarely occur apart from simultaneous disturbances in word-language. From this fact, and from the close topographical relation of the cortical structures involved in speech and music, we may be disposed to conclude that the beginnings of music have been derived from speech. It would be safer, however, to conclude that both have been evolved from a mechanism designed for the vocal "expression of meaning." Psychologists now recognise that words are not necessary for the awareness of meaning; they are indeed but an imperfect means of formulating and conveying it. Further, musicians now recognise that music has a meaning of its own, which is spoilt, or at least, imperfectly rendered, by translation into words; indeed, "meaning," in the sense of what can be conveyed in *verbal* language, is by no means essential for musical enjoyment. At most what is common to two or more individuals listening to the same music is a common attitude, a common mood, or a common emotion. Even the most modern "programme music" requires a printed programme in order that the audience may interpret it in the precise "objective" manner desired by the composer.

In their fully-developed states, speech and music present very decided contrasts. Speech has a precision and a utilitarian character, opposed to the vaguer artistic influence of music. Speech serves for the communication primarily of cognitive experiences (what we *know*), whereas music primarily communicates affective experiences (what we *feel*). Music employs definite intervals precisely hit by the executant, and regular rhythmic periods; speech is relatively independent of pitch. What changes there are in the pitch of speech occur as a rule continuously and without uniformity; while its "rhythm" (in prose) is irregular. The most primitive music and the most primitive speech which are available for examination at the present day are perfectly distinct from each other. Nevertheless traces, perhaps, may be detected of their earlier approach to one another. In the most primitive music the intervals are only imperfectly defined; the slow *portamento* sung between widely different notes may be reminiscent of a long wail. The fact that in certain languages the same word may have different meanings according to the way in which it is intoned also brings speech and music more closely together. But even if it be true that both speech and music have been developed from a common mode of expression, it is clear that this common mode cannot properly be termed speech or music.

The prime function of musical expression is then to communicate certain emotions or feelings. The regard for beauty *per se* in Art only begins at a much later stage of mental development. For primitive peoples, and even for the masses in civilised countries, beauty and pleasure are practically synonymous. What pleasant purpose, then, has music served? Some have believed that music has developed from its employment for the facilitation of work or as an accompaniment of the dance. It is true that most primitive peoples find great delight in rhythmical expression, but an examination of their tunes shows that the use of definite rhythm is by no means universal or necessary. Others have believed that music has evolved from its service-ableness as a means of sexual attraction. But it has yet to be shown that even in birds this is the *origin* of their song. Certainly the sounds emitted by animals serve to communicate other feelings than those of love, *e.g.*, pain, alarm, contentment and anger. And so doubtless in ourselves music has arisen from efforts to express not merely sexual love, but such general feelings as joy, sorrow, tenderness and ecstasy.

A series of experiments, which I published[1] after this chapter was written, shows very clearly how differently music appeals to different individuals at the present day. Some when they hear music translate it into words, others are led by association to think of similar sounds in nature or else-where; in others again the emotional element predominates; while yet in others there is a strong tendency to movement. To such individual differ-ences, I believe, are to be attributed the rival hypotheses of different writers, which variously ascribe the beginnings of music to speech or to the imitation of the sounds of nature, or which lay stress on the importance of sex or of rhythm.

Note

1 "Individual Differences in Listening to Music," *British Journal of Psychology*, 1922, vol. xiii, pp. 52–71.

4

The boundaries of speech and song

George List

George List, 'The boundaries of speech and song',
Ethnomusicology, 7:1 (1963), pp. 4–13.

For this article List made extensive use of the spectrograph, a machine for generating visual displays from sound recordings. List used the spectrograph – which has long since been superseded by computer software – to aid him in the accurate transcription of pitch contours: the vertical axis in his figures refers to a voice's pitch (frequency), measured in cycles per second (cps, also sometimes written Hz or Hertz).

When speech is heightened in a socially structured situation, such as a dramatic production or in the telling of a tale, two opposite tendencies appear. The first is the negation or the leveling out of intonation into a plateau approaching a monotone. The second is the amplification or exaggeration of intonation, especially of the downward inflection that serves in most languages as a phrase, sentence, or paragraph final.

[. . .]

The classification system which we shall now develop is based to a great extent upon these two divergent modifications of speech intonation. The chart or graph, Figure 4.1, is analogous to a hemispheric map of the world. At the north pole is placed casual speech. Song, as previously defined, is found at the south pole. The forms found north of the equator are those which seem to have more characteristics of speech than song. The forms south of the equator exhibit to a greater extent the traits associated with song.

Movement to the east represents the diminution or negation of the influence of speech intonation. Movement to the west represents either the expansion of intonational contours or of scalar structures. Modification is continuous along the diagonals and each area marked extends its

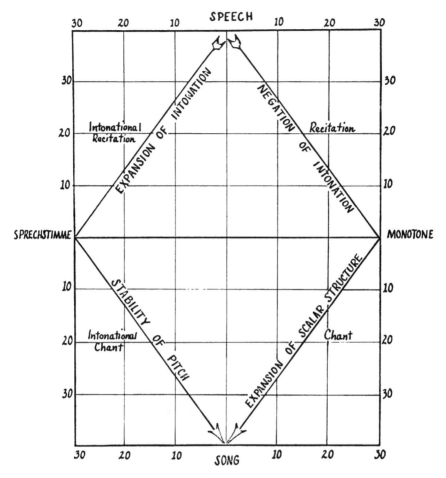

Fig. 4.1 Chart for classifying forms intermediate to speech and song

influence with decreasing magnetism in the three possible directions. Thus, the use of lines of latitude and longitude permits the placement of forms at midpoints both horizontally and vertically.

[. . .]

At latitude 20° north, midway on the diagonal moving to the southeast, we shall place forms such as the counting out or jumping rope rhymes of American children. These forms, while basically speech, make limited use of intonation. What intonation is present, usually short terminal glides, revolves around a central speech monotone which is ornamented with one or two auxiliary tones. The form is described here as "recitation." Figure 4.2 is a transcription of the first section of a jumping rope rhyme as recited

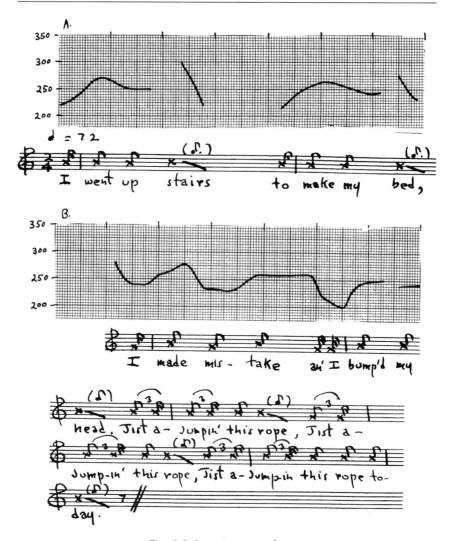

Fig. 4.2 Jumping rope rhyme

by an eight-year-old American child. The recitation of poetry by small children in our culture is comparable form.

When the line representing the continuous negation of speech intonation reaches the equator, the area of the complete monotone is reached. Certain Buddhist chants in Thailand exhibit pure monotone (Figure 4.3).

The midway point between the north pole and the equator on the diagram moving to the southwest has been assigned to forms displaying amplification of speech intonation. This type has been designated

Fig. 4.3 *Thai*, Buddhist chant

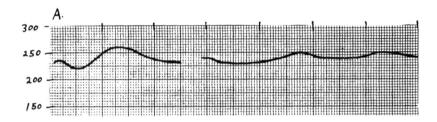

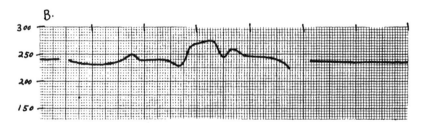

Fig. 4.4 *Palau*, intonational recitation

"intonational recitation." This communication form is found, for example, in the singing of the women of Palau, one of the Caroline Islands in Micronesia (Figure 4.4). In group singing the leader customarily recites a short text which several women then repeat in an improvisatory type of part singing. The "lining out" by the leader is what is termed here "intonational recitation."

At the point where the westwards moving diagonal meets the equator is found not merely the greatest amplification of intonation contours but their development into a free melodic form. This area has been labelled *Sprechstimme*. The term refers to the type of elevated or heightened speech characteristic of the melodrama and is best known by its application by Arnold Schoenberg to the type of vocal communication displayed in his *Pierrot Lunaire*. The Maori *haka* (Figure 4.5) is an example of *Sprechstimme*.

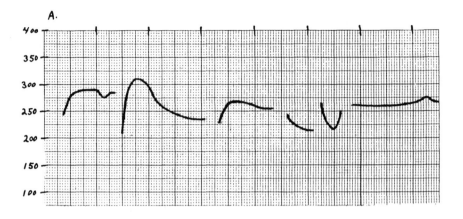

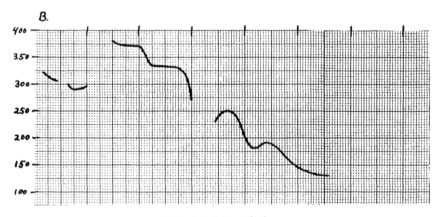

Fig. 4.5 *Maori*, haka

It will be noted that the range of the Palauan "intonational recitation" is approximately 220 cps to 275 cps, or approximately a major third. In contrast the Maori *haka* has a range of 130 to 380 cps, approximately an octave plus a perfect fifth. The latter therefore has an ambitus more than four times larger than the former.

The forms found to the southwest of monotone along the diagonal leading to SONG all display reasonably stable pitches. The influence of the monotone pervades until the halfway mark, to the area marked "chant." Along the diagonal to this point will be placed monotonic chants displaying an increasing number of auxiliary tones. Figure 4.6, a transcription of

Fig. 4.6 Tobacco "auctioneering"

excerpts from a recording of a tobacco auction in North Carolina, is an example of a fully developed form of "chant." Four auxiliary tones are utilized.

From this point south to SONG will be placed forms increasingly independent of monotonic influence and exhibiting increasing complexity of scalar structure, ditonic songs of the Vedda, tritonic taunts of American children, tetratonic Bulgarian folk songs, etc.

Along the diagonal moving southeast from the equator to latitude 20° south will be placed chant-like forms exhibiting contours related to speech intonation. They will be placed here in descending order of intonational complexity and increasing order of pitch stability. The Hopi "announcement" (Figure 4.7) is an example of "intonational chant."

Further south on this diagonal will be placed song-like forms which exhibit instability of pitch or some aspects of speech intonation. Since the songs of the Australian aborigines simultaneously exhibit a reasonably clear scalar structure such as the pentatonic and considerable instability of pitch and use of glides, they find their place here at latitude 30° south. The following American Negro song (Figure 4.8) will be placed at the same latitude on the central axis.

Fig. 4.7 *Hopi*, Announcement of a Rabbit Hunt

Fig. 4.8 American Negro Song

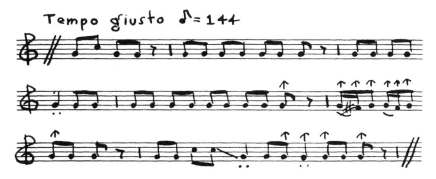

Fig. **4.9** *Hopi*, Owák Kachina Song

Fig. **4.10** *Hopi*, Buffalo Dance Song

Of the two Hopi songs discussed above, the Kachina song (Figure 4.9); a monotone embellished with one auxiliary, would be placed on the east diagonal a few degrees south of "monotone". The second (Figure 4.10), which possesses a pentatonic scale and exhibits few vocal glides, would be

Fig. 4.11 *Maori*, Ritual Chant

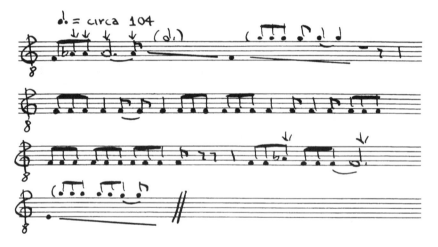

Fig. 4.12 *Maori*, Sentinel Song

placed on this diagonal at latitude 30° south. The Maori chant (Figure 4.11) and song (Figure 4.12), both exhibiting monotone, a limited number of auxiliaries, and a highly developed use of terminal intonation, would be placed on the central axis, a few degrees south of the equator.

5

The separation of speech and song

Jacques Derrida

Jacques Derrida, *Of Grammatology*, trans. G. Spivak (Baltimore, MD: Johns Hopkins University Press, 1967), from Part II, Ch. 3, Section II, pp. 195–200.

In this item Derrida refers to the music chapters – from 12 onwards – of Rousseau's *Essay* (chapters 12–14 are reproduced in Item 2, above). The references to the *Essay* and to Rousseau's *Dictionary of Music* are in the original text, as are most of the square brackets. As this passage illustrates, the critique of Rousseau's theories was an important springboard for the development of Derrida's own philosophy. Put simply, Rousseau had argued that language and music emerged together with the first society, and over the course of human history had separated and, in so doing, had degenerated. Music's effects depended on imitation. Derrida's critique argues that if so, primordial speech and song must *always already* – a favourite term of his – have begun to separate; and moreover, song is caught in a contradictory position since it must *transcend* nature in order to become song, and yet depends for its effects on the *imitation* of that very nature.

The themes of the first eleven chapters [of the *Essay*] are the genesis and degeneration of language, the relationships between speech and writing, the difference between the formation of the languages of the north and the languages of the south. Why is it necessary to treat these problems before proposing a theory of music? For several types of reasons.

1. There is no music before language. Music is born of voice and not of sound. No prelinguistic sonority can, according to Rousseau, open the time of music. In the beginning is the song.

This proposition is absolutely necessary within Rousseau's systematics. If music awakens in song, if it is initially uttered, *vociferated*, it is because, like all speech, it is born in passion. That is to say in the transgression of need by desire and the awakening of pity by imagination. Everything proceeds from this inaugural distinction: "it seems then that need dictated the first gestures, while the passions wrung forth the first words."

If music presupposes voice, it comes into being at the same time as human society. As speech, it requires that the other be present to me as other through compassion. Animals, whose pity is not awakened by the imagination, have no affinity with the other as such. That is why there is no animal music, One speaks of animal music only by looseness of vocabulary and by anthropomorphic projection. The difference between the glance and the voice is the difference between animality and humanity. Transgressing space, mastering the outside, placing souls in communication, voice transcends natural animality. That is to say a certain death signified by space. Exteriority is inanimate. The arts of space carry death within themselves and *animality* remains the *inanimate* face of *life*. The song presents life to itself. In that sense, it is more *natural* to man but more foreign to a nature which is in itself dead nature [still life]. One sees here what difference – at the same time interior and exterior – divides the significations of nature, life, animality, humanity, art, speech, and song. The animal who, as we have seen, has no relationship to death, is on the side of death. Speech, on the other hand, is *living* speech even while it institutes a relation to death, and so on. It is presence in general that is thus divided. "From this it is evident that painting is closer to nature and that music is more dependent on human art. It is evident also that the one is more interesting than the other precisely because it does more to relate man to man, and gives us some idea of our kind. Painting is often dead and inanimate. It can carry you to the depth of the desert; but as soon as vocal signs strike your ear, they announce to you a being like yourself. They are, so to speak, the organs of the soul. If they also paint solitude for you [*s'ils vous peignent aussi la solitude*], they tell you you are not there alone. Birds whistle; man alone sings. And one cannot hear either singing or a symphony without immediately acknowledging the presence of another intelligent being" (Chap. XVI).

Song is at the orient of music but it does not reduce itself to voice any more than voice reduces itself to noise. In the *Dictionary of Music*, Rousseau confesses his embarrassment in the article *Song* [*chant; tune* in the contemporary English translation]. If the song is indeed "a kind of modification of the human voice" it is difficult to assign to it an absolutely characteristic [*propre*] modality. After having proposed the "*calcula [tions] of intervals*" Rousseau advances the most equivocal criterion of "*permanence*," and then of melody as "*imitation* of the accents of the speaking or passionate voice." The difficulty is that the concepts of an intrinsic and systematic description must be found. No more than the voice does the song disclose its essence in an anatomical description. But vocal intervals are also alien to the system of musical intervals. Rousseau therefore hesitates, in the *Dictionary* as much as in the *Essay*, between two necessities: of marking the difference between the systems of vocal and musical intervals, but also of reserving all the resources of song in the original voice. The notion of *imitation* reconciles these two exigencies within ambiguity. The first chapter of the *Essay* corresponds in part to this passage in the article *Song*:

> It is very difficult to determine in what the voice which forms the words, differs from that which forms the song. This difference is sensible, but we cannot very clearly perceive in what it consists, and when we seek to find it, we find it not. Mons. Dodart has made anatomic observations, by favor of which he thinks really to discover, in the different situations of the larynx, the cause of two kinds of voice. But I do not know if these observations or the consequences drawn from them, are to be depended on. There seems to be wanting to the sounds which form the discourse, no more than *permanence*, to form a real *song*: It appears also, that the different inflexions which we give to the voice in speaking, form intervals which are not at all harmonic, *which form no parts of the system in our music*, and which consequently not being expressed in notes, are not properly a *song* for us. *The song does not seem natural to mankind.* Tho' the savages of America sing, because they speak, yet *a true savage never sung.* The dumb don't sing, they form only accents without permanence, a disgustful [*sourds* – muted] bellowing which their wants draw from them. I should doubt, if the Sieur Pereyre, with all his ingenuity, could ever draw from them any musical air. Children scream, cry, but they don't sing. The first expressions of nature have nothing in them melodious or sonorous, and they [children] learn to sing, as to speak, from our example. The melodious and appreciable tune, is only an artificial imitation of the accents in the speaking or passionate voice. *We cry, we complain, without singing; but, in song, we imitate cries and laments; and as, of all imitations, the most interesting is that of the human passions, so of all the methods of imitating, the most agreeable is the song.* (Only the word song [*chant*] is italicized by Rousseau.)

Through that example one may analyze the subtle functioning of the notions of nature and imitation. On several levels, nature is the ground, the inferior step: it must be crossed, exceeded, but also rejoined. We must return to it, but without annulling the difference. This difference, separating the imitation from what it imitates, must be *almost nil*. Through the voice one must transgress the nature that is animal, savage, mute, infant or crying; by singing transgress or modify the voice. But the song must imitate cries and laments. This leads to a second polar determination of nature: it becomes the unity – as ideal limit – of the imitation and what is imitated, of voice and song. If that unity were accomplished, imitation would become useless: the unity of unity and difference would be lived in immediacy. Such, according to Rousseau, is the archeo-teleologic definition of nature. *Elsewhere* is the name and the place, the name of the non-place of that nature. Elsewhere in time, *in illo tempore*; elsewhere in space, *alibi*. The natural unity of the cry, the voice, and the song, is the proto-Greek or the Chinese experience. The article *Voice* analyses and amplifies the same debate around the theses of Dodart and of Duclos (in the article *Déclamation des anciens* in the *Encyclopaedia*). The differences among languages are measured by the distance which, in the system of each language, separates the voice of speech from the voice of song, "for as there are languages more or less harmonious, whose accents are more or less musical, we take notice also, in these languages, that the speaking and singing *voices* are connected or removed in the same proportion. So, as the Italian language is more musical than the French, its speaking is less distant from song; and in that language it is easier to recognize a man singing if we have heard him speak. In a language which would be completely harmonious, as was the Greek at the beginning, the difference between the speaking and singing voices would be nil. We should have the same voice for speaking and singing. Perhaps that may be at present the case of the Chinese."

2. We have just accepted two pieces of evidence: the unity of nature or the identity of origin is shaped and undermined by a strange difference which constitutes it by breaching it; we must account for the origin of the *voice of speech* – therefore of society – *before* assigning, and *in order to assign*, its possibility to music, that is to say to the *voice of song*. But since in the *beginning* of the *all-harmonious* voice, word and song are (were) identified, *before and in order to* have perhaps a juridical or methodological meaning; they have no structural or genetic value. One might have been tempted to accord a structural value to the difference between speech and song, since Rousseau recognized that the latter comes to "modify" the former. But the archeoteleological concept of nature also annuls the structural point of view. In the beginning or in the ideal of the all-harmonious voice, the modification becomes one with the substance that it modifies. (This scheme has a general value and governs all discourses, from the moment that they make the smallest appeal to any of these notions, no matter which one: nature and its other, archeology and eschatology, substance and mode, origin and genesis.)

Of course, the methodological or juridical point of view has no rigorous value the moment the difference of value between the structural and

genetic points of view is annulled. Rousseau does not notice this consequence but we should recognize that it would wreak havoc to more than
one discourse.

We must now study the consequence. It is a matter of presenting, with
reference to the origin of language and society, a certain number of oppositions of concepts indispensable for understanding at the same time the
possibility of both speech and song. And above all for understanding the
tension or the difference that, in language as in music, operates at once as
opening and menace, principle of life and of death. Since *the first* speech
must be *good*, since the archeo-teleology of the nature of the language and
the language of nature dictate to us, as does "the voice of nature," that the
original and ideal essence of speech is song itself, one cannot treat the two
origins separately. But as the method of the discourse must retrace its path
and take into account the historical regression or degradation, it must
separate the two questions provisionally and, in a certain manner, begin
with the end.

This then is the story. For the history that follows the origin and is added
to it is nothing but the story of the separation between song and speech. If
we consider the difference which fractured the origin, it must be said that
this history, which is decadence and degeneracy through and through, had
no prehistory. Degeneration as separation, severing of voice and song, has
always already begun. We shall see that Roussau's entire text *describes*
origin as the beginning of the end, as the inaugural decadence. Yet, in spite
of that description, the text twists about in a sort of oblique effort to act *as if*
degeneration were not prescribed in the genesis and as if evil *supervened upon*
a good origin. As if song and speech, which have the same act and the same
birthpangs, had not always already begun to separate themselves.

Here one reencounters the advantages and dangers of the concept of the
supplement, and also of the concept of "fatal advantage" and "dangerous
supplement."

The growth of music, the desolating separation of song and speech, has
the form of writing as "dangerous supplement": calculation and gram-
maticality, *loss of energy and substitution*. The history of music is parallel to
the history of the language, its evil is in essence graphic. When he under-
takes to explain *how music has degenerated* (Chapter 19), Rousseau recalls
the unhappy history of the language and of its disastrous "perfecting": "To
the degree that the language improved, melody, being governed by new
rules, imperceptibly *lost* its *former energy*, and the *calculus of intervals was
substituted for nicety of inflection*" (italics added).

Substitution distances from birth, from the natural or maternal origin.
Forgetfulness of the beginning is a calculation that puts harmony in the

place of melody, the science of intervals in the place of the warmth of accent. In this weaning of the voice of speech, a "new object" comes at once to usurp and compensate for the "maternal traits." What suffers then from this is the "oral accent." Music thus finds itself "deprived of its" proper, that is to say natural and moral, "effects": "Melody being *forgotten*, and the attention of musicians being completely turned toward harmony, every-thing gradually came to be governed according to this *new object*. The genres, the modes, the scale, all received new faces. Harmonic successions came to dictate the sequence of parts. This sequence having *usurped the name* of melody, it was, in effect, impossible to recognize the *traits of its mother* in this new melody. And our musical system having thus *gradually* become purely harmonic, it is not surprising that its *oral tone* [*accent*] has *suffered*, and that our music has lost almost all its *energy*. Thus we see how singing *gradually* became an art entirely *separate* from speech, from which it takes its origin; how the harmonics of sounds resulted in the *forgetting* of vocal inflections; and finally, how music, restricted to purely physical concurrences of vibrations, found itself *deprived* of the moral power it had yielded when it was the *twofold voice of nature*" (italics added).

The points italicized in the passage should guide a subreading of this text and of many analogous texts. On each occasion one would notice:

1. That Rousseau weaves his text with heterogeneous threads: the in-stanteous *displacement* that *substitutes* a "*new object*," which institutes a substitutive supplement, must constitute a history, a progressive becom-ing *gradually* producing the *forgetting* of the voice of nature. The violent and irruptive movement that *usurps*, *separates* and *deprives* is simultane-ously described as a progressive implicating of, and a gradual distancing from, the origin, a slow growth of a disease of language. Weaving together the two significations of supplementarity – substitution and accretion – Rousseau describes the replacement of an *object* as a deficit in *energy*, the production of a re-placement as effacement by forgetting.

2. The adverb "doubly" [twofold] summons up in its own condition of possibility the metaphor of the voice of nature: "gentle voice," maternal voice, song as original voice, sung speech conforms to the prescriptions of natural law. In every sense of this word, nature speaks. And to hear and understand the laws formed by her gentle voice – which, as we recall, "no one is tempted to disobey," but which one must have been tempted to disobey – it is necessary to find again the "oral accent" of sung speech, take possession again of our own lost voice, the voice which, uttering and hearing, understanding-itself-signifying a melodious law, "was the twofold voice of nature."

6

Poetry and music

Richard Wagner

From Richard Wagner, *Gesammelte Schriften und Dichtungen*
(Leipzig: E. W. Fritzsch, 1887–8), reprinted Hildesheim: Georg
Olms, 1976, 10 vols., *Oper und Drama* (vol. III, p. 222–vol. IV,
p. 229), 'Dichtkunst und Tonkunst im Drama der Zukunft',
vol. IV, Part III, pp. 103–5, 108–12, 115–17.

New translation for this volume by W. Edgar Yates.

Wagner's theoretical writings have achieved a considerable reputation, despite being rather turgidly written – and unavailable to the
English reader in a modern translation. We commissioned this translation of a part of Wagner's argument on the relationship between
poetry and music in order to give English readers a comprehensible
taste of Wagner's thought. The reference towards the end of this item
to the composer of 'songs without words' is to Mendelssohn.

Hitherto poets have sought in two respects to make the language of words,
the self-sufficient medium of the intellect, compatible with the expression
of feeling – for which they have wanted to use it as a means of communication directed at the emotions: in *rhythm*, by the use of *metre*, and in *melody*,
by the use of *terminal rhyme*.

In respect of metre the poets of the Middle Ages still took close account
of *melody*, both in the number of syllables and especially in the stress. The
dependence of verse on a stereotyped melody, to which it was related only
superficially, degenerated into slavish pedantry, as in the schools of the
Mastersingers; then more recently a metre generated from prose and completely independent of any actual melody was created by taking as a model
the rhythmic metrics of the Greeks and Romans as transmitted in ancient
literature. Attempts to imitate and adopt this model, at first holding on to
what was most familiar, developed so gradually that we could not become

completely aware of the fundamental error on which they were based until inevitably we not only attained an ever better understanding of the rhythms of the ancients but also, through our attempts to imitate them, came to realise the impossibility and barrenness of this imitation. We know now that what produced the limitless variety of Greek metre was the integral living connection of the gesture of dance with the sound of verbal language, and that all the verse forms generated in this way were exclusively conditioned by a language that had been formed in just this interconnection, so that from the starting point of *our* language, whose cultural motivation was quite different, we are barely capable of grasping their rhythmic character.

What was distinctive about Greek culture is that it gave so strong a priority to the purely physical appearance of Man that we have to regard this as the basis of all Greek art. Through the medium of language, lyrical and dramatic works of art gave spiritual life to this physical appearance in motion, while monumental plastic art was ultimately its undisguised deification. The Greeks felt driven to develop the art of music only to the extent that it supported gesture, whose content was expressed verbally in language itself. By being used to accompany the movement of dance, the sound of verbal language acquired a fixed prosodic measure, that is, a purely physical weighting in the heaviness and lightness of the syllables, in accordance with which their relative length was determined. Though the basis of this was purely physical, it was not arbitrary, for even in respect of language it was derived from the natural properties of the vowels in the root-syllables, or the relation of those vowels to strengthened consonants; and it so definitely determined the rhythm that the accentuation of syllables – even of syllables without natural stress – ceded to it, this however being compensated in the melody by the emphasis of linguistic stress.

[...]

Where no attempt had been made to create a rhythm for verse based on a prosody of long and short syllables, as was the case in the Romance nations, and where in consequence the line of verse was based entirely on the number of syllables, terminal rhyme established itself as an indispensable condition of verse.

[...]

This momentum driving towards the final syllable was entirely in keeping with the character of the language of the Romance nations. After the multiple fusion of alien and obsolete elements, this language had developed in such a way that any understanding of its original roots was completely inaccessible to feeling. We can see this most clearly in French, in which the accentuation of the spoken language has become the very opposite of that emphasis on root-syllables that would feel natural in any residual connection with the linguistic roots. The French never emphasise any syllable other than the final one in a word, however early the true root may lie in longer or compound words, and however insignificant the final syllable may be. Within a phrase, they compress all the words into a monotonous, ever-accelerating assault on the final word, or rather the final syllable, which they then dwell on with a strongly increased accentuation, even when – as is usually the case – that final word is by no means the most important in the phrase. For in complete contradiction to this spoken accentuation, a phrase in French is constructed with its determining elements brought together at the beginning, whereas in German, for example, these determining elements are held back to the end of the phrase. It is not hard for us to trace this conflict between the content of the phrase and the accentuation of its expression back to the influence of terminal rhyme in verse on ordinary language. As soon as ordinary language starts to express a special emotion, it involuntarily adopts the character of that verse, a relic of the older melody, while German in a similar situation adopts alliteration, as in "*Zittern und Zagen*" ("shiver and shake") or "*Schimpf und Schande*" ("stigma and stain").

But the principal characteristic of terminal rhyme is, therefore, that without meaningful connection with the phrase it has the effect of a mere device for manufacturing verse, a last resort to which ordinary language feels driven whenever it seeks to express a heightened state of emotion. By comparison with the mode of expression in everyday speech, verse with terminal rhyme is an attempt to express an elevated subject in such a way as to make a corresponding impression on feeling by communicating in a way that differs from everyday expression. But precisely this everyday expression was the medium of intellectual communication from mind to mind; by using a different, more elevated medium, the human being doing the communicating wanted to some extent to avoid the intellect, to address feeling as distinct from intellect. He sought to do this by reawakening in the ear, the sensual organ of language-reception (which accepted intellectual communication automatically, unselfconsciously), an awareness of its own activity by stimulating a purely sensual pleasure in the expression itself. Verse with terminal rhyme can, it is true, hold the attention of the organ of hearing to the extent that, when listening, it feels tied to the recurrence of the rhyme; but the ear is drawn only into attentiveness, that is, it is drawn into a heightened expectation, which must be fulfilled to the entire capacity of the ear if it is to evoke such lively sympathy and satisfaction in the ear that it can communicate the delight of its reception to the

entire human capacity for feeling. Only when the whole emotional capacity of the human being has been completely roused into sympathy with a
subject communicated to him by the receptive sense can that emotional
capacity attain power enough to expand from a state of complete compres-
sion – to expand, that is, inwards, so as to provide the mind with infinitely
enriched and seasoned nourishment. The sole aim of every process of communication is *understanding*; the aim of the poet is in the last analysis communication with the mind, but in order to attain the intended understanding
with certainty he does not start by fixing the mind at the point he is aiming
at. Rather, he wishes the mind itself to some extent to work creatively in
the process of understanding. And the organ giving birth to this creative
process is, so to speak, Man's own emotional capacity. But that emotional
capacity is only favourable to this productiveness when moved by conception to the supreme excitement in which it attains the power to give birth.
This power, however, arises only from necessity, and that necessity from
the growing superabundance of what has been conceived. For what forces
an organ to give birth is only its overpowering fullness, and the act by
which the understanding of poetic intention gives birth is the communication of that intention by the receptive feeling to the inner mind. It is this
act that we must regard as bringing to a close the necessity for the productive creative feeling.

If the poet is unable to communicate his intention to the immediate
organ of hearing so fully that his communication generates the supreme
excitement that drives the communication forward to the whole human
capacity for emotion, he has only two possibilities open to him. Either he
can debase and blunt that organ by making it, as it were, forget its infinite
power of conception; or he can completely forgo its infinite powers of co-
operation, let go the bonds of its sensual sympathy, and use it again only
as slavishly dependent, communicating thought to thought, mind to mind:
that is, in effect the poet will give up his intention, he will stop creative
writing, he will excite the receptive mind only to combine what it knows
already, what is old, what has already been transmitted to it by sensual
perception, and will no longer transmit to it any new subjects at all. By
merely intensifying his language into rhymed verse he can only force the
receiving sense of hearing to an indifferent, childishly superficial attentiveness to inexpressive rhyme, incapable of extending inwards. The poet's
intention was not just to arouse an indifferent attention of that kind, but
he is finally driven to abandon any participation by feeling and to dispel
its fruitless excitement completely, in order to return to undisturbed communication with the intellect. We shall learn to recognise more clearly
that supreme productive excitement after we have first tested in what rela-

tion our modern music stands to the rhythmic or terminally-rhymed verse of present-day poetry and have observed the influence this verse has been able to exercise on it.

[. . .]

If ever any poet really aspired to elevate the means of linguistic expression available to him to the convincing fullness of melody, he would always first of all have had to try to use as the sole determining driving force for verse the accentuation of speech, in such a way as to establish precisely in its pattern of regular recurrence a healthy rhythm essential both to the verse and to the melody. But not a trace of this is to be seen anywhere, or if any trace can be recognised at all, it is only where the writer of verse abandons from the outset any poetic intention – writing, in fact, not as a poet at all but as a mere journeyman, serving the absolute authority of the musician by counting out and assembling rhyming syllables, with which the musician, profoundly contemptuous of the words themselves, can then do whatever he pleases.

How indicative it is, by contrast, that certain beautiful verses by Goethe – verses, that is, in which the poet sought so far as possible to create a certain melodic momentum – are generally described by musicians as being too beautiful, too perfectly finished, to be set to music. The truth of the matter is that for the meaning even of these verses to be completely captured in a musical composition they would first have to be reduced to prose and then re-created, on the basis of that prose, as an independent melody; for to our musical feeling it seems instinctive that the *verse* melody is similarly only something that has been *thought out*, a seductive form invented by the imagination, and in that sense quite different from musical melody, which has to express itself in a clearly realised sensual form. If therefore we regard such verses as too beautiful to be set to musical composition, that only means that we regret having to destroy them as verses – something we allow ourselves with less unease when what we are confronted with is a literary effort commanding less respect. We thereby admit to ourselves that we are completely unable to imagine an authentic relationship between verse and melody.

The modern melody-maker, who had an overview of the fruitless attempts to establish a suitable mutually complementary and creative relationship between the language of verse and tonal melody, and who was in particular aware of the malign influence on melody – distorting it into musical prose – exercised by accurate reproduction of the accentuation of the spoken language, felt forced, rejecting the distortion or complete denial of verse by trivial melody, to compose melodies from which he completely avoided any troublesome contact with verse (which he respected for its own sake but found too irksome in the context of melody). He called them "songs without words". And quite rightly songs without words gave rise to disputes, which could be settled only by leaving them undecided. The "song without words", which is now so popular, is the authentic translation of our entire music to the realm of the piano, for comfortable manipulation by the travelling salesmen of our art. In the song without words the musician says to the poet: "Do whatever you like, and I too will do what I like. We get along best when we have nothing to do with each other!"

Let us see now how we can reach this "musician without words" in such a way that by the compelling power of the highest poetic aspiration we lift him down from his cushioned piano stool and transport him into a world of the highest artistic potential, which will reveal to him the creative power of the word – which, weak as a woman, he gave up without a struggle, and to which Beethoven himself gave life through the painful birth-pangs of Music.

7

Oral mnemonics for the Japanese *noh* flute

David Hughes

David Hughes, 'No nonsense: the logic and power of acoustic-iconic mnemonic systems', *British Journal of Ethnomusicology*, 9:2 (2000), pp. 93–102.

In Hughes' essay, square brackets are used to distinguish vowel and consonant sounds, according to common practice in linguistics. See Hughes' note on page 55 for details.

Introduction

In the *New Grove dictionary of music* (Sadie, 1980), solmization is defined as the "use of syllables in association with pitches at a mnemonic device for indicating melodic intervals." The paragraph goes on to claim: "Such syllables are, musically speaking, arbitrary in their selection . . ." (in Sadie 1980:458; unsigned).

The present article demonstrates that many systems of syllables for transmitting melodic intervals are far from being "musically speaking, arbitrary": on the contrary, in such cases the particular choice of vowels to represent melodic flow is acoustically well motivated, highly regular and shows consistency across numerous music cultures. In addition, there are syllabic systems that transmit information other than or in addition to intervals, such as duration, loudness, resonance, timbre, attack and decay; most of these similarly use vowels and consonants in non-arbitrary ways. Since the latter are not, strictly speaking, solmization systems, a broader term is needed to embrace all systems where there is a close and highly regular connection between sonic aspects of the mnemonic syllables and of the corresponding musical phenomena. I propose the admittedly awkward term *acoustic-iconic mnemonic systems*. This reflects the fact that certain phonetic features of the syllables – both vowels and consonants – are in an iconic relation to the musical sounds they represent; that is, they mimic or resemble them closely acoustically, as onomatopoeic words imitate sounds. But the connection between an onomatopoeic word and its referent is often far from obvious to someone who does not already know, whereas the principles behind acoustic-iconic systems (though not their precise application) are universally accessible to human experience. Thus we shall see that musicians from Japan and Uganda might well be expected to find each others' mnemonic systems mutually intelligible.

The term "nonsense syllables" is often used to describe such mnemonics. This article, however, endeavours to show that, although lexically meaningless, such syllables make eminent sense once their logic is understood.

Such systems depend for their effectiveness upon their orality: to fully experience the impact of the syllables, one must sing or recite them, preferably aloud but at least in one's head. Such systems have often come to be written down as well, as we shall see, but even in these cases their oral use is likely to continue in parallel.

The basic logic underlying acoustic-iconic mnemonic systems allows them to function successfully and with impressive consistency even though the users are generally unaware of the full details of this logic. Consciousness is not necessary for these systems to function, because they are based on perceptions that are universally available, even if subliminally. It is a major aim of this article to demonstrate that these perceptions do exist, and then to explain why. This discussion may have some practical relevance. In Japan, for example, there is some resistance among younger students to the use of such mnemonics. As I believe in their utility, I would like to have the evidence to convince such learners that the traditional method is still useful.

Oral mnemonics in Japanese music

Let me describe my first few lessons on the *nōkan*, the flute of Japan's Noh theatre, in 1979. The teacher was Fujita Daigorō, a "Human National Treasure." At the first of our 25-minute weekly lessons, I proudly showed him the Noh flute that I had just bought. He looked it over, said "Very nice", and to my surprise handed it back without even trying it. Then we spent the rest of the session singing the syllables in Figure 7.1. This is the melody of the four-line repeated flute motif central to the "Chū no mai" dance. The flute was not used.[1]

At our next lesson, once he was satisfied that I had memorized these lines, he handed me a folded Japanese fan and had me imitate his finger movements on a similar fan while I sang the mnemonics. The fan was held more or less as the flute would be, but not against the mouth.

Fig. 7.1 Noh flute solmization for "Chū no mai" repeated section. Pitches are notional: both pitches and intervals can vary each time they are sung

Finally in the third lesson he allowed me to pick up my flute. We then practised as we had with the fan, singing the mnemonics over and over yet again, only this time with me fingering on the flute. It was not until the fourth week, however, that I was at last allowed to actually blow into the flute. At no time during these four weeks did my teacher ever pick up his own flute.

Playing the flute for that first time, "thinking" the mnemonics as I did so, the melody seemed to come out naturally (although not with the subtle ornamental detail of a mature version). The fingers knew where to go, and the syllables continued to course through my mind. The pitches and intervals were doubtless different, since we had never sung at any specific pitch, and as I already knew, there was no standard pitch or tuning pattern for Noh flutes anyhow, as they never need to accompany other melodic instrument or singer. But I felt a very close identity between what we had sung and what I was now playing. Eventually I learned the entire "Chū no mai" by the same method. No written notation was offered by my teacher at any time.

Mnemonics of this type in Japan are most commonly called *shōga* (or *kuchi-shōga* by modern scholars). They exist for many instruments, both melodic and rhythmic. Singing of *shōga* is standard in learning not only the Noh flute but also, for example, the wind instruments of *gagaku* (court music). And it is equally valued in the latter case, as the following example shows.

In the late 1980s a group of London-based musicians had been striving to perform *gagaku*, using five-line staff notations and recordings, with some guidance from myself. When an ensemble of *gagaku* musicians conducted workshops at my university, we performed our two pieces for them. Their leader charitably claimed to be impressed with how close we had come to the sound, considering that our instruments were mostly Chinese rather than Japanese. But he remarked that it was obvious that we had not learned in the traditional way, namely by first singing the *shōga*: had we done so, he said, the entire flow of the music would have been different – more natural and correct. Even today, beginning court musicians may spend not weeks but years learning pieces via *shōga* before playing the relevant instrument.

Why is *shōga* considered – and indeed why is it – so valuable in learning Japanese music? On one level it could be merely that singing the melody in advance, with much of its ornamental detail, implants it firmly in your mind. But then, why not just sing "la la la" (or "ra ra ra")? It is clearly because the acoustic-iconic nature of the vowels and consonants adds an important dimension to the memorization process, one that (from my own experience) seems to translate easily into direct performative action on the instrument. Let us now consider the elements that make such mnemonic systems effective.

The nature of acoustic-iconic systems

Both the consonants and the vowels of *shōga* and other acoustic-iconic systems help the learner internalize the sound of the desired musical output and often its technique of production. They can do this because each choice of consonant and vowel is likely to reflect some feature(s) of the musical sound in a relatively direct and intrinsic way. This is in sharp contrast to, say, tonic sol-fa, where the choice of "do, re, mi . . ." to represent particular scale degrees is truly "musically speaking, arbitrary", a historical accident; or to North Indian *sargam*, whose syllables were also selected for reasons other than their sound. Each type of system has its advantages. Sol-fa is arbitrary but 100% consistent; acoustic-iconic systems are rarely 100% consistent, but what they lose in precision they gain in relevance.

Space will not permit extensive notated examples (for which see Hughes 1989, 1991), but here are a few observations, beginning with the role of consonants. For wind instruments, initial consonants generally mimic the attack or onset of a pitch. In Figure 7.1, the lack of a consonant before the opening [o] indicates a relatively smooth onset rather than an abrupt tongued attack (An [h] begins many breath phrases whose first note falls on a downbeat, and is similarly non-abrupt.) The following [hy-] does not interrupt the air flow, and nor does the flautist do so, but the two-element sound reflects the fact that there is usually a grace-note ornamentation at this point linking the first two main notes. The ensuing [r] between identical vowels, which is pronounced as what acousticians call a "flap", indeed marks a simple finger-flap to articulate the beat, with no breath pulse. The *shōga* for the superficially similar flute (*ryūteki*) of *gagaku* has some differences: thus the attack at the start of a phrase is similarly gradual, yet unlike the Noh flute it is marked in *shōga* by a [t], with its inevitable abrupt onset as the tongue tip is pulled away from the roof of the mouth: [taa-fa'a-roru ta . . .]. The [t] may not mimic the attack with precision, but it does mark a cutting of the air stream that distinguishes this note's attack from those of the subsequent notes of the phrase ([fa, ro . . .]).

Looking at other cultures as well, we find that "stop" consonants such as [p, t, k, b, d, g] generally mark the sharp attack of a plucked string or struck membranophone or idiophone. The deeper pitches are more commonly marked by the voiced consonants [b, d, g]; thus the open bass string of Japan's *shamisen* lute is sung as [don] vs. the [ton] of the higher-pitched open middle string, and [d] represents a deeper, more resonant sound than [t] or other voiceless sounds in mnemonics for Javanese drums ([tak dung dhah]), many Middle Eastern drums ([dum tek]), Brazilian musical bow *berimbau* ([chin don]) and so forth. There are acoustic-phonetic reasons underpinning this which cannot concern us here.

To reflect a two-element sound, a consonant cluster may be used: a rapid two-hand sequence on the Javanese *ciblon* drum is called [dlang]; the octave chord on a Javanese *gambang* xylophone is expressed as [klèng] or [klong] in a nineteenth-century poem (Poerbatjaraka 1987:267). Or a chord on a string instrument can be marked by a more complex fricative or affricate [sh] or [ch] rather than a simple stop consonant, as in *shamisen* double-stop [chan, shan] vs. single-string [ten, ton].

Final consonants often help show decay. In many drum mnemonics, a final [k] (or other stopped sound) represents a damped stroke, while a final nasal or vowel shows that the sound is left to resonate and decay naturally. Since a wind or bowed instrument generally can sustain a note with little or no decay or timbral change, their solmization tends simply to prolong the vowel. But a longer note on a plucked string or a struck instrument is often distinguished from a shorter one by adding a nasal consonant [n, m, ng].

In sum, consider then finally a *shamisen* passage such as [tereren don]: [t] for normal pluck, [r] for gentler left-hand pizzicato or up-pluck, [d] for deeper pitch, [n] to indicate that the last two sounds are prolonged but decay noticeably. Thus every consonant has an acoustic-iconic role to play. But what about the vowels?

Vowels, mnemonics and relative pitch

The remainder of this article will focus on the role of vowels and on homologies between their acoustic features and those of the musical phenomena they represent. In general, the use of consonants in mnemonics strikes me as being fairly straightforward and common-sense. With vowels, the factors determining their use seem less immediately apparent to most people, although after explanation many people suddenly do find them relatively intuitive or obvious. Vowels are often used in accordance with any of three characteristics: what phoneticians call their Intrinsic Pitch, Intrinsic Duration and Intrinsic Intensity.

Let us look first at Intrinsic Pitch, which is by far the most powerful and interesting of these three. In a sonogram, each (normal, voiced) vowel appears as a fundamental (the pitch at which the vocal cords vibrate) plus various relatively dense regions of overtones reflecting that vowel's characteristic resonance pattern (just as for a musical instrument). These latter regions are called formants, and they are crucial to "forming" the vowel's acoustic profile. To simplify the situation for our purposes, we can consider the vocal tract, from larynx to lips, as consisting of two primary resonating chambers: one between the larynx and the point of narrowest constriction between the tongue and the roof of the mouth; the other between this point of maximum constriction and the lips. Figure 7.2 shows the approximate shape of the vocal tract for the vowel [i]. The deeper chamber, marked "F1 [first formant] area", can be called the throat cavity, and the other (F2 = second formant) the mouth cavity.

Although in normal speech the tension on the vocal cords determines the vowel's most clearly heard pitch, its fundamental, these two cavities also resonate in response to certain harmonics of the vocal cords, producing pitches which are at least subliminally perceived – necessarily so, or else the vowel would lose its identity. The pitch of the fundamental can vary freely, but the sizes of the mouth (F2) and throat (F1) cavities, and hence their vibrational frequencies, remain fairly constant for a particular vowel. The resonant frequency is, of course, in inverse proportion to cavity size, and due to the structure of the vocal tract, F1 will always be lower

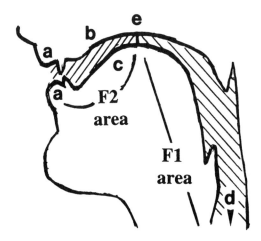

Fig. 7.2 Shape of vocal tract for vowel [i], showing the F2 and F1 resonating chambers (a = lips; b = palate; c = tongue; d = to the larynx; e = point of maximum constriction)

		i	e	a	o	u
Spanish	F2	2300	1900	1300	900	800
	F1	275	450	725	450	275
Japanese	F2	2200	1900	950	750	900
	F1	250	450	600	450	300
Korean	F2	2031	1834	1292	840	920
(ŭ = 1155, ŏ = 999)						

Fig. 7.3 Frequencies in Hz of first formant (F1) and second formant (F2) of Spanish, Japanese and Korean vowels (from Delattre 1965:49, Han 1963:56 and Onishi 1981:672). Spanish and Japanese figures = average male voice; Korean figures = one male speaker. Absolute pitch will vary, but relative pitch patterns persist.

than F2. Figure 7.3 shows typical F1 and F2 values for five standard vowels in three languages.

Of course, the vowels are not quite the same in each language, but you will notice a similarity in ordering. In any language, a vowel close to [i] will have an F2 value higher than a vowel close to [e], and both will be considerably higher than for [a], and so on. For F1 a different pattern obtains. The reasons for these patterns, though too complex to explain here, make good physiological sense.

The values shown in Figure 7.3 will also vary somewhat with the individual speaker, and under influence of neighbouring sounds, and of course with the specific dialect. For example, Japanese [u], which in the standard language is pronounced with minimal lip-rounding, has an F2 value closer to 750 Hz when more rounded, as often in *shōga*, in most dialects, and when adjacent to the more rounded [o].

Now let us return to the *shōga* of the Noh flute. It turns out that there is a remarkably regular correlation between the ordering [i a o u] of the four vowels used and the relative pitches of their associated notes. To demonstrate this, I made a matrix as shown in Figure 7.4, with the four vowels used listed on both axes. Next I compared the *shōga* and the melody: for each successive pair of syllables, I made an entry in the matrix showing whether the associated melody pitches ascended (+), descended (−) or stayed the same (=). For example, the first two syllables [o hya] in Figure 7.2 are linked to a rise in pitch, so I add one point after the plus sign in row [o], column [a]. An examination of five representative Noh flute compositions yielded the data in Figure 7.4.

This table shows, for example, that when a syllable containing [i] was followed by one with [o], the melody at that point descended in 34 of 35 cases in our sample. It can be seen from Figure 7.4 that [i] represents the highest position in this hierarchy: in pairs involving [i] and another vowel, the former's corresponding pitch is higher in 160 of 167 cases (96%). (Let us ignore the repeated pitches for now.) The vowel [a] ranks second: it is lower than [i] in 58 of 62 cases, and higher than [o] in 44 of 45 pairs (the exception falling across a phrase boundary). The vowels [o] and [u] are not clearly ranked in relation to each other: they seem to share the bottom rung. Notice that the sequence [a u] represents a falling interval in 17 of 22 cases, whereas the reverse sequence [u a] is equally often rising or

2nd vowel 1st vowel	i	a	o	u
i	+1	+0	+1	+0
	−0	−28	−34	−23
	=7	=1	=0	=1
a	+30	+4	+0	+4
	−4	−0	−13	−17
	=0	=17	=1	=1
o	+17	+31	+0	+11
	−0	−1	−0	−8
	+0	=0	=4	=0
u	+28	+8	+5	+2
	−0	−9	−6	−4
	=0	=8	=0	=2

Fig. 7.4 Vowel pitch succession in Noh flute solmization

falling. Intrinsic Intensity or Duration may be the reason in the latter case [. . .]. Overall, then, we can say that the four vowels of this system are ranked in pitch from high to low as follows: [i], then [a], then [o/u] together, with some exceptions.

Is this an arbitrary ordering? Could we switch, say, [i] and [a] through-out Noh flute *shōga* with no disruption to the learning process? No: the vowels must be correlated with melodic direction in close correspondence to their F2 ordering. I base this claim on a number of similar examples [. . .] where relative pitch is indicated by syllables whose vowels are in approxi-mate F2 order. Figure 7.5 is a summary chart of several of these, but others could also be cited.

What all of these systems have in common is that there is no extrinsic reason why the vowels in each case should be in this order, unlike the origins of Western solmization with Guido of Arezzo and a certain poem text. The systems in Figure 7.5 owe their existence, structure and utility

Intrinsic Pitch (F2)	i e a o u
1 Noh flute	i a o/u (see above)
2 *hichiriki* (*gagaku* oboe)	i e a o u (unpubl.)
3 *ryuteki* (*gagaku* flute)	i a o u (1989:6)
4 *p'iri* (Korean oboe)	i e a ŭ o u; or: i e a/ŭ/o u(1991:313)
5 *chŏk* (early korean flute)	i a/o ŏ /u (1991:313ff.)
6 Kim kisu's notation system for Korean ornamentation	i e a/ŭ o ŏ (1991:315ff.)
7 *berimbau* (Brazilian musical bow; Hélène Rammant personal communication, December 1999)	i o (as in [din don])
8 Sundanese gamelans' comparative overall pitch levels	i e a o u (1989:11)
9 Scots bagpipes *canntaireachd* oral notation (fixed pitches)	i e a o ʌ (1989:11)
10 Lesotho drurns (Joe Legwabe personal communication 5/92)	i a/u (as in [digidagididum]); also: e o
11 Thai drums	i a o (as in [ting t'am / cha cho])
12 Middle East drums	e u (as in [dum tek])
13 Manding drums (discography D5)	i a u (as in [ba di nin kun])

Fig. 7.5 F2-based relative-pitch syllabic systems. Vowels listed from high to low; see Hughes 1989, 1991, pages shown, for details and original sources. Korean ŭ = [ɨ], ŏ = near [ɔ].

precisely to their close adherence to F2 ordering. I say only "close adherence" because in both Japanese and Korean, as Figure 7.3 shows, [u]
generally has a higher F2 value than [o], yet [u] overwhelmingly represents a lower pitch. [. . .] In any case, it will be convenient and not too
misleading to call these "F2 systems".

The systems shown are varied in their functions. The F2 principle can
be found operating to represent: relative pitch of successive melody notes
(examples 1–7 in Figure 7.5); relative pitch of the tuning systems of entire
gamelans (example 8); fixed scale degrees (example 9); relative pitch of
different drumstrokes (examples 10–13); and yet other possibilities not
discussed here.

Note that the majority of F2 systems indicate *relative* pitch relations, not
absolute pitch. For example, in Noh flute solmization (Figure 7.1), the
vowel [i] can occur in conjunction with several different absolute pitches,
and so can the other three vowels. There is no one-to-one association of a
vowel and a pitch (unlike, say, the names of Western pitches). Unlike the
Noh flute, the two melodic winds of *gagaku* are tuned to specific pitches and
operate within a fixed-pitch system, and yet here too there is no regular
connection. Figure 7.6 shows how often each vowel is associated with
each pitch in a varied sample of *gagaku* pieces.

It can be seen that in *ryūteki* mnemonics, which follow the order [i a o
u] 98% of the time, the vowel [i] is linked to nine different pitches over a

	hichiriki	*ryūteki*
d″	-	5i
c″	-	2i
b′	-	18i, 5a
a′	13i	10i, 23a
g′	5i, 4e	19i, 7a, 10o, 3u
f(♮)′	1i, 31e, 20a	6i, 15a, 17o, 11u
e′	41a, 2o, 2u	35a, 9u
d(♮)′	17i, 1a, 3u	4i, 4a, 29o, 2u
c(♮)′	16i, 1a, 8o, 5u	6o, 8u
b(♭)	43o, 2u	32o
a	1i, 11o, 10u	13o, 4u
g	-	2i, 1o
f(#)	6u	1i, 4u
e	-	1u

Fig. 7.6 Relation between vowels and absolute pitches for *hichiriki*
and *ryūteki*. *Hichiriki* sounds one octave higher than shown; *ryūteki*
sounds two octaves higher

range of nearly two octaves; in the *hichiriki* with its narrower range, it is linked with six of the nine possible pitches. The other vowels are also promiscuous, if less so. This sort of variation is characteristic of what I have called "vowel-pitch solfège systems" but perhaps could have better named "relative-pitch F2 systems". It relates directly to the fact that the users of such systems are almost never consciously aware of the acoustic logic behind them [. . .].

Note

1 In this article, vowels in square brackets indicate a loose usage of the International Phonetic Alphabet (IPA), sufficient to our needs but with some typographical substitutions for a non-specialist readership. The symbols [i I e a ʌ ɔ o u] are to be pronounced approximately as in American English "beat, bit, bait/bet, bah, but, bought, boat, boot" respectively, though never as diphthongs; [ɨ] is as in "book" but with the tongue somewhat farther forward and less lip-rounding; [ü] is like [i] but with lips rounded; [y] represents its normal English value as in "yet", and [ng] is as in "sing".

References

Delattre, Pierre (1965) *Comparing the Phonetic Features of English, French, German and Spanish: An Interim Report* (London: George G. Harrap).

Han, M. S. (1963) *Acoustic Phonetics of Korean* (Los Angeles: University of Southern California Press).

Hughes, David W. (1989) 'The historical uses of nonsense: vowel-pitch solfège from Scotland to Japan', in M. L. Philipp (ed.), *Ethnomusicology and the Historical Dimension* (Ludwigsburg, Germany: Philipp Verlag), pp. 3–18.

—— (1991) 'Oral menemonics in Korean music: data, interpretation and a musicological application', *Bulletin of the School of Oriental and African Studies*, 54:2, 307–35.

Onishi, Masao (ed.) (1981) *A Grand Dictionary of Phonetics* (Tokyo: Phonetic Society of Japan).

Poerbatjaraka (1987) 'Radèn inu main gamelan: bahan untuk menerangkan kata pathet', in Judith Becker et al. (eds), *Karawitan*, vol. 2 (Ann Arbor: Center for South and Southeast Asian Studies, University of Michigan), pp. 261–84 (in English).

Sadie, Stanley (ed.) (1980) *New Grove Dictionary of Music and Musicians*, 6th ed. (London: Macmillan).

8

Drum signalling in a West African tribe

George Herzog

George Herzog, 'Drum-signaling in a West African tribe', *Word*,
1 (1945), pp. 217–38, reprinted in Thomas A. Sebeok and
Donna Jean Umiker-Sebeok (eds), *Speech Surrogates: Drum and
Whistle Systems. Part I* (The Hague: Mouton, 1976), pp. 553–8.

Although this item refers to Herzog's work in Liberia, he also refers to
the 'Togo Mandate': at this time Togo was administered by the French
and British governments under a League of Nations mandate, the
British-governed part later joining the independent state of Ghana.

The use of musical instruments for purposes of signaling is very widespread, and definite systems of communication are or were based on it in
native Africa, Middle and South America, and the Pacific. The African
systems are the most elaborate and often serve for free conversation; their
existence is well known to the anthropologist and the traveler, but they
have been little investigated from the linguistic point of view, and still less
in their social setting. The few studies we have establish beyond doubt that
in Africa this signaling, usually on drums, is based on a direct transfer into
a musical medium of spoken language-elements: pitch or tone, which is of
fundamental importance in most African languages, and some other phonetic features. Consequently, we do not deal here with a code such as the
Morse code, in which the ascription of meaning to a series of symbols is
purely conventional, nor with an intertribal code (as has been reported
erroneously time and again). Communication between tribes speaking different dialects or languages is, of course, feasible, and is practised, but all
it requires is that the drummers in the border-area be to some extent bilingual. They can even learn to identify a number of signals in the neighboring language together with their approximate meanings, without knowing
the text in the other language, or its exact translation. In exceptional cases,

however, signaling does function like a conventional code. For instance, the Ewe of the Togo Mandate who learned drum signaling from their Twi neighbors do not transpose the Twi signals into Ewe; they drum Twi signals, but give them Ewe meanings. If the drummer is bilingual, or if he understands at least the Twi texts, he is not involved with a code; otherwise he is, and so are his listeners. Naturally, signals constitute a code for any native listener who is not sufficiently familiar with the technique.

I had the opportunity in 1930 to study the signaling of a West African tribe, the Jabo of Eastern Liberia, in full detail. The late Edward Sapir began a study of this language with the assistance of a native speaker resident in the United States who came from the township of Nimiah, a politically independent subdivision of the Jabo. Sapir found unusually complex tonal phenomena not reported from Africa hitherto – 4 tone-registers, utilization to an unusual degree of tone-differences for grammatical purposes, a large number of tonal changes due to the interaction of neighboring tones, and the existence of 'tone-classes' (morphophonemic word-classes displaying differences in tone-behavior). He felt that these findings should be checked with other speakers in Africa and had the inspiration, characteristic of his particular imagination, that an investigation of drum-signaling would also serve as a further check on the language data. The subsequent expedition in which Sapir's informant participated substantiated Sapir's brilliant work on both levels, and added a considerable body of new linguistic material.

The main results of this study are: signaling in Eastern Liberia follows linguistic features closely and in unusual detail; it is practiced on a great variety of instruments, some of which do not serve for communicating over a distance, but only for other purposes; signaling as a technique is intricately interwoven with phenomena of social life and structure; it displays the same type of sophistication which we know of African music and folklore; and it shows complex and subtle transitional forms between language and music. The language of signaling is, to some extent, a technical language. It is highly poetic, which is connected with the heroic connotations of warfare in this region, and with the elevated style of the language-symbols that surround offices of wordly authority or are embodied in dealings with supernatural powers. Signaling is employed in all these contexts. But, curiously enough, the very requirements of rational intelligibility also call for the employment of poetic forms. In Jabo, as in many languages of the Sudanese family, most stems are monosyllabic. Thus the bare occurrence in a signal of a beat for the name of a person, an animal, or an object could mean a large number of different things, so that it becomes exceedingly useful to expand the context of the word with a paraphrastic formula, such as a proverb or an honorary title which characterizes the person or animal. Then it is no longer a single beat, but a particular rhythmic and melodic motif which identifies the subject. The rich African development of honorary appellations, names, titles, and proverbs, highly poetic in themselves and used extensively in songs and stories, thus saturates the style of signaling; but even so, and partly just because of the high aesthetic requirements, the bulk of signaling is apt to be practiced and fully understood only by specialists.

These observations are likely to hold, on the whole, for much, if not most, of Negro Africa. It is probably a specialized local phenomenon that in Eastern Liberia a very large number of signals have texts which are or pretend to be in neighboring languages; and this also makes signaling difficult for the average person. The predilection for foreign material may indicate that signaling spread comparatively recently in this region; it may reflect comparatively recent population movements. Yet it is also bound to be connected with the constitution of the population; the region is thickly studded with innumerable small tribes who hold intensive intercourse with each other, and regard the stronger tribes with wholesome respect. Much of the Jabo signaling and poetic material is in Kru or in *soi-disant* Kru, the language of a powerful tribe to the West; much of it in Grebo, a tribe to the East who settled on the coast before the Jabo and influenced the culture of the latter in many ways. Jabo drummers of Nimiah are still supposed to go for the study of signal-drumming to Trembo, where a different Jabo dialect is spoken. In the following study, only the summary results are submitted. Since differences between the systems on the different instruments are not negligible, only drum-signaling is treated here [. . .].

The signal-drums of Eastern Liberia are of two types. The first are the wooden forms without a skin head, usually hollow cylinders, which are found in so many places of the world, with or without a signaling function. Technologically, they are not drums, but bells. The others are skin-covered drums, single-headed. In contrast with much of West Africa, the use of skin-covered drums for signaling is quite restricted in Eastern Liberia, but that of the wooden drums is elaborate.

The wooden signal-drum or 'slit-drum' consists of a hollowed-out tree-trunk with a longitudinal slit, the lips of which vary in thickness between themselves and in different places of the same lip, thus providing a number of points for producing various tones. Two straight sticks are used for beating, and different tones are also produced by different positions of the sticks in the hands, or by striking with a different part of the stick. A large instrument, over eight feet in length, may be used alone or in conjunction with a smaller drum about half of its size, but both played by the same drummer. The drums are the property of the military and policing organization of the town which includes all males, and which holds periodic assemblies and social gatherings. The drummer, a regular official of this organization, signals to a distance when he summons a member who may be in the fields to come to the village, or when an assembly is called unexpectedly. But the main duty of this drum is to serve somewhat like a chairman's gavel. The drummer regulates the meetings; he calls for order or dismisses the meeting, and so on, with special signals. In addition, on special occasions when war-like celebrations are held, he plays the praising titles of warriors or eminent men, who then advance and boast of their deeds, holding a dialogue with the drum, in which a horn-player may also join. Their female relatives are expected to come forth and offer gifts to the instrumentalists. Every mature man of some standing has a special title on this drum by which he is called, and which may refer to his deeds, character or social status; although the title may equally well be teasing or gossipy, in harmony with the fact that the men's organization functions also as a social dub. More martial and serious titles are given to men on the horn, in praising songs, and in formal greeting.

The bulk of the material which the drummer employs consists, then, of a large number of fixed formulas, variations, and additions to the fixed formulas. The latter are frequently repeated during one 'communication', with variants and other forms interspersed. There is no exchange of communications between villages on these drums, or on the skin-covered ones, a technique so common elsewhere in Africa. Single signals can be conveyed from village to village, but this is rare. Naturally, when a village hears these drums from the next village or tribe, it is at once clear that something is 'going on', either a meeting, or a war-like celebration, including a war dance, or actual preparations for war. A town or a small tribe will have only one set of these drums, and two or three individuals who play them well enough to be able to substitute for the regularly appointed drummer. The Jabo-speaking tribe of Nimiah, in which the study was made, consists of the Upper and the Lower Town (the latter on the seashore), with about 600 souls each, and a few smaller settlements. Although there is considerable rivalry and duplication of political institutions between the two towns, only the Upper Town, which is older and is the residence of the tribal chief, had these drums. The lower town could, technically, borrow them, but only against a sizable fee.

Signal-drumming is considered difficult by the natives. In the course of the study, I learned how to play every signal, first on one drum, then on two, wrote them down in notation, and recorded them also acoustically –

accomplishments equally astounding to the natives, although the finer points of variation and ornamentation were not mastered. The bare signals are fairly simple according to our musical standards, but local Whites or Americo-Liberians, unacquainted with the linguistic foundation, naturally cannot find their way in the system.

The skin-covered signal-drum is slightly personified; it has an honorary title. Elsewhere in West Africa, drums of this type have personal names and have sex ascribed to them according to their size. (The large Jabo wooden signal-drum has the name of God's wife.) The drum is a large hollowed wooden trunk, six to eight feet long; every village has one, and it is the official signaling instrument of the village, with its official player. It is usually lashed to the side of a house and slanted at an angle so that the player standing facing the skin head can play it. If need be, a similar drum may be used instead which, together with a set of smaller drums, is normally played for women's dances. In this case it stands upright on the ground, and the drummer stands behind it on a little platform. It is beaten with two quite heavy, straight wooden sticks. Different tones are produced by beating either the center of the head or a place nearer the edge, which gives a higher tone since the skin is more taut; and the two sticks are unequal in weight, which also enters into the tone-difference. Only a limited number of signals are used – the drummers knew only five – and no conversation is feasible. The signal is preceded by a series of evenly spaced rapid beats, to call for quiet and attention; this is repeated three times. Then comes the signal, three times, then again the call for attention, and so on as long as necessary. This call does not represent word-meaning. The signals are all short; some in surrounding languages.

Dance-drums. Various smaller drums of both types are used in dancing, with or without a large one. They play, for the most part, strictly musical rhythms without word-meaning; they 'sing' to use the native expression, although word-meaning has been read into some of these musical rhythms. Four wooden slit-drums and one small skin-covered drum are used, without the singing voice, to accompany the war-dance of the men, which is a highly acrobatic affair as far as the dancing and the drumming of the leading drummer are concerned. The natives take considerable pride in the excellence of these performances, good teams visiting neighboring tribes and performing for them in exchange for copious gifts, food, and acclaim. The leading drummer of such a team uses two small wooden drums, one of them being the optional adjunct to the signal-drum in signaling, and the large signal-drum itself being demoted in this ensemble to playing a purely musical, simple rhythmic role. Every piece consists of an arrangement of definite musical rhythms in a loosely fixed order, but before the end of the piece, as a signal of its approaching end, the leading drummer beats out a few times a set motif which has word-meaning, while the other drummers pause. As with the xylophone pieces, the text of this motif is the name of the piece itself; it is apt to revile enemy tribes and to refer to old, successful wars and battles. The leading drummer also signals brief snatches to the dancers in which he praises or teases them; these have reference to their manner of dancing. Other snatches, some of them purely musical, serve as signals for the dancers so that they may shift the dance-movements, the latter being regulated in all dancing by the drumming and the leading drummers. In other dances only skin-covered drums are used; the small ones are beaten by the hands and can convey brief signals.

Part II

Song, text and voice

9

The voice as a musical instrument

Simon Frith

Simon Frith, *Performing Rites: Evaluating Popular Music*
(Oxford: Oxford University Press, 1996), pp. 183–91. © Simon
Frith, 1996. Reprinted by permission of Oxford University Press.

This is an extract from Frith's chapter entitled 'The voice', in which
he considers the voice (mainly in popular music) from four different
perspectives – as a musical instrument, as a body, as a person and as
a character. This item focuses on the first of the four.

Look at a song's lyrics on the page: whose "voice" is there? Who's talking?
The answer seems to start with the pronouns, the "shifters," not just the
"I," the apparent speaker, but the "you" and "we" and "she" which reveal
various things about the speaker. Even without an explicit "I," that is, we
have an implicit one, someone who's doing the addressing: "*you've* got a
lot of nerve, to say that *you're* my friend." The "voice" in the printed lyrics
is thus articulated by the text itself, by a process that is both self-expressive
and self-revealing, both declared openly and implied by the narrative.

But even from the reader's point of view there's more to the voice than
this. The printed lyric is already a double act, both the communicative
process it describes or enacts – the "I" of the lyric speaking to the "you" of
the lyric – and the communicative process it entails, writing and reading.
As readers do we necessarily become the "you" of the writer's "I"? Do we
take onto ourselves her love or contempt? Do we have to take a place in
her story? The answer is obviously no; or, at least, there are certainly other
options. We can refuse to become involved at all, read the lyric as an over-
heard conversation between other people, take it to be reported speech, put
quotation marks around it. Or we can read it as if speaking it, become the
"I" ourselves. (I think it would be impossible to read Bob Dylan's "Posi-
tively 4th Street" as if we were the "you" at issue – and this is a song posi-
tively *obsessed* with the word. The pleasure of these lines is as a means of
sounding our *own* feelings of contempt and hauteur.)

How we read lyrics is not a completely random or idiosyncratic choice. The lyricist sets up the situation – through her use of language, her construction of character – in a way that, in part, determines the response we make, the nature of our engagement. But once we say that, we admit that there's another "voice" here, the voice of the lyricist, the author, the person putting the words in the "I's" mouth, putting the protagonists into their lyrical situation. And the authorial voice can be more or less distinctive; we may recognize – respond to – that voice (Cole Porter, Elvis Costello, Morrissey, P. J. Harvey) even when reading a lyric. "Voice" in this sense describes a sense of personality that doesn't involve shifters at all, but is familiar as the special way a person has with words: we immediately know who's speaking.

Now stop reading the lyrics, and listen to the song. Whose voice do we hear now? Again there's an obvious answer: the singer's, stupid! And what I argue [. . .] is that this is, in fact, the stupid answer. We hear the singer's voice, of course, but how that voice relates to the voices described above is the interesting question. To sing a lyric doesn't simplify the question of who is speaking to whom; it makes it more complicated.

In *The Composer's Voice*, Edward Cone asks whose voice we hear when we listen to a Schubert setting of a poem by Goethe. We hear a singer, Thomas Allen say, with a distinctive physical voice; we hear the protagonist of the song, the "I" of the narrative; we hear the poem's author, Goethe, in the distinctive organization of the words and their argument; and we hear Schubert, *in whose voice* the whole thing is composed. And this last definition of voice, as the stylistic identity of the composer, is undoubtedly the dominant definition of "voice" in classical music criticism: a Schubert song is a Schubert song, regardless of whose words he has set to music and which singer is singing them. Schubert's "voice" thus refers to a personal quality – a quality of his personality – apparent in all his musical work.[1]

Even in this phrasing, though, a new question is raised. What is the relationship between Schubert's characteristics *as a composer* (his distinctive use of musical language which can be traced across different works, enabling us to speak of his musical "identity" and "development") and his characteristics *as a person*? This is, of course, to raise the long-debated question (long debated in literary criticism, at any rate) of the relationship between someone's life and their work. This issue tends to be put aside in music criticism because of the belief that music is a more directly emotional form of expression than literature, and is therefore more directly (or unconsciously) revealing of the composer's character. One of Anthony Storr's casual comments can thus be taken as typical: "The listener doesn't even have to be able to read music to recognize Haydn's robustness and humour, combined with his capacity for deep feeling.[2] Is music really so transparently expressive of personality? Is a voice?

The same questions can be addressed to popular music. What is the relationship between the "voice" we hear in a song and the author or composer of that song? Between the voice and the singer? This relationship has, of course, different complications in different genres, but two general issues arise immediately. First there is, as in classical music, the problem of biography: what is the relationship of life and art? On the whole, pop fans are less simple-minded than classical music critics about this. While one can certainly find Hollywood biopix of pop stars (Oliver Stone's *The Doors*, say) to match its biopix of classical composers – the life pouring out in the sounds – this tells us more about Hollywood (and the attempt to turn Jim Morrison into a Real Artist) than it does about pop music.

The up-front star system means that pop fans are well aware of the ways in which pop performers are inventions (and the pop biographer's task is usually therefore to expose the "real" Bob Dylan or Madonna who *isn't* in their music). And in pop, biography is used less to explain composition (the writing of the song) than expression (its performance): it is in real, material, singing voices that the "real" person is to be heard, not in scored stylistic or formulaic devices. The pop musician as interpreter (Billie Holiday, say) is therefore more likely to be understood in biographical terms than the pop musician as composer (Mark Knopfler, say), and when musicians are both, it is the performing rather than the composing voice that is taken to be the key to character. As Robert O'Meally asks about Billie Holiday, "She was the greatest jazz singer of all time. With Louis Armstrong, she invented modern jazz singing. Why do these accounts [all the books about her], which tell us so much about her drug problems, no-good men, and supposedly autobiographical sad songs, tell us so little about Billie Holiday, artist?"[3]

And the answer is because as listeners we assume that we can hear someone's life in their voice – a life that's there despite and not because of the singer's craft, a voice that says who they really are, an art that only exists because of what they've suffered. What makes Billie Holiday an artist from this perspective is that she was able to give *that which she couldn't help expressing* aesthetic shape and grace. Compare Gregory Sandow on Frank Sinatra:

> Even before Kitty Kelley's unauthorized biography it was hardly a secret . . . that Sinatra hasn't always been the nicest of guys. So it's a commonplace of Sinatra criticism to separate Sinatra the artist from Sinatra the man. But I've always thought that his character slips through in his perfor-

mance . . . And in fact it slips through precisely because of his art. Because
he *is* an artist, he can't help telling a kind of truth; he can't help reaching
towards the root of everything he's felt. He makes his living singing love
songs; like any great popular singer, he can expand even a single sigh in those
love songs into something vast. But he's also got his own story to tell, a story
that goes far beyond what any love song could express: it's a story a little bit
about triumph, partly about a lust for power, often about loss, and very much
about humiliation and rage.[4]

The first general point to make about the pop voice, then, is that we hear
singers as *personally* expressive (even, perhaps especially, when they are
not singing "their own" songs) in a way that a classical singer, even a
dramatic and "tragic" star like Maria Callas, is not. This is partly a matter
of sound convention. As Libby Holman once put it, "My singing is like
Flamenco. Sometimes, it's purposefully hideous. I try to convey anguish,
anger, tragedy, passion. When you're expressing emotions like these, you
cannot have a pure tone."[5]

In classical music, by contrast, the sound of the voice is determined by
the score; the expression of anguish, anger, tragedy, and passion is a
matter of musical organization. As Umberto Fiore writes, "In this context,
the voice is in fact an instrument: bass, baritone, tenor, soprano and so
forth. Individual styles can only *improve* these vocal masks, not really
transgress them . . . the creation of a person, of a character, is substantially
up to the music as such; if truth is there it is a *musical* truth."[6]

But if we hear the pop singer singing "her self," she is also singing a song,
and so a second question arises: what is the relationship between the voice
as a carrier of sounds, the singing voice, making "gestures," and the voice
as a carrier of words, the speaking voice, making "utterances"? The issue
is not meaning (words) versus absence of meaning (music), but the relationship between two different sorts of meaning-making, the tensions and
conflicts between them. There's a question here of power: who is to be the
master, words or music? And what makes the voice so interesting is that
it makes meaning in these two ways simultaneously. We have, therefore,
to approach the voice under four headings: as *a musical instrument*; as *a
body*; as *a person*; and as *a character*.

I'll begin with the voice as a musical instrument. A voice obviously has
a sound; it can be described in musical terms like any other instrument, as
something with a certain pitch, a certain register, a certain timbral quality,
and so forth. Voices can be used, like any other instrument, to make a noise
of the right sort at the right time. Both these terms (right sort, right time)
are apparent in the most instrumental use of the voice, as "backup." Here
the singers' sound is more important than their words, which are either

nonsensical or become so through repetition; and repetition is itself the key to how such voices work, as percussive instruments, marking out the regular time around which the lead singer can be quite irregular in matters of pitch and timing, quite inarticulate in terms of words or utterances.

Even in this case, though, the voices can't be purely sound effects; at the very least they also indicate gender, and therefore gender relations (the aggressive-submissive attitude of the Raelettes to Ray Charles; the butch male choral support for Neil Tennant on the Pet Shop Boys' "Go West"), and it is notable that while rock conventionally uses other male voices, other members of the band, to sing close harmonies, backup singers are almost always female – and remarkably often black female at that. This raises questions about the voice as body to which I'll return; but in talking about the voice as musical instrument I'm not just talking about sound, I'm also talking about skill and technique: neither backup nor lead singers simply stand on stage or in the studio and open their mouths. For the last sixty years or so, popular singers have had a musical instrument besides their voices: the electric microphone. The microphone made it possible for singers to make musical sounds – soft sounds, close sounds – that had not really been heard before in terms of public performance (just as the film closeup allowed one to see the bodies and faces of strangers in ways one would normally only see loved ones). The microphone allowed us to hear people in ways that normally implied intimacy – the whisper, the caress, the murmur. O'Meally notes the importance of the mike for the development of Billie Holiday's singing style, "as she moved from table to table in speakeasies . . . Whether in clubs or on recording dates, she continued to deliver her lyrics as if only for one or two listeners whom she addressed face to face."[7]

The appearance of the female torch singer and the male crooner had a number of consequences both for musical sexuality (crooners were initially heard as "effeminate" and unmanly, for example; the BBC even banned them for a time) and for what one might call musical seduction (radio advertisers took immediate note of "the performer's capacity to make each member of the audience perceive the song as an intimate, individual communication;" and Rudy Vallee quickly became "one of the biggest radio and advertising successes").[8] As Bing Crosby, probably the greatest musical entrepreneur of the twentieth century (or at least the one with the best understanding of the implications of technology) realized, crooning made a singer the perfect salesman of his own song.

This wasn't a matter of singers just going up to a microphone and opening their mouths, either. Mike technique had to be learned. Take the case of Frank Sinatra:

As a young singer, he consciously perfected his handling of the microphone. "Many singers never learned to use one," he wrote later. "They never understood, and still don't, that a microphone is their instrument." A microphone must be deployed sparingly, he said, with the singer moving in and out of range of the mouth and suppressing excessive sibilants and noisy intakes of air. But Sinatra's understanding of the microphone went deeper than this merely mechanical level. He knew better than almost anyone else just what Henry Pleasants has maintained: that the microphone changes the very way that modern singers sing. It was his mastery of this instrument, the way he let its existence help shape his vocal production and singing style, that did much to make Sinatra the preeminent popular singer of our time.[9]

One effect of microphone use is to draw attention to the technique of singers *as singers* in ways that are not, I think, so obvious in classical music or opera, as they move with and around the instrument, as volume control takes on conversational nuances and vice versa. Another is to draw attention to the *place* of the voice in music, to the arrangement of sounds behind and around it, as the microphone allows the voice to dominate other instruments whatever else is going on [. . .]

Even when treating the voice as an instrument, we come up against the fact that it stands for the person more directly than any other musical device. Expression with the voice is taken to be more direct than expression on guitar or drum set, more revealing – which is why when drums and guitars are heard as directly expressive they are then heard as "voices." And this argument has legal sanction. Lawyers in cases of musical theft assume that a voice is a personal property, that it can be "stolen" in a way that other instrumental noises cannot (James Brown's vocal swoop is recognizably his immediately; a guitarist has to prove that a melodic riff, a composition rather than a sound, is unique). The most interesting legal rulings in this context concern soundalikes, cases in which the voices used ("Bette Midler," "Tom Waits") *weren't* actually theirs, and yet because they were recognizably "the same" could nevertheless be adjudged to invade the stars' "privacy;" to steal their "personality." To recognize a voice, the courts ruled, is to recognize a person.[10]

Notes

1 Edward T. Cone, *The Composer's Voice* (Berkeley: University of California Press, 1972), chap. 1.
2 Anthony Storr, *Music and the Mind* (London: HarperCollins, 1993), p. 117. Storr also tells us that "Wagner's personality was charismatic and so is his music" (p. 120).

3 Robert O'Meally, *Lady Day: The Many Faces of Billie Holiday* (New York: Arcade, 1991), p. 97.
4 Gregory Sandow, "Tough Love," *Village Voice*, January 13, 1987, p. 71.
5 Quoted in John Moore, " 'The Hieroglyphics of Love': The Torch Singers and Interpretation," *Popular Music* 8(1) (1989): 39.
6 Umberto Fiore, "New Music, Popular Music, and Opera in Italy," unpublished paper, n.d., p. 4. His emphasis.
7 O'Meally, *Lady Day*, pp. 31–2.
8 For the BBC see my "Art *vs* Technology: The Strange Case of Popular Music," *Media Culture and Society* 8(3) (1986): 263. For advertising see Roland Marchand, *Advertising the American Dream: Making Way for Modernity, 1920–1940* (Berkeley: University of California Press, 1985), p. 109.
9 John Rockwell, *Sinatra* (New York: Random House, 1984), pp. 51–2.
10 See Jane M. Gaines, "Bette Midler and the Piracy of Identity," in Simon Frith, ed., *Music and Copyright* (Edinburgh: Edinburgh university Press, 1993).

10

Working-class 'country'

Steven Feld, Aaron A. Fox, Thomas Porcello and David Samuels

Steven Feld, Aaron A. Fox, Thomas Porcello and David Samuels,
'Vocal anthropology', in Alessandro Duranti (ed.), *A Companion
to Linguistic Anthropology* (Oxford: Blackwell, 2004),
pp. 328–32.

This extract from a jointly-authored chapter draws most obviously on
the work of Aaron A. Fox (see his *Real Country: Music and Language in
Working-Class Culture* (Durham, NC: Duke University Press, 2004)).

In South-Central Texas, the art of singing "country" music is highly valued
and carefully cultivated, as are critical and aesthetic discourses about
singing (Fox 1995). Country singers are musical specialists, responsible –
like all folk artists – to their local communities for a wide range of performance skills (Bauman 1977); but they are especially respected for their
mastery over (and creative extensions of) a canonical catalogue of vocal
techniques. This case study focuses on several of those techniques, in order
to consider the larger significance of singing as a cultural practice that
presents ramifications for a general theory of music and language.

Many articulatory possibilities are available to working-class country
singers. Fully pitched, metrically regularized, and amplitudinally shaped
singing (with an expansive and exploitable range of voice qualities and
vibratos and phonetic indexes of different modes, registers, genres, and
dialects of "ordinary" speech) is of course a predominant "default" modality. Singers also produce heightened speech, which they call "recitation,"
and which mimics the less rigid meter of speech while retaining a song's
original versification (similar to some types of operatic "recitative" and
other quasi-spoken idioms in many musical drama traditions).

Country singing style also involves frequent importation of fragments of
metrically non-regular and non-pitched speech into song performance
(e.g., bits of dialogue between a singer and a "picker" in the band that are
performatively spoken against the background of a song). Of course, such

"fully spoken" discourse also shapes the boundaries around song performances. Stage patter, bandstand talk, and interactions with audience
members (using intonationally and dynamically heightened speech) can
also be used to move between the spoken frame of song performance and
full singing. Specific transitional gestures between speech and song include
"count-offs," which establish the meter of the song, introductory words
summoning full attention from audiences (for example, many singers
begin songs with the formulaic expression "I said . . ."), and stylized formulae for marking reported speech, including elaborate techniques of
voice imitation, reflecting a strong preference among Southern working-
class Americans for direct discourse over indirect discourse.

Competent singers are often quite consciously aware of this range of
articulations. They may refer to a corresponding set of ethnotheoretical
concepts to describe specific formulae, articulations, and voice qualities.
More commonly, both among singers and among listeners, metamusical
discourse proceeds by analogy (usually comparing one singer's style to
another well-known singer's example), or through a metaphorical vocabulary that emphasizes qualities of "hardness," "sweetness," "sadness,"
"volume," "power," "precision," "ordinariness," and appropriateness of
singing style to textual content and sociomusical context.

All such evaluations are oriented toward the master-tropes of musical
evaluation in South Texas, the sociomusical categories of "feeling" (as
noun and verb) and "relating" (as a mode of telling and a mode of social
and aesthetic engagement). Singers who perform "with feeling" are said
to "relate to" their material, their traditions, and their communities. Likewise, audiences say they can "relate to" singers who sing "with feeling"
(or "feel"). In turn, such evaluative tropes are further summarized through
strongly inflected tropes of genre identification, typically in phrases like
"that's *country*," or (most assertively), "that's *real* country." Such tropes
resonate with a matrix of cultural sensibilities and practices for which
musical style is a summarizing symbol. Evaluations of song performance
thus extend pervasively into assertions of rural, working-class, Southern
social identity and cultural continuity.

Vocal style in Texas country singing can be approached analytically
through a fine-grained description of particular techniques employed by
singers. Many properties of vocal sound (e.g., vibrato, amplitude, articulatory noise, melodic shape, etc.) can be measured and correlated with the
communicative and expressive features of song texts (e.g., explicit affective
verbs, specific references to feeling states, canonical moods of particular
poetic (sub)genres). Similar correlations, considered quite important by
most Texas country singers, can be made between vocal techniques and

the language-structural properties of song texts (many vocal inflections, such as "cry breaks," appear to be conditioned equally by phonological environments and by affective connotations of the referential text).

A continuum of intonational markedness, ranging from unpitched, metrically irregular, but intonationally heightened speech to full pitched, metrically regular singing, is routinely employed to mark structural divisions in song texts, changes of point of view and narrative voice, contrasting affects, and degrees of expressive engagement by the singer. Timbral quality deserves special attention; Texas singers evoke important affects and moods through distinctive changes in the site and manner of voice production. A pharyngealized tone, for example, can be iconic of the ravaged voice of a character textually narrated explicitly or implicitly as "crying." "Crying" itself can be iconically represented with specific inflections known categorically as "cry breaks" – sharp deformations of the melodic line effected through intermittent falsetto or nasalization, pulsing articulations achieved through glottal stops or diaphragmatic tensing, or the addition of articulatory vocal "noise" to an otherwise "smooth" tone. An enormous range of rhythmic and metric possibilities are suggested by the intertwining of musical and linguistic form in country singing as well, ranging from a relatively "natural" delivery that mimics the variable meters of ordinary speech, to the rigidly metrical delivery characteristic of other locally familiar oral genres such as auctioneering.

Working-class singers (and listeners) themselves often attend to these various dimensions of singing style as analytically and technically distinct. But of course the art of singing well involves a less consciously considered blending of these techniques into expressive syntheses that can be drawn upon for specific aesthetic purposes. Most typically, musicians and listeners use a shorthand terminology for such gestalts that refers to the names of canonical singers like George Jones, Merle Haggard, Patsy Cline, Johnny Cash, and Marty Robbins.

'He stopped loving her today'

Since much of the repertoire performed by local singers in Texas comprises "covers" of the classic country canon, the default local practice is to apply (or imitate) the style of the original recording artist associated with each particular song. This is especially true for less accomplished singers, and for those still learning their craft. As Texas singers become more competent and develop individual styles, and as they acquire a repertoire of original songs or covers by obscure artists whose styles are not familiar, they increasingly apply their own distinctive stylistic signature to everything they perform. Eventually they may be said to have "made (even a well-known 'cover') song their own" by fully restyling a canonical song, sometimes with dramatic modifications in affect and meaning from the canonical recording.

Typically, however, such singers retain a special affinity for one or two major stars' styles (and repertoire), and these styles can be instantly recognized as "influences" on their personal styles: Thus, a singer might be classified as singing "in a Marty Robbins (or Merle Haggard, etc.) style." This would not necessarily imply that the singer in question was simply competent in a derivative sense. A rich cultural conception of voice and orality, reminiscent of Bakhtin's theory of voicing in literary discourse (1981), is the basis for such tropes of classification, resonating with the pervasive elaboration in working-class Texas discourse of direct and quasi-direct discourse and extensive voice-imitation in reported speech constructions.

Movements within this range of possible articulations are ubiquitous expressive resources. A careful listening to George Jones's 1980 recording "He Stopped Loving Her Today,"[1] for example, reveals why Jones is widely regarded as the greatest vocalist in the history of country music, especially by his fellow Texans, and why this particular performance is almost universally acclaimed by working-class country fans as among the most important in the history of the genre. What follows is a description of Jones's complex vocal stylization of this song, from beginning to end. Interested readers should have little difficulty locating an audio recording of this legendary song (first released on Jones's 1980 Epic recording "I Am What I Am," but subsequently reissued on many compilations and greatest hits recordings) to supplement the verbal descriptions below.

Jones begins the narration, which is introduced as reported speech ("*He said* 'I'll love you 'til I die' . . . ") by singing lightly, at times coming close to a spoken articulation, glancing off each word with a breathy tone and very delicate vibrato. Subtle changes in pitch quality and metric feel mark the boundaries between verbs of speaking and directly reported discourse. A subtly pharyngealized tone, in which one can hear the ravaging effects of crying on the narrator's voice, conveys the ethos of elegiac sadness that dominates this song. The stressed vowel in the word "slowly" is mimetically elongated as Jones's narrator describes the passage of years during which the protagonist cannot forget his beloved.

Over the course of the song's unusually long sequence of four verses prior to the first refrain, Jones uses modulations in voice quality to intensify the abject poetic scene. These become ever more claustrophobic as the narrator gradually reveals the depth of the male protagonist's obsession with a lost love, as he lives out his "half crazy" life surrounded by objects that serve as shrines to the memory of his beloved (her picture on his wall; her letters, which he keeps by his bed with every "I love you" underlined in red). The vocal line gradually acquires more intensity, with increasingly sustained and amplitudinally shaped notes (i.e., the amplitudinal envelopes of sustained vowels become more elaborate). Jones gradually develops a richer timbre and a broader vibrato as these verses progress. The song modulates up a half-step at the third verse, after Jones reaches for a high note on the desperate line in which we learn the protagonist never stopped "hoping she'd come back again." Jones also gradually increases the use of his trademark melismas, and the entire sequence of verses is characterized by steadily increasing amplitude. These effects combine to create extreme tension and anticipation of a remarkable textual and performative *denouement.*

Finally, in the fourth verse we find out that the narrator has gone to see the protagonist as he is "all dressed up to go away," and finally smiling (marked by the most melismatic articulation yet in the performance) for the first time "in years." At this point, the anticipation of an explosive release of tension is literally unbearable for many listeners.

The long-anticipated refrain, from which the song takes its title, arrives in fullthroated, elaborately melismatic, sustained, and vibrato-rich tones as Jones at last reveals the reason why the protagonist "has stopped loving her today": he has died. He is dressed up and smiling because he is at his own funeral. At last, the somber, elegiac tone of the previous melodramatic verses is narratively justified. However, the song contains an additional poetic relaxation and release, in the following verse and refrain.

Withdrawing, after the refrain, to observe the arrival of the protagonist's long-lost beloved at the funeral, Jones suddenly reverts, with an eerie effect, to what country singers call "recitation" – a loosely metric spoken articulation (breathy, with elongated vowels and heightened intonational movement) which preserves the poetic structure of the composition (rhyme, line breaks, and scansion). This sudden distancing of the narrator from the poetic *mise en scène* demands, as it were, a third vocal persona to emerge from Jones's performance: that of the wry observer, personally uninvolved in the immediate emotional drama of the song. Behind this recitation, in which Jones describes the funeral scene, a wordless female voice laments in an operatic melodic descant, layering the most extreme form of singing (fully pitched, wordless, rich vibrato) behind Jones's move into a quasi-spoken recitation, a juxtaposition of non-referential pure song and song straining toward referential speech that is almost didactic in its representation of the speech/song continuum as it is understood in this musical tradition.

This recitation moves, in a manner typical of the genre, from a description of the scene to the first reported inner speech of the narrator himself (who has otherwise been merely a relatively dispassionate reporter of events). This thought is couched as wordplay – indeed, as reported inner speech – and it delivers the final refrain on the heels of a vertiginous joke that plays on a trite romantic cliché: "This time, he's over her for good." But just as this comic moment seems to break the morbid spell of the tale, the refrain returns, one last time, more fully and powerfully sung than previously, in an all-out quasi-operatic apotheosis in which Jones sweeps grandly through his entire vocal range until relaxing on the final line.

Such masterful examples of vocal style lie at the center of an extremely dense network of vocal practices and expressive ideologies that constitute the discursive and experiential world of working-class Texas communities extending from the most casual forms of talk through a rich range of verbal art genres to song. This network is focused and attended to explicitly in singing practice, but it extends well beyond the boundaries of song *per se*. An analysis of the techniques of Texas country singers reveals the dense relationships between song and speech in this culture. When the focus is expanded to incorporate verbal art, ordinary talk, and the soundscapes of everyday working-class life, one sees, or rather hears, a vivid acoustic refraction of a particular form of sociality materialized in every act of vocalization, and every act of listening. Singing is especially privileged in this community because it allows for a ritualized, explicit consideration (both by community members and by analysts) of the voice as the material embodiment of social ideology and experience. Song stands in an explicitly critical and denaturalizing relationship to "ordinary" speech in rural Texas, as in many other societies.

The parameters and microstructural details that emerge from an analysis of Texas singers' technical practice represent only a small portion of the "voice consciousness" of working-class Texans. And this consciousness, in turn, represents only one perspective, either local or ethnographic, on the social life of these communities. But it is a locally privileged perspective, one that is highly cultivated and deeply valued by community members. This suggests that theorists of the speech/song relationship should engage more fully with local understandings of vocal practice across a wide range of expressive genres. It suggests also that close attention to vocal practice and to the speech/song relationship can provide vital insights into the life of language in human society.

Note

1 "He Stopped Loving Her Today" by Bobby Braddock and Curly Putnam. Copyright 1978, 1980 by American Music. Copyright renewed, assigned to Unichappell Music, Inc. (Rightsong Music, publisher).

References

Bakhtin, M. (1981) *The Dialogic Imagination: Four Essays*, ed. M. Holquist, trans. C. Emerson and M. Holquist (Austin: University of Texas Press).

Bauman, R. (1977) *Verbal Art as Performance* (Rowley, MA: Newbury House).

Fox, A. (1995) "Out the Country;" Speech, Song and Feeling in Texas Rural Working-class Culture. PhD dissertation, Department of Anthropology, University of Texas at Austin.

11

Music, voice, language

Roland Barthes

Roland Barthes, *The Responsibility of Forms: Critical Essays on Music, Art and Representation*, trans. Richard Howard (New York: Hill & Wang, 1985), pp. 278–85.

This item comprises the complete published version of a 1977 lecture: the Swiss-born baritone Charles Panzéra (1896–1976) described here had died in the previous year.

There will be something a little paradoxical about the reflections which follow: they have for their object a unique and special endeavor: that of a singer of French art songs whom I loved a great deal, Charles Panzéra. How can I involve the auditors of a Colloquium whose theme is a general one in what is perhaps only a very personal taste, my enthusiasm for a singer absent from the musical scene for the last twenty-five years and thereby, no doubt, unknown to most of you?

In order to justify or at least excuse so egoistic an enterprise, and one no doubt unsuitable to the customs of such Colloquia, I should like to remind you of this: any interpretation, it seems to me, any discourse of interpretation is based on a positing of values – upon an evaluation. However, most of the time, we conceal this basis: either by idealism or by "scientism," we disguise our evaluation: we proceed "*indifferent* [= without difference] *as to what is valid in itself, as to what is valid for everyone*" (Nietzsche, Deleuze).

It is from this *indifference* of values that music wakens us. About music, no discourse can be sustained but that of difference – of evaluation. As soon as someone speaks about music – or a specific music – as a value *in itself*, or on the contrary – though this is the same thing – as soon as someone speaks about music as a value *for everyone – i.e.*, as soon as we are told we must love all music – we feel a kind of ideological cope falling over the most precious substance of evaluation, music: this is "commentary." Because commentary is unendurable, we see that music compels us

to evaluation, imposes difference upon us – or else we fall into futile discourse, the discourse of music-in-itself or of music for everyone.

Hence, it is very difficult to speak about music. Many writers have spoken
well about painting; none, I think, has spoken well about music, not even
Proust. The reason for this is that it is very difficult to unite language,
which belongs to the order of the general, with music, which belongs to
the order of difference.

If then, on occasion, one can risk talking about music, as I am doing
today, it must not be in order to "commend" scientifically or ideologically,
i.e., *generally* – according to the category of the general – but in order
openly and actively to affirm a value and to produce an evaluation. Now
my evaluation of music involves the voice, and very specifically the voice
of a singer I have known, one whose voice has remained in my life the
object of a constant love and of a recurrent meditation which has often
carried me, beyond music, toward the text and toward language – the
French language.

The human voice is, as a matter of fact, the privileged (eidetic) site of
difference: a site which escapes all science, for there is no science (physiol-
ogy, history, aesthetics, psychoanalysis) which exhausts the voice: no
matter how much you classify and comment on music historically, socio-
logically, aesthetically, technically, there will always be a remainder, a
supplement, a lapse, something non-spoken which designates itself: the
voice. This always *different* object is assigned by psychoanalysis to the category of objects of desire: there is no human voice which is not an object
of desire – or of repulsion: there is no neutral voice – and if sometimes that
neutrality, that whiteness of the voice occurs, it terrifies us, as if we were
to discover a frozen world, one in which desire was dead. Every relation to
a voice is necessarily erotic, and this is why it is in the voice that music's
difference is so apparent – its constraint to evaluate, to affirm.

I myself have a lover's relation to Panzéra's voice: not to his raw, physical voice, but to his voice as it passes over language, over our French language, like a desire: no voice is raw; every voice is steeped in what it says.
I love this voice – I have loved it all my life. At twenty-two or twenty-three,
wanting to learn to sing and knowing no teacher, I intrepidly applied to
the best singer of art songs of the period between the wars – to Panzéra.
This man generously worked with me until illness kept me from continuing my apprenticeship to singing. Since then, I have not stopped listening
to his voice, on the rare, technically imperfect records he has made: Panzéra's historical misfortune is that he ruled over French art songs between
the wars but no testimony to this reign can be directly transmitted to us:
Panzéra stopped singing at the very advent of the long-playing record; we

have only some 78 rpm's of his work, or imperfect rerecordings. Nonetheless, this circumstance retains its ambiguity: for if listening to these records may disappoint today, it is because these records are imperfect, and perhaps more generally because history itself has modified our tastes, so that this way of singing has lapsed into the indifference of the out-of-fashion, but also, more topically, because this voice participates in my affirmation, my evaluation, and because it is therefore possible that I am the only one to love it.

We lack, I believe, a historical sociology of the French *mélodie*, that specific form of music which developed, by and large, from Gounod to Poulenc but of which the eponymous heroes are Fauré, Duparc, and Debussy. This *mélodie* (our word is not a good one) is not exactly the French version of the German lied: through romanticism, the lied, however cultivated its form, participates in a German form of existence at once popular and national. The ecology, one might say, of the French *mélodie* is different: its milieu of birth, formation, and consumption is not popular, and it is national (French) only because other cultures are not much concerned with it; this milieu is the bourgeois salon.

It would be easy, by reason of this origin, to reject the French *mélodie* today, or at least to ignore it. But History is complex, dialectical, especially if we shift to the level of values: as Marx had clearly seen in detaching the "Greek miracle" from the social archaism of Greece, or Balzacian realism from Balzac's theocratic convictions. We must do the same thing with the French *mélodie:* seek out how it can interest us, despite its origins. Here, for my part, is how I should define the French *mélodie:* it is the field [*champ* or *chant*] of celebration of the cultivated French language. At the period when Panzéra sings these songs, such celebration is coming to its end: the French language is no longer a *value*; it is entering upon a mutation (whose characteristics have not yet been studied, or even consciously perceived); a new French language is being born today, not exactly by the action of the "working classes," but under the action of an age class (marginal classes have today become political realities), the young; there is, separate from our language, a young parlance, whose musical expression is *Pop.*

In Panzéra's period, music's relation to the old French language is in its extreme refinement, which is its last refinement. A certain French language is dying out: this is what we hear in Panzéra's singing: it is the perishable which glistens so heart-breakingly in this singing; for an entire art of speaking the language has taken refuge here: *diction* is to be found among singers, not among actors subservient to the petit-bourgeois aesthetic of the Comédie-Française, which is an aesthetic of *articulation* and not of *pronunciation*, as was Panzéra's (to which we shall return).

Panzéra's musical phonetics involves, it seems to me, the following features: (1) vocalic purity, particularly apparent in the French vowels par excellence: the *ü*, a forward, *exterior* vowel, one might say (as if it summons the Other to enter my voice), and the closed *é*, which serves us, semantically, to oppose future to conditional, imperfect to *passé simple*; (2) the distinct and fragile beauty of the *a*'s, the most difficult vowel of all when it must be sung; (3) the grain of the nasals, a little harsh, as though spiced; (4) the *r*, rolled of course, but in no way obedient to the somewhat heavy roll of peasant speech, for it is so pure, so brief, that it merely affords the *idea* of a rolled *r*, as if its – symbolic – role is to virilize gentleness without abandoning it; (5) lastly, the patina of certain consonants, at certain moments: consonants which have "alighted" rather than fallen, sounding "induced" rather than marked.

This last feature is not only deliberate but indeed theorized by Panzéra himself: it constituted part of his teaching, this necessary patina of certain consonants, and served him, according to a project of *evaluation* (once again), to oppose *articulation* and *pronunciation*: articulation, he used to say, is the simulacrum and the enemy of pronunciation; one must *pronounce*, never *articulate* (contrary to the stupid watchword of so many singing manuals); for articulation is the negation of *legato*; it seeks to give each consonant the same phonic intensity, whereas in a musical text a consonant is never the same: each syllable – far from being the result of an Olympian code of phonemes, given in itself and once and for all – must be set (like a precious stone) in the general meaning of the phrase.

And it is here, on this purely technical point, that the scope of Panzéra's aesthetic (and I should add: ideological) options suddenly appears. Articulation, in effect, functions abusively as a *pretense of meaning*: claiming to serve meaning, it basically misreads it: of the two contrary excesses which kill meaning, the vague and the emphatic, the latter is the most serious and the most consistent: *to articulate* is to encumber meaning with a parasitical clarity, useless without being, for all that, sumptuous. And such clarity is not innocent; it involves the singer in a highly ideological art of expressivity – or, to be even more precise, of *dramatization*: the melodic line is broken into fragments of meaning, into semantic sighs, into effects of hysteria. On the contrary, *pronunciation* maintains the perfect coalescence of the line of meaning (the phrase) and of the line of music (the *phrased*, as we call it in French: *le phrasé*); in the arts of articulation, language, poorly understood as a theater, a staging of meaning that is slightly kitsch, explodes into the music and deranges it inopportunely, unseasonably: language thrusts itself forward, it is the intruder, the nuisance of music; in the art of pronunciation, on the contrary (Panzéra's), it is music which enters the language and rediscovers there what is musical, what is "amorous."

For this rare phenomenon to occur, for music to enter language, there must be, of course, a certain *physique* of the voice (by *physique* I mean the way in which the voice behaves in the body – or in which the body behaves in the voice). What has always struck me in Panzéra's voice is that through a perfect mastery of all the nuances imposed by a good reading of the musical text – nuances which require knowing how to produce *pianissimi* and extremely delicate "dis-timbres" – this voice was always *secured*, animated by a quasi-metallic strength of desire: it is a "raised" *voice – aufgeregt* (a Schumannian word) – or even better: an erected voice – a voice which gets an erection. Except in the most successful *pianissimi*, Panzéra always sang with his entire body, *full-throatedly*: like a schoolboy who goes out into the countryside and sings for himself, as we say in French *à tue-tête* [to kill the head] – to kill everything bad, depressed, anguished in his head. In a sense, Panzéra always sang with *the naked voice, à voix nue.* And it is here that we can understand how Panzéra, while honoring the art of the French *melodié* with a last luster, subverts that art; for to sing *à voix nue* is the very mode of the traditional folk song (today often edulcorated by unwarranted accompaniments): Panzéra, in secret, sings the cultivated song as though it were a folk song (the singing exercises he assigned were always borrowed from old French songs). And here, too, we recognize the aesthetic of meaning I so love in Panzéra. For if the folk song was traditionally sung *à voix nue*, that is because it was important *to understand the story*: something is being told, which I must receive without disguise: nothing but the voice and the telling: that is what the folk song wants; and that – whatever the detours imposed by culture – was what Panzéra wanted.

Then what is music? Panzéra's art answers: a *quality of language.* But this quality of language in no way derives from the sciences of language (poetics, rhetoric, semiology), for in becoming a quality, what is promoted in language is what it does not say, does not articulate. In the unspoken appears pleasure, tenderness, delicacy, fulfillment, all the values of the most delicate image-repertoire. Music is both what is expressed and what is implicit in the text: what is pronounced (submitted to inflections) but is not articulated: what is at once outside meaning and non-meaning, fulfilled in that *signifying* [*signifiance*], which the theory of the text today seeks to postulate and to situate. Music, like signifying, derives from no metalanguage but only from a discourse of value, of praise: from a lover's discourse: every "successful" relation – successful in that it manages to say the implicit without articulating it, to pass over articulation without falling into the censorship of desire or the sublimation of the unspeakable – such a relation can rightly be called *musical.* Perhaps a thing is valid only by its metaphoric power; perhaps that is the value of music, then: to be a good metaphor.

12

'Hey Jude'

Tim Riley

Tim Riley, *Tell Me Why: A Beatles Commentary*
(London: The Bodley Head, 1988), pp. 249–55.

"Hey Jude" began as an improvised song of encouragement to Julian
Lennon, John's son by Cynthia, as Paul was driving him home one day.
The Lennons were getting a divorce, and Paul's compassion was directed
toward the child who found himself caught in the middle. With unfinished
lyrics, he brought the song in and played it for Lennon. The two of them
remember the demo session differently:

> I remember I played it to John and Yoko and I was saying, "These words
> won't be on the finished version." Some of the words were "the movement
> you need is on your shoulder," and John was saying, "It's great! 'The move-
> ment you need is on your shoulder.'" I'm saying "It's crazy, it doesn't make
> any sense at all." He's saying "Sure it does, it's great." I'm always saying that,
> by the way. That's me. I'm always never sure if it's good enough. That's me,
> you know. (*Paul McCartney in His Own Words*, p. 23)

> Well, when Paul first sang "Hey Jude" to me – or played me the little tape
> he'd made of it – I took it very personally. "Ah, it's me!" I said. "It's *me*." He
> says, "No, it's *me*." I said, "Check, we're going through the same bit," so we
> all are. Whoever is going through that bit with us is going through it, that's
> the groove. (*The Ballad of John & Yoko*, p. 50)

John read himself right into Paul's song: his involvement with Yoko and
the ensuing divorce with Cynthia happened at the same time that Paul
split from his longtime girlfriend, actress Jane Asher. The lyrics are atypi-
cally self-referential in that way ("You're waiting for someone to perform
with"), as Nicholas Schaffner points out. What's more telling is how
Lennon insisted that Paul keep the lyrics just as they were – Paul introduced them as dummies (like "Yesterday"'s "scrambled eggs"), but Lennon
stamped them completed. This documented instance of who wrote what
and how the other responded shows just how sympathetic they were
to each other's temperaments. They often doctored up one another's
sketches, but "Hey Jude" was so good that Lennon didn't touch it.

As usual, the biographical concerns reveal only so much of what the record is all about; the high spirits resonate beyond any immediate personal references. The communal overtones that were atomized in "She Loves You" are expanded in "Hey Jude"; the singer is singing as much to himself as he is to Jude, but Paul hones in on the joy of that earlier thunderbolt and stretches it into an anthem. The beat is grand rather than manic, and the choral refrain coda outlasts the song itself. "Hey Jude" reflects a larger realm of experience, and conveys a richer vision of how good life can get.

Paul starts the song alone with an immediacy of feeling, an urgency he can no longer suppress. He sings with the hope that something just may come of his effort, and by the end a sad song *is* made better. Part of this transformation lies in the journey from a lone voice to a chorus of others singing with him – the implicit message is faith in other people, the rejuvenating effect of shared singing. But in trying to cheer someone else up, Paul discovers his own capacity for healing. The process of singing the song testifies that uplifted spirits are *earned*, not just willed: no peace is possible without struggle, "Hey Jude" tells us, and although the journey must be shouldered alone, the strength of community sees the singer through. Instead of escape ("Tomorrow Never Knows") or withdrawal (the alternative world of *Sgt. Pepper*), "Hey Jude" declares human experience as the only path toward enlightenment. (That it accomplishes this much on one side of a hit 45 makes it all the more encompassing.)

The solo vocal opening is Paul's balladic answer to Lennon's naked outbursts (in "No Reply" and "You're Going to Lose That Girl"). As with the solo vocal that trips "Penny Lane," the emotional tone is engaging from the first few seconds. The compassion lies in the gentle fall between the two title words, and the sound has a hue that radiates warmth and empathy. Paul holds the pedal down to let the simple piano chords ring fully; their rhythmic cadence is ripe with feeling. By the end of the first verse, the melody is an old friend.

The suppleness of Paul's voice couldn't be sweeter – he caresses the words, soaring through the contours of a line as if in free flight, hugging its curves and gliding on its plateaus. The cut-off delivery of "re-mem-bah" is soft, not clipped; he enjoys singing through the consonants as much he enjoys holding the vowels. Like all great singers, he invites the listener into the song without conceit; the artistry lies in the seeming ease with which he greets us.

The second verse adds guitar (left) and a single tambourine (center) as the understated grace gains fluency. The vocal harmonies ("ah") that enter during the second half of this verse (behind the words "the minute") hint at the glory to come and help ease the groove for the drum fill into the first bridge. As Ringo offers a restrained tom-tom and cymbal fill, the piano shifts downward to add a flat seventh to the tonic chord, making the downbeat of the bridge a point of arrival ("And any time you feel the *pain*"). The singer arrives a split second before the downbeat does, making the moment well up with anticipation. Paul's bass enters here, and the song bursts wide open, just as it will on a larger scale during the transition to the coda.

The downward bass motion that defines the harmony of the bridge settles the groove into a steady pace. The bridge consists of two stanzas, separated by the same piano figure that introduces them. As relief to the midrange of the verses, Paul's voice shoots upward: the bridge begins high and ends low; the verse melody arcs in a rainbow curve. At the end of the bridge (in the subdominant), the "na-na-na"s reorient the harmony for the verse as the piano figure turns upside down into a vocal aside (two steps downward become two steps upward toward the original dominant seventh, a musical question mark). The transition glows with feeling as it reorients the harmony.

To sustain interest in a four-verse, two-bridge song, details are added: tambourine on the third verse, subtle harmonies to the lead vocal. After he sings "Now go and get her," a distant but audible Paul sings "So let it out and let it in, hey Jude," telescoping the lyric of the second bridge in the background. John joins Paul beneath his lead on the line "Remember to let her into your heart" and leaps above him on the next line on the words "start to make it better." When these vocal lines intersect on the line "Remember to let her into your heart," the musical interplay jells into a full-bodied blend. The basic rock ensemble gets colorful long before the choir comes in.

Paul arrives a hair early again at the second bridge ("So let it out and let it in"), but by now he's more at ease with the music – he doesn't have to define this moment the way he did before, he just lets it happen. Like the stage metaphors McCartney sets up in *Sgt. Pepper*, expectation and obligation are weighed; "You're waiting for someone to perform with" casts Jude as a nervous actor overplaying the part. A guitar lick enters in contrary motion to the piano after the words "perform with" (the piano moves downward as the guitar shifts upward). This brief juxtaposition sets Paul off – he sings the next line ad libitum, free from the melody, inspired by the splendor of sound that surrounds him. This is where the most encouraging lines of the song come: "Don't you know that it's just you/Hey Jude, you'll do/The movement you need is on your shoulder" – a tidy compendium of pop clichés that expresses the value of self-reliance and self-trust. Since Paul is singing not only to Jude and himself but to his audience, the metaphorical message is larger: he's telling us that we all share an intuitive talent for living. After the "na-na-na" transition back to the final verse, Paul adds a modest "yeah" beneath the piano's echo to prepare for the final stretch.

The last verse arrives with a strong sense of return – it's like the song has come back home again. This is the last time Paul sings the title line in the verse setting, and he strings it out delicately, with real affection. The single-line harmony that John sings with Paul on this verse, a repetition of the first verse, is more expressive than the harmony he supplies in the third verse. It's their best duet since "If I Fell," not only for its sense of shared experience but for its similarly effortless intricacy – the harmony is just as affecting as the melody it complements. Lennon's presence on the last verse makes what would have been a great solo more of a *band* experience, strengthening the power of what would have been a solo tour de force.

As the last verse comes to a close, a mood of expectancy pervades – the song isn't ending, even though it's supposed to be. Something even bigger is around the corner; and as it slowly begins to appear, the anticipation heightens even further. When Paul begins his ascent on the repeated word "better," the whole mood is transformed from quiet reassurance to liberated ecstasy. The screams that send off the coda are the joy that has been building up throughout the entire song; all hesitation is set loose, and the coda springs to life from beneath the singer's cries with a new commitment. (The repeated progression [I–♭VII–IV–I] answers all the musical questions raised at the beginnings and ends of bridges. The flat seventh that posed dominant turns into bridges now has an entire chord built on it.)

For the remainder of the record, the three-chord refrain provides a bedding for Paul to leap about on vocally. The Beatles asked the forty-piece orchestra to sing along for the chorus, making the seemingly nonsensical "na-na-na"s sound like the spontaneous anthemic climax Paul must have imagined. If ever a trivial pop snippet was apotheosized, it is here. "Yeah, yeah, yeah" may be the early Beatles' cries of romantic enchantment; "na-na-na" is the mature version of the same intoxication with life. Both spring from a desire to say more than can be said with words, and both convey far more than words could ever express.

The seemingly endless string of ad-libbed hoots, hollers, screams, wails and asides that Paul turns in atop this communal glory speaks for his sense of the moment. He has a way of off-handedly inserting a lick or a phrase that gives everything around it a new shape, a new shade of meaning. This is no small talent. By recombining what has come before with new inflections, ornamenting the already sturdy refrain with lines of soaring beauty, he makes "Hey Jude" not only a masterpiece of melodic invention but a recording of unrivalled vocal ingenuity. It becomes a tour of Paul's vocal range: from the graceful, inviting tone of the opening verse, through the mounting excitement of the song itself, to the surging raves of the coda. In seven and a half minutes he goes from refinement to abandon in a continuous escalation of pitch. If the song is about self-worth and self-consolation in the face of hardship, the vocal performance itself conveys much of the journey. He begins by singing to comfort someone else, finds himself weighing his own feelings in the process, and finally, in the repeated refrains that nurture his own approbation, he comes to believe in himself. The genius lies in the way he includes the listener in the same pilgrimage.

13

The voice of Egypt

Virginia Danielson

Virginia Danielson, *The Voice of Egypt: Umm Kulthūm, Arabic Song, and Egyptian Society in the Twentieth Century* (Chicago: University of Chicago Press, 1997), pp. 138–44.

Danielson's study of the legendary Egyptian singer Umm Kulthūm (1904–75) necessarily uses much Arabic terminology, most of which is explained within the text. The terms used but not explained here (having mostly been defined earlier in the book) are as follows: *khanaafa* is a colloquial term for *ghunna* or 'sweet nasality'; *mawwal* (pl. *mawawil*) is a type of colloquial song; *mashayikh* is the plural of *shaykh*, a title conferred on public figures – in this case singers – usually with religious connotations; *qasida* (pl. *qasa'id*) is a genre of sung poetry; *mujawwad* is a style of Quranic recitation; and *asil* means authentic (as in authentically Egyptian or Arab).

Umm Kulthūm's voice itself brought sighs of appreciation. Ordinary listeners used ordinary language for the sound of her voice. For them it was simply "powerful," "beautiful," or "amazing." The speech of experts directs attention to its more specific qualities. They speak of the power, clarity, and bell-like resonance of her voice. Their words offer ways of hearing the nuances she learned and cultivated.

The power of her voice – its volume, resonance, and resilience – that was noticed with amazement by listeners in the 1920s remained a salient characteristic of her sound throughout her life. But she also deployed many colors, among them *bahha* (hoarseness), *ghunna* (nasality), falsetto, and an array of pretty and affective frontal resonances that constantly varied her sound and added impact to the sung text. Her listeners identify *ghunna* as an important marker of authentic singing. A writer for *Rūz al-Yūsuf* devoted a full page to praise of nasality, calling it "what pleases us in the voices of Sayyid Darwīsh, Muḥammad 'Abd al-Wahhāb, and Umm Kulthūm." He likened Umm Kulthūm's voice to the "tones of a *mizmār*" (a double-reed instrument) and concluded that "the sweetest [quality] in her voice is that of *khanaafa.*"[1] When Western culture accrued influence in Egypt, *ghunna* was one of the musical qualities that came to be considered undesirable among those interested in emulating the West. Partisans of European classical music apparently considered all kinds of nasality to be rustic, countrified, or unsophisticated. Racy identifies changes from nasal to nonfrontal resonance in the early twentieth century with Westernization: accordingly, the nasal voice is the local voice and tone color an indicator of identity.

Baḥḥa served at once as a beautiful feature of Umm Kulthūm's rendition and as a way to heighten the emotional impact of the text. It contributed to her most compelling performances, such as that of the religious *mawwāl* "Bi-Riḍaak," and was part of her rendition of almost every song in her repertory for as long as her voice was capable of producing it. Falsetto was linked with a trill, producing vibrant ornaments for the upper range of a line.

Still, listeners rarely reacted to the first note she sang but, rather, to the first phrase. Her rendition of the words was what mattered.

"The song depends before all else on the words," Umm Kulthūm said. "If the words are beautiful, they will inspire the composer and the singer, and the composition will turn out beautifully and the rendition excellent. The more affective the text, so will be the song." "The words, in my opinion," she said, "are what is important [*al-fā'ida*] in music."[2]

Throughout her career Umm Kulthūm was known for her mastery of Arabic language and poetry. To her, it was fundamental: "The singer who does not articulate accurately cannot reach the heart of the listener and is not capable of perfect artistic rendition."[3] It was said that she "tasted each word."

Asked to explain *ṭarab*, the state of "enchantment" wherein the listener is completely engaged with a performance, Umm Kulthūm said that it was attained when the listener "felt" the meaning of the words.[4] Usually she sought to evoke meaning(s) in indirect ways, drawing the listener closer to the themes and emotions of the text, *taṣwīr al-ma'ná*.

Her skills in diction and *taṣwīr al-ma'ná* were invariably noted and appreciated by critics as well as by her larger audience. Bayram al-Tūnisī remarked that "Simple words acquire depth and beauty when she sings them." The scholar Ṭāhā Ḥusayn said that he "listen[s] to her a great deal. I enjoy her excellent delivery of the Arabic language, and I very much like the depth of her sensitivity to its meaning." Umm Kulthūm's artistry was "the art of the word, and the art of rendition, beyond her gift in singing."[5]

It was frequently said that even one who did not speak Arabic would understand the meaning of a text from listening to her sing it, and this statement succinctly expressed perceptions, widely shared in Egypt, of Umm Kulthūm's particular skill.

Aḥmad Zākī Pāshā's vivid simile captures the essence of an important conceptualization with long roots in Arab culture, that of the closeness of poetry and music: "Poetry and music are two entities in the human soul having a single meaning, or two meanings for a single thing, as flowers and their scent."[6] Umm Kulthūm's linkage of text to melody pulled this conceptual wire into the twentieth century and electrified it in new uses.

Ibn Surayj (ca. 634–726), in his discussion of the expectations of a good singer, included good pronunciation and correct inflection of the Arabic case endings.[7] Surveying the history of Arabic song, Ibrahim Boolaky wrote that "Verses – countless in number – were admired not merely for their poetical content but also for their exquisite diction. The overall quality of the vocal expression of the time depended as much on the choice of words as on the skillful use of the human voice."[8] Musical genres often shared the names of the poetic genres to which their texts belonged, for instance the *mawwāl* and the *qaṣīda*. In the mid-nineteenth century Lane noted that "distinct enunciation . . . [was] characteristic of the Egyptian mode of singing."[9] Al-Khulaʿī devoted a long paragraph to pronunciation, urging professional singers of his day, whom he believed frequently were illiterate, to hire teachers to school them in language and grammar so as to avoid obvious errors in articulation and inflection.

A good comprehension of texts was also expected of singers and composers. The singer, according to al-Khulaʿī, must understand the syntax, grammar, and meaning of poetry, and choose songs appropriate in their texts to the tastes and understanding of the audience.[10] In practice, Racy found that "despite the elaborate melismas occurring frequently in the vocal line, the dynamic accentuation of the text [of *qaṣāʾid*], for example, the degree to which each text syllable was elongated or emphasized, was often reflected in the duration of the notes."[11] Clever plays on words (for instance, successive puns); allusions to historical, legendary, or religious figures or events; allusions to local happenings; and metaphors all contributed to the well-loved text. So too did rhyme, alliteration, and skillful use of sounds characteristic of the Arabic language, especially the emphatic consonants (*ḥ, ṣ, ḍ,* etc.).

Ultimately the link of word to music was the essence of *ṭarab* in Umm Kulthūm's idiom. It explained why she was a paragon of Arabic singing, representing a turn away from the process of enchantment (*taṭrīb*) based on melodic invention alone,[12] a quality associated by Egyptian listeners with Turkish singing.

Egyptian listeners often link the various skills associated with proper delivery of the text – pronunciation, correct inflection, informed delivery, and *taṣwīr al-maʿná* – with the training required to recite the Qurʾān, thus investing these aesthetic requirements with age and weighty significance.

[. . .]

Although it is not considered to be song (and conservative Muslims reject any connection between the two), recitation and song share fundamental principles. Egyptian observers have argued that Qurʾanic recitation is the foundation of Arabic song, although its sound is unique.

[. . .]

The elements shared by the recitation of the Qurʾān, the singing styles of the *mashāyikh*, and Umm Kulthūm's style of rendition include correct pronunciation, sensitive expression of textual meaning, attention to the unity of the textual phrase, and use of vocal tone colors.

Recitation is governed by an elaborate system of rules known as *tajwīd*. According to a modern manual, "Tajwīd, in the technical sense, is articulating each letter from its point of articulation, giving it its full value."[13] Rules mandate the nasalization of certain syllables when they appear in the context of particular combinations of consonants. Rules for duration require the reader to regulate the length of syllables by counting two to six beats. Nasalization affects the duration of the syllables, and the entire system produces rhythms particular to the recitation of the Qurʾān, unlike the meters of poetry.

A secondary aim in the melodically elaborate *mujawwad* style of recitation is *taṣwīr al-maʿná*. For the singer and composer, the affective treatment of a text often involved the depiction, shaping or heightening of its meaning, sense, or idea. Nelson observes that *taṣwīr al-maʿná*, as applied in recitation of the Qurʾān, refers "more to mood or emotion than to meaning," and that "techniques for correlating melody with meaning [are] limited only by the imagination of the reciter."[14] Correct treatment of text, including *taṣwīr al-maʿná*, produced an effect perceived as the fusion of sound and meaning:

> Ultimately, scholars and listeners recognize that the ideal beauty and inimitability of the Qurʾan lie not in the content and order of the message, on the one hand, and in the elegance of the language, on the other, but in the use of the very sound of the language to convey specific meaning. This amounts

to an almost onomatopoeic use of language, so that not only the image of the metaphor but also the sound of the words which express that image are perceived to converge with the meaning.[15]

Clear articulation was essential to the correct recitation of the Qur'ān and also to many prayers. "The word," according to popular understanding, "is the foundation of religious song."[16] The link between treatment of text in singing and recitation of the Qur'ān formed a fundamental piece of the conceptual framework for discussions of musical competence: "If [recitation of] the Qur'ān is the foundation [of musical training], [then] the tongue is properly trained, and spreads in its possessor good execution, vibrant tone, melodiousness, and correct shortening of final consonants."[17]

During the twentieth century, the reciters and singers of religious song came to be viewed as the principal repository of Arabic song and singing. Their style and repertory were identified as historically Arab and *aṣīl*.

[. . .]

With performers such as Salāma Ḥijāzī and Zakariyyā Aḥmad moving readily between the world of recitation and religious song and that of urban stage and theater, careful treatment of text became linked with Muslim classicism conceptually and practically.[18] Zakariyyā explained this quality in Umm Kulthūm's idiom:

> By virtue of her memorization and reading of the Qur'ān, she acquired experience that made her capable of giving to each word or each letter what was appropriate to correct pronunciation. From habit over the years, it became part of her nature, and her delivery of the letters was perfected to the point where her listener can clearly perceive every word she sings.[19]

When the rendition of a song features the type of clear pronunciation associated with the recitation of the Qur'ān, it strikes a familiar chord for the listeners, establishing a link of shared experience between the singer and themselves. Listeners may not be capable of articulating the rules of recitation but often they can hear when others apply them or break them.

[. . .]

Shared knowledge produced the assessment of Umm Kulthūm as "naturally gifted," listeners and singer alike having been slowly familiarized with constitutive elements of an aesthetic. In this case, however, what was learned was not the cultural property of the privileged few, but was and is widely shared by all strata of society. Significantly, folk repertories, which would be equally familiar throughout the society, are not, in this case, what is claimed as the source of cultural authenticity. The learned poetry and linguistic skill of the best of the *mashāyikh* claimed greater authority.

El-Hamamsy captures the central place of the sound and idea in the shared culture of Arabic speakers:

> By perpetuating a community of language the Qur'ān kept alive a commu-
> nity of culture – a process which was reinforced by the use of the Qur'ān as
> a basic teaching text throughout the Arab world. . . . Reverence for the
> Arabic language transcends sectarian considerations so that one finds an
> Egyptian Copt such as Makram Ebeid acknowledging that his powerful
> oratory owed much to the study of the Qur'ān.[20]

In an eloquent discussion, Timothy Mitchell writes that "the force of the phrase gathers not simply from the various references of the separate words, but from the reverberation of senses set up between the parts of the phrase by their differing sounds." Mitchell argues, correctly in my view, that pleasure in the sounds and meanings of words, and even the power of words of comfort, instruction, or charm against the powers of evil textures the lives of ordinary people.[21] My own experience suggests that it is nearly impossible to overestimate the impact and relevance of the sound of recitation in Egyptian cultural practice.

Qualities shared with Qur'anic recitation formed the stable core of Umm Kulthūm's singing styles, to which other "new," "modern," or even foreign qualities were added as musical fashions changed. In relying on this fundamental style, Umm Kulthūm linked herself artistically to the *mashāyikh*. Through her performances, she and her audience maintained and strengthened the presence of the *mashāyikh* and the associated practices and concepts about culture within Egyptian society. This practice of performing and listening at once drew from and advanced a particular set of values and a view of culture and its potentials grounded in Muslim, Egyptian, and Arab practices.

Notes

1 *Rūz al-Yūsuf* no. 195 (November 9, 1931), 21.
2 *Umm Kulthūm: Qiṣṣat Ḥayātihā, Majmū'at Agānīhā wa-ba'ḍ Nukātihā
   wa-Wafātuhā* (Umm Kulthūm: the story of her life, collection of her songs
   and some of her jokes, and her death). Beirut: Maktabat al-Ḥadīth, ca. 1975,
   53.
3 Umm Kulthūm, quoted in Rajā' al-Naqqāsh, "Liqā' ma'a Umm Kulthūm" (A
   meeting with Umm Kulthūm), *al-Kawākib* (1965). Reprinted in *Lughz Umm
   Kulthūm.* Cairo: Dār al-Hilāl, 1978, 44.
4 "Al-Ḥadīth al- Ākhir," Ṣawt al-Qāhira cassette tape no. SC76015.
5 Ni'māt Aḥmad Fu'ād, *Umm Kulthūm wa-'Aṣr min al-Fann* (Umm Kulthūm and
   an era of art). Cairo: al-Hay'a al Miṣriyya 'l-'Āmma lil-Kitāb, 1976, 393; Abd
   al-Fattāḥ Ghaban "Bayram Yataḥaddath 'an Umm Kulthūm," *Rūz al-Yūsuf*

(March 24, 1975); Ṭāhā Ḥusayn quoted in "Innahā Ajmal Ṣawt" (The most beautiful voice), *al-Idhā'a wa-'l Tilīfizyūn* (February 8, 1975).

6 Aḥmad Zākī Pāshā, quoted in Sāmī al-Shawwā, *Mudhakkirāt Sāmī al-Shawwā* (The memoirs of Sāmī al-Shawwā), ed. Fu'ād Qaṣṣāṣ. Cairo: Maṭābi' al Sharq al-Awsaṭ, 1966, 141.

7 Ibn Surayj, quoted in Kristina Nelson, *The Art of Reciting the Qur'an*. Austin, Texas: University of Texas Press, 1985, 37.

8 Ibrahim Boolaky, "Traditional Muslim Vocal Art," *Arts and the Islamic World* 1 (Winter 1983–84): 52–5; 52.

9 Edward William Lane, *An Account of the Manners and Customs of the Modern Egyptians, Written in Egypt during the Years 1833–1835*. 1836. Reprint, The Hague and London: East-West Publications, 1978, 364.

10 *Kitāb Mu'tamar al-Mūsiqá 'l-'Arabiyya* (Book of the conference of Arab music). Cairo: al-Matba'a al-Amīriyya, 1933, 88.

11 Ali Jihad Racy, "Musical Change and Commercial Recording in Egypt, 1904–1932," Ph.D. diss., University of Illinois, 1977, 262.

12 Maḥmūd Aḥmad al-Ḥifnī et al., eds., *Turāthunā 'l-Mūsīqī min al-Adwār wa-'l Muwashshaḥāt* (Our musical heritage of Adwār and Muwashshaḥāt). 4 vols. Cairo: al-Lajna al-Mūsīqiyya al-'Ulyá, 1969, 1:78.

13 Nelson, 15.

14 Ibid., 64, 65.

15 Ibid., 13.

16 Muḥammad al-Gharīb, "al-Ughniyya al-Dīniyya Tastahdif al-Qalb" (Religious song aims at the heart), *al-Idhā'a wa-'l Tilīfizyūn* no. 2633 (31 August 1985), 18–19.

17 Fu'ād, 348.

18 Habib Hassan Touma, "Die Musik der Araber im 19. Jahrhundert," in *Musikkulturen Asiens, Afrikas und Ozeaniens im 19. Jahrhundert*, ed. Robert Günther. Studien de Musikgeschichte des 19. Jahrhunderts, Band 31 (Regensburg: Gustav Bosse, 1973), 52.

19 Zakariyyā Aḥmad, quoted in Maḥmūd 'Awaḍ, *Umm Kulthūm allatī lā Ya'rifuhā Aḥad* (The Umm Kulthūm nobody knows). Cairo: Mu'assasat Akhbār al-Yawm, 1971, 111.

20 Laila Shukry El-Hamamsy, "The Assertion of Egyptian Identity," in *Ethnic Identity: Cultural Continuities and Change*, ed. George DeVos and Lola Ranucci-Ross. Palo Alto, Calif.: Mayfield, 1975, 302.

21 Timothy Mitchell, *Colonising Egypt*. Cambridge: Cambridge University Press, 1988, 143.

14

Siddheshwari Devi sings

Sheila Dhar

Sheila Dhar, *Here's Someone I'd Like You to Meet: Tales of Innocents, Musicians and Bureaucrats* (Delhi: Oxford University Press, 1995), pp. 129–34.

Siddheshwari Devi (1907–76) was one of the finest exponents of *thumri* and related genres of north Indian song. Sheila Dhar's first-person account – albeit written several decades after the events described – offers a vivid account of musical performance in the 1930s, an era when most female singers belonged to the courtesan, or *bai* community (or *baiji*, -*ji* being an honorific suffix), and were accomplished dancers as well as singers. Other italicised terms are as follows: *salaam* (greeting), *pandal* (marquee), *halwais* (sweet makers), *jalebi* (a kind of sweet), *sarangi* (a bowed lute), *achkan* (a kind of coat), *mujra* (a traditional performance context for music and/or dance) and *taan* (a melodic figure). The phrase 'to have salt in one's face' means to be sexy and flirtatious (rather similar to the way the adjective 'saucy' is used in English). I have added rough translations to the comments quoted in Hindi.

When I was about eight, it seemed much more important to belong to an 'old family' than to a good school. The term was used as though it meant an exclusive tribe, which it certainly did in a way. We took for granted that we belonged to this tribe. At the time we knew only a dozen or so other old families in the city of Delhi. They all greeted one another when they passed in their horse carriages or cars on the roads. But there was not much of what was called 'inter-dining' in those days, probably because each family was large and socially self-sufficient.

The only occasion when an old family might have to go outside itself and relate to the entire tribe was a marriage celebration. When my grandfather was invited to a wedding outside the community with all the members of his household, it was something of an event. It was a welcome acknowledgement of 'old family' status and therefore had to be responded to but it was considered bad form to take it literally. So there was no question of the entire brood going to a wedding outside the community. But if one or two children were taken along by the elders, it was usually seen as a token of genuine warmth in the relationship between guest and host.

In our household there was a rough and ready system by which its thirty-odd children took turns at treats of this kind. My cousin and her mother had gone to the last wedding with my father so this time it was my turn. As the outcome of some such calculation, I found myself holding my grandfather's finger and trailing behind him at a glittering celebration in Kashmiri Gate, dressed in an incongruous yellow silk frock with embossed gold patterns which my mother had stitched overnight out of a sari in honour of the occasion. The silk smelt of sandalwood and roses and I felt rather grand altogether. The shiny maroon shoes of which my grand-father's clerk had bought several pairs 'for the girls' at a Chandni Chowk sale fitted only approximately, loose at the back and pinching badly at the toes. But to me this was less important than the beaded brass buckles that adorned the shoes, making me feel like a princess. When my mother said she felt the shoes didn't fit, I vehemently denied it lest it jeopardize my chances for what was clearly a visit to fairyland.

The access to the scene of the festivities was through a narrow lane which fanned out into an enormous courtyard. I remember my amaze-ment at seeing a caparisoned elephant standing comfortably in the area, greeting guests by lifting its trunk into a *salaam* and trumpeting occasion-ally. Huge silver platters of hot savouries and fragrant, freshly made sweets were being passed round by a large number of harassed but still obsequious family retainers who seemed more involved in the details of hospitality than the senior members of the family. The only function of the hosts seemed to be to bow, smile and fold their hands continuously as guests poured in. I was struck by the fact that though the newly-married couple were the reason for the celebrations, no one seemed to be particularly interested in them. They sat side by side on a sofa in the vast *pandal*, still and silent, smothered in brocade, gold ornaments and flowers, heads bent and faces invisible. I was dying to lift the curtain of flowers from the bride-groom's face and the veil of gold cloth from the bride's to see for myself whether this was really the happy ending of a romantic fairy tale. I wanted it very much to be, but something, including the harrowed expressions of the over-worked and sweaty *halwais* frying *jalebis* behind a colourful arras, told me it wasn't likely.

We were ushered into the main area of the *pandal* where at least fifty upholstered sofas and armchairs were arranged around a huge flowered carpet on which a striking woman in red sat apart, smiling and twinkling winningly at the guests. She was flanked by an emaciated drummer in a frayed *achkan* and a wizened old *sarangi* player with startlingly blue-black hair. There was also a modest harmonium player who had the air of a button waiting to be pressed. 'This is Siddheshwari Bai, the celebrated *thumri* singer from Banaras', someone whispered as the music began. She had been laughing and joking informally with whoever among the guests greeted her, but with the first strains of the *sarangi*, her expression became more focused, more collected. She seemed to be weighing something in her mind, probably what she should open her concert with. She closed her eyes for an instant, then nodded her head in silent approval, bent towards the players to give them some instructions and vigorously cleared her throat. She covered her left ear with the palm of her hand, stretched out her other arm in a gesture of appeal to the listeners and began to sing. Her rich, resounding voice needed no amplification in that space. She established instant rapport by hitting some high notes which sent a ripple of excitement among the listeners.

The music did not mean much to me at this point but I was hypnotized by her face and her voice. The two together sent such powerful signals of warmth and reassurance that I was reminded of my mother, to my own great surprise.

The languorous beat of the *thumri*, and the passionate and persuasive words of the song in which Siddheshwari Bai begged Krishna, the apple of Yashoda's eye, to come home because night was falling drew in the friendly audience immediately. Gradually her face and arms began to move as though she was acting as well as singing. The hand gestures and mime tried to paint different versions of the picture described in the *thumri* she was singing. I discovered later that this was no novelty but a routine part of the traditional '*mujra*'. I had come across something like this in the performance of a dancer who had been invited to our school but this was the first time I had ever seen someone 'dance' while sitting down. It was also the first time I had seen one person exercise so much control, so effortlessly, over hundreds of people. I was sure she could make her audience feel whatever she wished.

Soon there was rapt silence, except for awed remarks about the excellence of the performer. 'She is no beauty, but my God how much salt she has in her face!' someone hissed from the row behind us. I asked my grandfather what salt in the face meant and he said 'Hush! We will talk later.' With each song, the atmosphere in the *pandal* became more and more informal. The audience expressed their appreciation with loud cries of '*wah, wah, kya kehne*' ['Wow – what can one say?'] or '*jawab nahin hai*'

['There's no answer'], not by clapping. After some time, an uncle of the bridegroom called out to her with a request to dance. *'Baiji, zara thumke ke saath ho jai!'* ['Baiji, do it with the (dance) movement']

She smiled radiantly, said something that made everybody laugh and began to tie her ankle bells. This was obviously a stage of the entertainment which was most eagerly awaited because the audience hailed it with glad cries. She stood up and tried the bells by striking each foot on the ground. Now I knew why the white sheet which is invariably spread for musicians was absent. When the atmosphere warmed up, this was meant to turn into a dance recital. The *sarangi* player secured his small instrument to his waist with a padded, belt-like contraption and also stood up behind her, ready to follow her around the improvised stage as she danced. The *tabla* player did the same, The ensemble became mobile within minutes and was now able to address and delight each section of the audience intimately in turn. At long last Siddheshwari Bai came near us. I felt I was drowning. Her eyes were fixed on my grandfather but to my great discomfiture, he was not responsive of appreciative enough, or so it seemed to me.

This time her song described a beautiful young woman drawing water from the well, filling her pot, balancing it on her head and walking home while the onlookers, marvelled at her grace and loveliness. Siddheshwari Bai's mime, hand gestures and body movements painted the picture for me very clearly. But for that I would not have been able to decipher the meaning of the words which were in an unfamiliar dialect and blurred for me by the musical embellishments. I was electrified by the sequences of brilliant footwork and explosions of sound from the *tabla* which peppered the musical story-telling.

In the middle of this number, when she was singing the intriguing words *jhama jham* again and again, trying to recreate the sound of overflowing water, there was a flurry of excitement at the far end of the marquee. All eyes and ears turned away from the performer and the magic she had woven evaporated. Some very special guests were being escorted in with loud and deferential exclamations by a group of the host party. They were led to the biggest sofa in the centre of the central row. When they were seated, and the fawning cloud of attendants and ushers dispersed I was able to see that the special guests were an elderly British couple. He was dressed in a black suit which looked as though it had been fashioned out of metal. She wore a long white satin gown, furs and a gracious smile. 'It is the Chief Commissioner and his lady', our host told my grandfather as he bustled past, beaming with satisfaction at the superb eminence of the guests he had the power to summon.

The dancer also received enough signals from diverse sources to know that the occasion had now become even more grand than it had been. She decided to do something about it at once, and abruptly changed the song she was singing from '*jhama jham*' to 'my love is like a little bird', I discovered later that this was the opening line of a musical hit in London. She sang the words with such a strong Indian accent that the British guests were none the wiser. However, many of the local people expressed their admiration and pride at such versatility and inventiveness. "Like a little bird" she sang in many different ways, as though it were a traditional *thumri*. 'That flies, that flies, that flies from tree to tree e e e e e e . . . .' The last syllable stretched into a masterly *taan* that swept two and a half octaves, leaving the listeners gasping for breath. The style of the miming also changed abruptly. The languorous, elephantine walk of the village belle denoted by sinuous gestures and coy looks gave place to a high-heeled look and jerky, almost comic hand movements suggesting the erratic flight of the British bird. Siddheshwari Bai's impromptu confection in honour of the Chief Commissioner was clearly the highlight of the festivities and was talked about in Delhi for months afterwards.

15

Text and performance in *thumri*

Peter Manuel

Peter Manuel, *Thumri in Historical and Stylistic Perspectives*
(Delhi: Motilal Banarasidass, 1989), pp. 16–19, 30–3, 140–2.

In these extracts from his book on the Indian genre of romantic song, Manuel compares the *ṭhumrī* (in Hindi) with the Urdu *ghazal* (a form of sung poetry), as well as with the classical *khayāl* (*khyal*). *Śṛṅgāra rasa* – the amatory or erotic sentiment – describes the predominant mood of *ṭhumrī* performance. The term *bol banao* refers to the technique, typical of *ṭhumrī*, by which individual words and phrases are repeated with different inflections in order to bring out different nuances of meaning; a *tān* is a kind of improvised melodic phrase (cf. *taan* in Item 14). *ś* is pronounced sh, *ć* as ch.

While the erotic, *śṛṅgāra rasa* predominates in ṭhumrī, it is the pangs of unrequited longing rather than the joys of union that are portrayed. The tradition of depicting the protagonist (in Urdu as well as Hindi verse) as perpetually forlorn and distressed contrasts with artistic conventions in many other cultures (e.g., Western pop), which balance laments with optimistic and jubilant songs. Two approaches may be taken in attempting to explain this concentration on unrequited love. From a purely aesthetic viewpoint, the artists' choice to dwell endlessly on one theme – that of separation – can be seen as a deliberate limitation which affords a singular depth of sentiment and expression, and which further provides a conventional stylistic framework which highlights the individual artists' contribution. Indeed, this approach is manifest in many other aspects of Indian art: just as the Hindi poet may devote his entire output to describing subtle nuances and shades of unrequited love, so may a ṭhumrī singer perform lengthy interpretative passages on a single text phrase; and a *khayāl* singer may spend ten minutes of a performance elaborating three or four notes of a *rāga*, developing their melodic potential in extreme depth.

While the concentration on a single theme may be a deliberate artistic device, the choice of the particular theme of separation cannot be regarded as entirely arbitrary. While that theme is certainly meaningful to all cultures, some scholars (e.g., Russell and Islam 1968: 3) have argued that it is particularly expressive of the Indian condition. First, actual physical separation of couples is common in Indian, where economic hardship often obliges the husband to live and work away from this family; disease and other natural accidents may also prematurely claim the life of a marriage partner. Moreover, in much of rural India, men and women generally sleep separately, while in the cities the entire joint family may sleep crowded into one or two rooms, or, in the summer, on the rooftop. Naturally, due to perpetual lack of privacy in such situations, sexual intercourse may take place only infrequently, causing frustration to both parties. Hence, in some ṭhumrīs, the heroine begs her husband to spend the night with her rather than in the courtyard with the menfolk.

At a broader level, the theme of separation and frustration may be particularly meaningful to the Indian whose interests and aspirations are frequently subjugated to the customary demands of family, caste, and society at large. Traditionally, the family, rather than the individual, has been regarded as the unit of the social and economic system (Basham 1959: 155). Hence, social cohesion, convention and order have been stressed at the expense of the individual's autonomy. In marriage, a degree of formalization between the sexes often occurs, and the concept of the importance of marital duty may overshadow that of love. Marriages often assume the character of parentally arranged financial contracts, where bargaining over dowries receives more attention than the potential compatibility of the bride and groom. (The increase in reported "dowry murders" in recent decades would seem to suggest that this trend is increasing, especially among the middle classes.) Such a rigid social structure, conducive as it may be to a sort of cohesion and order, may naturally generate some frustration at the level of the individual, and when his personal hopes are so often thwarted or narrowly channelled, it should not be surprising that poetry, music, dance, and even painting tend to dwell upon the pain of separation (Russell and Islam 1968: 3).

The fear of social castigation is depicted in the numerous ṭhumrīs and *khayāls* portraying the anxiety of the heroine that her jingling anklets may awaken her sleeping mother-in-law as she furtively sneaks off to meet her lover at night. Other texts portray Krishna teasing the cowgirl heroine, while she pleads with him to release her, lest they be seen together in daylight. An example is the following:

Example 21

Sab hī nār-nārī dekhat
Lāj na āve, nit uṭh kahe ko muskyat, aisi
Ab kī jāne de bāt, milūṅgī rāt, rahūṅgī sāth, sunūṅgī bāt
Ghar ko jāne de, ratīyā āne de, sās sunegī to degī gālī
(Telang 1977: 97)

All the women are looking, have you no sense of decency?
Why are you always leering so?
Let me go, I'll meet you tonight, and stay with you, and listen to you;
Let me go home, and come in the evening; if my mother-in-law hears she'll
abuse me.

The phenomenon of the predominance of the theme of separation has also
been discussed in relation to the Urdu ghazal and the two genres do invite
comparison. In ghazal, as in thumrī, expression and consummation of love
are always thwarted, and the lover is driven to near madness. Naturally,
ghazals, most of which are written as independent poetry rather than mere
song-texts, are more sophisticated, subtle, and rich than thumrī texts; but
aside from this, one may discern some important differences between the
kinds of separation depicted in the two genres. Ghazal is written from the
man's perspective, focusing solely on his wretched condition; in thumrī,
the female is the speaker and protagonist (although we may assume that
most thumrīs were composed by men). The beloved in ghazal is often
portrayed as cruel, disdainful, and generally heartless, occasionally even
wielding a scimitar with which to behead her lovers, who offer their necks
in meek abnegation. This sort of extremism is absent in thumrī; moreover,
while in thumrī the beloved is often reproached for his infidelity, he is not
portrayed as spiteful. Krishna is mischievous but not cruel, and he is
unfaithful but not uncaring.
  The difference in tone between the two genres is perhaps due to the even
greater social repression and inflexibility of heterosexual relations in medi-
eval Muslim society, and on the other hand, to the tradition of sensuality
in Hindu culture which has always pervaded Indian art, and has been
traditionally accorded a place in society. In general, the thumrī is less pes-
simistic than the ghazal; in the latter, there is seldom any faith that union
with the beloved will ever be achieved. On the other hand, in thumrī, while
the beloved may be out of town, it is implicit that he will return eventually.
[. . .] [T]he model of the *Gīta Govinda* may be cited: Radha spends one night
in the agony of longing, but the following night Krishna comes and they
consummate their love in a night-long ecstatic orgy. This felicitous conclusion may be contrasted with the fate of Majnun, the legendary lover in the

ghazal, who dies wandering mad and alone in the desert. Yet even in Hindi poetry, the tradition that Krishna is adulterer rather than husband to Radha may reflect a lack of faith in the institution of marriage as a source fulfillment.

The role of the text in singing

Judged [as literary works, ṭhumrī texts] are not great masterpieces of art; although many reflect ingenuity or quaint charm, they are generally stereotyped, simple, and often pedestrian. But it must be remembered that they were not written as poems, but as song texts, and should be appreciated as such. For when a poem is set to music, it loses its literary status and becomes part of the music, with a purely musical function and value. Suzanne Langer (1953: 153) has articulately described this phenomenon, which she calls "the principle of assimilation." It is because the song-text becomes a musical rather than poetic element that, in Langer's words, "trivial or sentimental lyrics may be good texts as well as great poems." Ṭhumrī texts are fine examples of verse which is in itself undistinguished, but which forms an excellent vehicle for musical elaboration. Here we are discussing their meaning, more than their mere sound-value, for the goal of ṭhumrī is the musical expression of the sentiment of the text.

The simplicity and breadth of ṭhumrī texts are assets rather than a hindrance to expression. Langer (1953: 154) has noted how a great poem may not lend itself to musical rendering, as the text is so complete, autonomous, and self-contained that it "will not give up its literary form." Ṭhumrī singer Rita Gangoly made a similar observation:

> If there is a lot of concrete poetic imagery, then the obligation of the poetry to be expressed in music may become so great that the musician loses his freedom to improvise. That's why the text has to be simple, and that sort of simplicity is difficult to acquire in music, and in life . . . and that's why a simple *sāhitya* [poem], full of scope, is the ideal composition in *khayāl* and ṭhumrī. Since the aim is music, not literature, if the literature is complete, then there's no scope for the singer. So the literature used is of such a type that it leaves a lot of area to be filled in.[1]

Thus, the most popular and effective ṭhumrī texts are simple, open-ended statements expressing often in oblique terms a relatively broad and general emotional condition which a good singer can illuminate and present in an infinite variety of shades and forms. Typical examples are excerpts such as "*piyā bin nahīn āvat ćain*" – "I find no peace without my lover"; "*ras ke bhare tore nain*" – "your eyes are filled with passion"; or even more suggestive and oblique, "*bājū band khul khul jāe*" – "my bracelets have slipped off."

Munawar Ali Khan has aptly likened the text to a telegram, such as "So-and-so has died," which in itself may convey little emotion, but can become a vehicle for prodigious emotional expression in the course of melodic elaboration.[2]

The general, broad nature of the ṭhumrī text may be illustrated by contrasting it with some verse more specific, concrete, and explicit in imagery. The two lines below, for example, express in simple terms a general feeling of longing and distraction:

> *Kaṭe na birhā kī rāt*
> *Maiṅ kāse kahūṅ jiyā kī bāt.*
>
> I cannot endure this night of separation
> To whom shall I explain the state of my mind?

Contrast these lines with Shakespeare's sonnet no. 27, which conveys more or less the same emotion, but with incomparably greater prolixity, specificity, and artifice.

> Weary with toil, I haste me to my bed,
> The dear repose for limbs with travel tired;
> But then begins a journey in my head
> To work my mind when body's work's expired;
> Or then my thought, from far where I abide,
> Intend a zealous pilgrimage to thee,
> And keep my drooping eyelids open wide,
> Looking on darkness which the blind do see;
> Save that my soul's imaginary sight
> Presents thy shadow to my sightless view,
> Which, like a jewel hung in ghastly night,
> Makes black night beauteous and her old face new.
>   Lo, this by day my limbs, by night my mind,
>   For thee, and for myself, no quiet find.

Although superior as poetry, such verse would not be suitable for rendering in ṭhumrī, whether in part or in its entirety, because the imagery and thoughts are so specific and closely interrelated that a vocalist would be unable to elaborate a single line and highlight different shades of interpretation.

In the process of *bol banāo*, which we shall examine in greater detail below, the singer may elaborate and develop a single line or phrase for as long as five minutes. Hence, there is no need for ṭhumrī texts to have strict internal cohesion; in fact, if the different lines depend on each other for coherence, musical elaboration would become difficult, as the singer would be obliged to improvise simultaneously on a clumsy two- or more-line segment of text. As a result, most *bol banāo* ṭhumrīs tend to have an atomistic structure, where although the lines are interrelated in so far as they may express the same general sentiment, each single line is complete and self-contained, and thus can be used by itself as a basis for improvisation. *Bol banāo* elaboration and reinterpretation often occur on a single phrase, such as *"khelat gend"* ("playing with the ball") or *"koel bole"* ("the cuckoo cries") or even a single word, such as *"dard"* ("pain") or *"ćain"* ("happiness"). Thus, in ṭhumrī texts, the "patchy" quality, or the lack of sustained development of a single idea, is not the result of the poet's inability to stick to one thought, but is rather a deliberate (whether ingenuous or not) effect rendering the text suitable for *bol banāo*.

To clarify and summarize – a good ṭhumrī text is "incomplete" in that its expression of emotion is sufficiently broad, simple, and general so that the singer can interpret it in innumerable ways. At the same time, each line is "complete" and autonomous in that the emotional thought, however simple, is expressed within that one line, and does not require two or more lines in order to be clear.

In this respect, ṭhumrī may again be contrasted with ghazal, where the meaning extends over two full lines (a couplet); as the singer develops a line, he builds up suspense in anticipation of the final dramatic moment when the closing rhymes (*radīf* and *qāfiya*) are delivered and the sense and rhyme of the couplet at once become clear. This sort of suspense is essential to the ghazal-song, but is totally absent in ṭhumrī.

Further, in ghazal, the text is of higher and more autonomous *poetic* quality, and, consequently, it retains more of its purely literary significance in singing. The text is less assimilated, less a part of the *musical* product than in ṭhumrī. Thus, ghazal texts are longer, more complex, and more independent than ṭhumrī text, while the melodic substance of a ghazal-song is much more limited than that of a ṭhumrī. For this reason, ghazal does not exist as an instrumental form, but ṭhumrī, whose interest is more ingerently musical, is an important musical genre. (Conversely, ṭhumrī, unlike ghazal, does not exist as a literary form.) The contrast is even more marked in *tarannum*, in which a ghazal is recited, without accompaniment, to a simple, strophic, un-elaborated melody. Here the melody serves only to render the text more accessible and its meter more apparent, though it has minimal aesthetic interest in itself.

Correspondingly, ṭhumrī may also be contrasted with the vocal form *khayāl*, where the text is important less for its meaning than for its sound. Text delivery is often blurred, broken, and generally unintelligible, for what is required is more a "semblance of speech" and not a coherent semantic expression; the emphasis, rather, is on pure, abstract, melodic improvisation. That is, the *khayāl* singer is interested in a phrase like "*piyā bina*" ("without my lover") only as a set of phonemes, whereas the ṭhumrī singer will explore the meaning in this phrase.

[. . .]

Writers like Hanslick (1957: 29), Langer (1953: 126) and Meyer (1956) have argued persuasively that the expressive power of music lies in its ability to suggest the passage of emotions in organic, humanly perceived time, and that music's waning, waxing, surging, lingering, and complex layers of tension and relaxation convey emotional states and processes in ways not possible through verbal or plastic arts. Such melody, by presenting the illusion of the kinetic ebb and flow of emotion, is inherently expressive; the presence of a text, as in ṭhumrī, naturally colors the impact, so that the attentive listener perceives the emotional content within the context of the lyric. The *bol* [text], then, renders the expressive content of the melody slightly more concrete and specific; but, as we have seen, most texts are broad and simple in meaning, and their stock themes of longing and separation lend themselves naturally to expansive melodic elaboration, and to assimilation into the musical dimension.

Again, the artist conceives and depicts the text not as a literary element, but as he experiences it – often at a semi-conscious level – in the dimension of musical, aesthetic emotion (except for particularly literal cases of word-painting.)

In interpreting the text, the singer uses the musical material at his disposal, including the various melodic phrases, motives, and *tāns* which he has learned or acquired in the course of years of practice; he might originally have learned and conceived of the motifs as abstract musical ideas, without any accompanying text. In *bol banāo*, these melodic phrases are enlisted in the service of text expression; naturally, it is essential that the vocalist has sufficient mastery and facility with these phrases, that they be at his fingertips, as it were, so that when he is actually concentrating on the musical sentiment of the text for inspiration, they emerge naturally, spontaneously, and with continuity and feeling.

[. . .]

Musicians naturally develop a repertoire of favorite motifs and *tāns*, and when a listener becomes very familiar with the music of a given artist, one invariably notices that many motifs recur in almost every performance of a given ṭhumrī *rāga* by that artist. The question thus arises: How is it that these same recurring melodic phrases can be used to express different texts? Does not their very recurrence imply that the vocalist is concentrating on exposition of the *rāga* rather than of text? The ability of a musical phrase to accommodate different shades of emotional meaning enables us to answer the latter question in the negative. The affective import of such a melodic motive is sufficiently general and imprecise so that it can be expressive in different (textual) contexts. A musical phrase can in fact assume different emotional meanings depending on its text, or its musical context.

A parallel phenomenon has been noted by Bukovzer (in Schwadron 1971: 95) in reference to musical figures in Baroque music:

> . . . the musical figures were in themselves necessarily ambiguous and took on a definite meaning only in the musical context and by means of a text or title . . . musically identical figures lent themselves to numerous and often highly divergent meanings.

Thus, we should have no reason to doubt Munawwar Ali Khan when he insists that his fundamental inspiration in ṭhumrī is the text. He admits that he may sing the same phrases in two different Bhairvī ṭhumrīs, but he insists that these identical phrases may have different inspiration, and different musical meaning, depending on whether the text is, say, "Ā jā sānvariya" – "Come to me, my beloved" – or "Ab na mānūṅ torī batiyāṅ" – "I won't believe your words any more." Munawwar Ali emphasizes, "The *rāga* may be the same, some of the phrases may be the same, but the inspiration and feeling are different."[3]

Rita Gangoly, an unusually articulate ṭhumrī singer, has described at length her conceptualization of the *bol banāo* process, emphasizing the numerous and varied possible conceptual interpretations of a single line of text – interpretations which are themselves sufficiently broad in scope and subtle in content as to lend themselves naturally to assimilation into music through melodic elaboration. Rita's explication is worth quoting at length.

> Suppose the bol is "*Piyā bin nahīn āvat ćain*" ["I find no peace without my lover"]. First, "*piyā bin*": what is *piyā* ["beloved"]? What is the shape, the temperament of *piyā*? What was the environment when you met *piyā*? What is your relationship with *piyā*? When is he coming? When did he leave you? All these possibilities are in just one word: *piyā*. You're thinking of him in a bad, sad mood, in a nostalgic mood, you're angry with him, you're conversing with him, you're separated . . .
>
> Then "*piyā bin*" ["without my lover"]. It's clear that he's absent. "*Nahīṅ*" ["not"]: the very concept of denial itself has so much scope. Then "*nahīṅ āvat*" ["doesn't come"]: you can do *āvat nāhiṅ āvat, piyā bin nahīn āvat*. Even then it's complete. Then at the last image, the singer has the obligation of elaboration of another personal image: "*ćain*" ["peace", "happiness"]. The person who has made you restless, it's he only who gives you peace, around which you've established so many incidents, nostalgic memories. You're depressed at the moment, but there's no peace – there's only peace when he's there. So "*ćain*" alone can be elaborated for hours.
>
> There's a well-known bandish my *gurū-jī* used to sing: "*Sānjh bhaī ghar ā jā Nand Lāl*" ["Evening has fallen, come home, Nand Lal"]. *Sānj* – evening, when

the cows are going back, when there's twilight, dusk, or the dusk of your life, or a transition period from adolescence to adulthood. It can be welcome, alarming, sad, or joyful. Look at the scope, the way a musician can elaborate a hundred ways within that *rāga* . . .

It is the same with *"Bājū band khul khul jāe"* ["My bracelets have come off"] . . . Every rendering of this ṭhumrī is totally different, every *"bāju band"* experience is different . . . It means "my life is going out of my grip." It's not just the bracelet of a frail woman, rather, "my whole fantasy and romance, my whole image I've woven around me, it's all slipping out of my hand; my total concept of life has changed, because the beloved has cast a spell over me; he has changed and challenged the basic concept and questions of my life." That's why ṭhumrī singing requires intelligence.[4]

Rita's explanation suggests that the step-by-step elaboration of the text may resemble and parallel the methodical development of melodic regions in *khayāl* and, to an extent, in ṭhumrī. Her concept of text development is similar to that described by Munawwar Ali Khan, who likens the text to a telegram; the message itself – for example, "So-and-so has died" – is simple and plain, but there may be a pathetic and moving story behind the message, which the ṭhumrī singer endeavors to bring out through his melodic elaboration.[5]

Notes

1 Personal communication, 4/81.
2 Personal communication, 4/81.
3 Personal communication (in Urdu) in 4/81.
4 Personal communication in 4/81.
5 Personal communication in 3/81.

References

Basham, A.L. (1959) *The Wonder that was India* (New York: Grove Press).
Hanslick, Eduard (1957) *The Beautiful in Music* (New York: Liberal Arts Press).
Langer, Susanne K. (1953) *Feeling and Form* (New York: Charles Scribner's Sons).
Meyer, Leonard (1956) *Emotion and Meaning in Music* (Chicago: University of Chicago Press).
Russell, Ralph, and Khurshidul Islam (1968) *Three Mughal Poets* (Cambridge, MA: Harvard University Press).
Schwadron, Abraham (1971) "On words and music: toward an aesthetic conciliation", *Journal of Aesthetic Education*, 5:3, 91–108.
Telang, Gangadhar Rao (1977) *Thumari Sangrah* (Lucknow: Uttar Pradesh Sangit Natak Academy).

Part III

Song performance and society

16

The meaning of song

Victor Zuckerkandl

Victor Zuckerkandl, *Man the Musician (Sound and Symbol: Volume 2)*, trans. Norbert Guterman, Bollingen Series 44/2 (Princeton, NJ: Princeton University Press, 1973), pp. 23–30.

Imagine a hillside in a warm country; it is morning and the sun is shining brightly. A young man is up in a pear tree, picking the fruit, and as he picks he sings. Why is he singing? I suppose most of us would say, Because it is a beautiful day, and it is good to be young on a beautiful day in a beautiful countryside, picking luscious pears. All this may be so, but there is another, deeper, more essential reason for song in this situation. Our young man might not sing as he picked if the day were not so fine or if troubles weighed on him, but if he sang at all as he picked pears, he would sing the same song – and a different song if it were grapes. The song he sings is the immemorial pear-picking song in his part of the world, a tune that musically makes fruit and picker one, that "brings" the pears to the picker's hands and consecrates his harvesting of them. It is as though the picker's hands did not reach out for the fruit but surrendered to it, as though the fruit, instead of resisting the hands, were meeting them halfway, dropping into them of its own accord. Instead of opposition, distinction, we have togetherness, unity.

It might be objected that not every type of activity is furthered or enhanced by music. Thus, scientists and scholars need yield to no one in capacity for self-abandon, and it is a fact that they do not sing as they work. Faust alone in his study, singing, as Gounod portrayed him, strikes us as ludicrous. A game like chess, similarly, does not lend itself to a musical setting: imagine a chorus of kibitzers! Hunters, too, sing only in operas, and then only before or after they shoot (if the composer knows his business). In real life, hunters keep still, not just so as not to alert the quarry – they would keep still even if the birds or animals they seek had no sense of hearing. In the kitchen you hear singing only from persons doing routine tasks, like peeling potatoes, never from the chef nervously preparing a delicate sauce. What the objection overlooks is that the kind of person-object relationship characteristic of thinking, study, or any other activity requiring concentration is not correctly designated by the term "self-abandon." For here the opposite is true: self and object are sharply distinguished. When engaged in such activities we are wholly with ourselves and wholly with the object at the same time. True, we do not focus on ourselves, yet we are entirely absorbed in observing the object, concentrating on it, and in doing this we keep the object away from ourselves, distinct from ourselves. This is an attitude incompatible with any sounds. The man singing in the pear tree does not focus on the fruit. Nor does Orpheus act like a hunter when he encounters wild beasts.

Thus music is appropriate, is helpful, where self-abandon is intended or required – where the self goes beyond itself, where subject and object come together. Tones seem to provide the bridge that makes it possible, or at least makes it easier, to cross the boundary separating the two.

There exists a type of music making at this level which does not – or, at any rate, not as obviously as other types – serve as a means to an end. Wherever folk music is still alive, people come together to sing. To be sure, many songs, such as dance tunes, lullabies, martial airs, religious chants and hymns, have a specific, immediate purpose; but there are also others which are sung for their own sakes, just for the sake of singing. What is the meaning of this practice?

A folk song is primarily a poem, that is, a verbal structure. It tells a story, evokes a situation, expresses feelings. There can be no doubt that the words of the song are all-important; the tune takes second place. The title of the song refers to what the words say, not to the melody; indeed, different songs are often sung to the same tune. In many collections of folk songs the main part of the book is given over to the verbal texts, followed by the indication "To be sung to the tune of . . ." What each text is sung to is usually given in an appendix; the number of tunes is invariably inferior to that of the texts.

It would seem, then, that even in those folk songs where the tune is not just a means to an end, its function is clearly secondary. It might even be maintained that in folk songs the contribution of the tune is less essential than in other forms of early music making. Dancing and celebrations without musical accompaniment lack something essential, whereas a poem is a self-contained whole, lacking nothing.

This is no doubt true of the unvocalized poem, the poem I think about or read silently, perhaps to recite it to myself or to someone to whom it is unfamiliar; it is not true of the poem that is actually meant to be vocalized, to represent the voice of a community. Can one imagine that people come together to *speak* songs? One can, but only as a logical possibility; in real life this would be absurd. It would turn something natural into something utterly unnatural. Looked at in this way, what the musical tones contribute to the folk song is essential: only in so far as it is sung does the folk song really exist. Take the tune away, and what remains is something entirely different.

A trivial explanation suggests itself: the naturalness of singing and the artificiality of speaking in chorus are supposed to be accounted for by the fact that meter regulates the temporal succession of tones but not that of words. It is argued that the meter alone makes possible orderly group performance, but that to keep time when speaking is unnatural. This explanation overlooks the fact that only with the advance to genuine polyphony – in other words, the advance to art music – did meter become an indispensable element of musical language. Music in its original state is free to comply or not to comply with a meter. Gregorian melodies which know no meter are nevertheless sung by choirs. In folk music outside the boundaries of the West, group singing and group playing without meter are nothing less than alien. We may marvel at the accomplishment, but it is taken for granted. On the other hand, there is no reason why a poem, an utterance in rhythmic language, could not be merely spoken metrically under certain circumstances. At any rate, the reason why it is unnatural to recite folk songs rather than sing them must be sought elsewhere, not just in the fact that tones have become inseparable from meter.

It seems that the spoken word is unsuitable in the situation naturally presupposed by the existence of folk songs. The spoken word presupposes a speaker and someone spoken to, is directed by one person to another, implies a communication. "All speech," we read in Bruno Snell's *Der Aufbau der Sprache*, "consists in this: that a sound reaches an ear, another being. . . . Speaking is always the speaking of someone to someone about something." The words of the folk song, however, are not directed by one person to another or by many persons to many others; the voice is that of the group, which includes all those present; here, there is no "other being," no mere listeners. More accurately, the speakers are also the listeners, not in the sense that every individual speaks to all the others, but in the sense that all of them together speak to themselves taken together. Nor can there be any question of communication: what is there to be communicated where everyone knows exactly – indeed, must know – what is to be said in order to take part in the collective speaking? If one member of the group happens to lead the chorus, his words are certainly not addressed to the others; each of the latter could say them as well. He does not tell them anything they don't know; he does not speak to the others but *for* them; he is still the mouthpiece of the group. Nor does a comparison with the special situation of the monologue get us anywhere: to soliloquize is merely to think aloud, to voice thoughts that could just as well remain unvoiced, whereas a song does not really exist until it has been voiced. People do not come together to think of songs silently, to imagine them in common. And so the question arises, What is the element of the tune whose addition to the words of the folk song turns something meaningless into something meaningful?

The answer must be sought in the difference between the human inter-relationships created by the word, or speaking, and those created by the tones, or singing. The spoken word presupposes "the other," the person or persons to whom it is addressed; the one speaking and the one spoken to are turned toward each other; the word goes out from one to the other, creating a situation in which the two are facing each other as distinct, separate individuals. Wherever there is talk, there is a "he-not-I" on the one hand and his counterpart, an "I-not-he," on the other. This is why the word is not the natural expression of the group. In the group, person and person are brought together, not separated; the barriers between individuals are not emphasized, they are minimized. An individual may certainly step in front of the group and speak to it; but when he speaks within the group from out of the group, as a member, and when the group includes all individuals present, when there is no "other," no "facing each other," then one of the conditions under which speaking is meaningful is canceled out by the realities of the situation. Now, if adding tones to the words results in transforming the meaningless into the self-evident, it is reasonable to assume that singing is the natural and appropriate expression of the group, of the togetherness of individuals within the group. If this is the case, we may assume that tones – singing – essentially express not the individual but the group, more accurately, the individual in so far as he is a member of the group, still more accurately, the individual in so far as his relation to the others is not one of "facing them" but one of togetherness.

A closer look at the situation involved in each case confirms this: the nature of tones expresses the situation of togetherness as closely as the nature of the word expresses the situation of "facing each other." Tones are not directed to others (Géza Révész's hypothesis that they originate in the call – that is, the caller's intention to give greater range to his voice – is just as well- or ill-founded as any other attempt to rationalize the primordial and to penetrate even behind the beginnings). Tones do not refer to things; they say nothing about anything. And yet they are not mere "expressions," either, are not merely emitted: they are also intended to be heard, namely, by the singer himself. Invariably, they are both outgoing and incoming. Whereas the word goes out from me, the speaker, and remains outside with the person spoken to, who replies with another word, I, as a singer, go out of myself with the tone and at the same time, as a listener, return to myself from outside with the tone. In the tone, and only in the tone, the singer encounters himself coming from the outside, and not just himself if the singer is the group. In the one tone that comes from all, I encounter the group as well as myself. The dividing line between myself and the others loses its sharpness. Here the situation is not one where two distinct parties face each other; here the others do not address their singing to me. Whereas words turn people toward each other, as it were, make them look at each other, tones turn them all in the same direction: everyone follows the tones on their way out and on their way back. The moment tones resound, the situation where one party faces another is transmuted into a situation of togetherness, the many distinct individuals into the one group.

If this is the case, why do not people simply sing songs without words? Why do the words in songs give way to the tones only for short moments, at the most? Why is there no folk song that is not a sung poem?

Mere melodies would be sufficient if the meaning of song were exhausted by the transmutation of the face-to-face encounter between persons into a togetherness, if the singer were concerned only with feeling at one with the community. Something else must be involved in a form of expression where words are necessarily linked to tones. The singer who uses words wants more than just to be with the group: he also wants to be with things, those things to which the words of the poem refer. A person using words only is never with things in this sense: he remains at a distance from them; they remain for him "the other," that which he is not, "outside" him. By contrast, if his words are not merely spoken but sung, they build a living bridge that links him with the things referred to by the words, that transmutes distinction and separation into togetherness. By means of the tones, the speaker goes out to the things, brings the things from outside within himself, so that they are no longer "the other," something alien that he is not, but the other and his own in one. Thus a form of speaking that is addressed to no one and communicates nothing becomes intelligible. So long as the words of the poem remain silent within myself, what they are intended to say is not yet "something other," a thing "outside" myself; I must utter them, project them out of myself, in order to transform what they say into a "thing" other than myself, encountered from the outside. Only then can the tones fulfill their purpose: remove the barrier between person and thing, and clear the way for what might be called the singer's inner participation in that of which he sings – for an active sharing, an experience of a special kind, a spiritual experience. This experience is not a dreaming-oneself-out-of-oneself, not a dreaming-oneself-into-something-other, as though one were different from what one is. The singer remains what he is, but his self is enlarged, his vital range is extended: being what he is he can now, without losing his identity, be with what he is not; and the other, being what it is, can, without losing its identity, be with him. This kind of experience is not to be confused with sympathy. Sympathy is directed at immediate action, like compassion meant to shorten or to allay another's suffering, whereas the active sharing of suffering – for instance, expressed in a song that tells a story of suffering – consists precisely in this, that the suffering is fully re-experienced in the singer's mind. Here the emotion is secondary, is the effect not the cause of the sharing, and together with the latter is spiritualized, "put into brackets." (This is why the evil to which the poet refers is just as good, just as lovable, as the good.)

Thus our question on the meaning of song has been given a preliminary answer: it lies in the transmutation of the twofold confrontation between person and person and between person and thing into a twofold togetherness: the I-not-he and I-not-it become the I-and-he and the I-and-it. The tones are the medium in which the transmutation takes place.

17

Hazara lullabies

Hiromi Lorraine Sakata

Hiromi Lorraine Sakata, 'Hazara women in Afghanistan:
innovators and preservers of a musical tradition', in E. Koskoff,
Women and Music in Cross-Cultural Perspective (New York:
Greenwood Press, 1987), pp. 85–95.

Sakata's article on Hazara women's music is based on her fieldwork
in Afghanistan during the periods 1966–67 and 1971–73. It hardly
needs pointing out that Afghanistan and its people have undergone
many traumatic changes since that time: this article stands, nonetheless, as a record of the situation she observed.

Afghanistan is an Islamic country situated in an area described at one time
or another as part of the Middle East, Central Asia, West Asia, and South
Asia. The country is populated by different ethnic peoples who are predominantly Sunni Muslims. The Hazaras living in the mountains of central
Afghanistan constitute the single largest group of Shi'a Muslims in the
country. Although the various groups speak different languages, adhere
to different customs, and belong to different religious sects, the general
precepts of Islam in Afghanistan are so prevalent and affect every aspect
of life that one finds a surprising amount of correspondence in the traditional conceptions and conventions of the many groups living there.

Afghanistan is a traditional Islamic society where the dichotomy
between public and private (where public remains in the domain of males
and private in the realm of females) is maintained as an ideal. Traditional
women are supposed to be kept, or keep themselves, in seclusion, cutting
off social relations with males who are not closely related to them. However,
circumstances often prevent strict adherence to the ideals of seclusion; or
more likely, symbols or expressions of seclusion and their use are reinter-
preted by outsiders and insiders alike.

Factors other than sex, such as age or social status, also play a key part
in determining the role of women (see Rosaldo, 1974:29). Young girls and

boys are often treated as one gender – that of children. As children, they often share private life with the women, yet are allowed or go unnoticed in the peripheral sphere of the public life of men. For example, before the 1973 establishment of the Republic of Afghanistan, all city buses in Kabul were segregated; the first three or four rows of seats were reserved for the women and the children, and the rest of the bus was reserved for the men. However, young boys or girls travelling with their fathers could sit in the rear of the bus with the other men.

Women's gatherings (such as the traditional New Year's outings in the city of Herat) are attended by boys and girls accompanying women and those men who sell sweets, tea, and other necessities for a celebration. Male servants or young children are sent out on errands to public as well as private places. It is often through the conduit of these children and servants that news of happenings in both private and public places is transmitted to the women. Thus, it sometimes happens that women have access to more information than men, who do not have access to private situations other than in their own homes. Strict segregation between the sexes is maintained after puberty. The only common exceptions to this segregation are the household servants, providers of essential services, older women of some influence and power, or outsiders to the community.

I write about the exceptions here because, first, exceptions to the rule are everyday occurrences that are much more common than one imagines from reading descriptions of Afghan society, and, second, because a broader picture of the relationships between the traditional men's world and women's world helps us understand how it is possible for women to play a dominant musical role in a predominantly male society.

The distinction between public and private or, in the words of Michelle Rosaldo, between the "domestic orientation of women and the extra-domestic or 'public' ties that, in most societies, are primarily available to men" (1974:17–18) are manifested in music as well. Musical instruments in Afghanistan are played mainly by men, while those generally played by women and children are not thought to be "real" instruments such as the *daira* (tambourine) and *chang* (jew's harp). When the gender of the performer changes, the status of the instrument or the performer may also change. For example, when a man plays the *daira* as an accompanying drum for an ensemble, it is considered to be a "real" instrument. However, if a man plays the *chang*, he is not considered a "real" man; he may be considered an old man whose distinction from old woman becomes as fuzzy as the distinction between young girl and young boy, or he is considered a somewhat deviant character (the joker, the outcaste). One other instrument that lacks the legitimacy of being "male" is the *nai*, a long, end-blown flute associated with shepherds. It is not my intent here to discover why the *nai* is thought to be less of a real musical instrument than other wind instruments, but I might suggest that it has something to do with the close association of shepherds and women to nature as well as the age and status of the shepherds (young boys, unmarried men). Whatever the reasons, these three instruments avoid the stigma that most musical instruments have in a strict Islamic society – that they are *muezzins* (the crier of the Islamic call to prayer) of the devil (Hitti 1970:274). The association with women, children, shepherds, and by extension, nature, seems to render the instruments unreal or harmless.

Genres of music (from the Western perspective) that are not considered real music by the Afghans are children's game songs and lullabies, both closely identified with the domestic or natural realm of women and children. Again, the status of women and children in society seems to deem the genres associated with them innocent, ineffectual, or in a sense, devalued within a musical value system. Whenever I made it known in the villages that I was interested in studying the music, villagers would assure me that I had come to the wrong place; there was no music there. But when I asked to hear specific genres, such as *lalai* (lullaby) or *kartugak* (a Hazara children's song style), they immediately complied, although they laughed and thought I was ridiculous to be interested in such trivia. They may have resolved the seeming contradiction by thinking that I had an interest in both music and in women's play.

The social and musical situation in the Hazarajat does not differ from that of Afghanistan in general. Some writers have observed the seeming ascendency of Hazara women compared to other women in the country (Elphinstone 1819:2:250–51), but many of the differences may be attributed to the fact that the whole of the Hazarajat is made up of a few, small rural communities or households. Because of the relatively small population, there may appear to be less of a dichotomy between public and private. Locations and occasions for public musical performances are rare. Most of the public music is played in the context of private celebrations such as wedding festivities.

I categorized Hazara songs into children's songs, lullabies, women's songs, men's songs, and accompanied songs in order to systematically study the repertoire. Although it originally was not my intent to study Hazara music according to men's and women's repertoires, an analysis based on separate repertoires sheds light on the possible development of a general Hazara musical style. There are two important issues under consideration here. One concerns a specific repertoire of songs and another a particular style of performance of songs. Some songs are sung exclusively by a certain group of people and share stylistic characteristics, while other songs are sung by a number of different groups and do not share a particular style.

Among the songs sung exclusively by a particular group and sung in a particular style are "girls' special songs" and *chang* melodies performed by girls and young women. Young boys and men, although familiar with this repertoire, do not perform these genres. Young boys and girls do sing other songs that are shared by men and women, but these songs do not seem to be restricted to any gender, age grades, or particular groups.

Lullabies can be divided into two kinds: "functional lullabies," and "stylized lullabies." Functional lullabies are sung by women to help soothe babies and put them to sleep; stylized lullabies are sung by men, often to the accompaniment of a *dambura* (a two-string, fretless, plucked lute). They are meant to be sung as social entertainment. Among the songs sung by men exclusively are the accompanied songs, exclusively a male genre because only men play the accompanying *dambura*, and the songs sung in a particular style and melody-type, which I have labelled "prototype melody." Women's songs and men's songs do not exist as special repertoires in Hazara conceptualizations. Neither the function of these songs nor the song texts identify them as particularly women's songs or men's songs; both men and women and boys and girls share knowledge of the repertoire. It is only the gender of the performer that determines the songs as belonging to one category or the other. Yet, when one looks closely at the musical structures as performed, one can also perceive a difference in style between the two. Generally, men and boys tend to use larger intervals and set their melodies within wider ranges than women or girls.

In an earlier work (Sakata 1968), I suggested a theory of gradual evolution of Hazara melody types, pointing to a general tendency to increase in size and complexity ranging from the simple lullaby, to songs sung by women, to songs sung by men, and finally to accompanied songs sung by men. I cited that as men had more outside contact than women, it was therefore understandable that their songs should be more developed and complex than the songs of women. In a sense, I was pointing to the often stated notion that women, more than men, were preservers of tradition. What I failed to indicate, however, was the affinity of all Hazara songs, whether sung by men, women, or children, to the repertoires exclusive to women and young girls. These songs contain the very elements that identify other songs as Hazara. The women seem to have identified the musical characteristics that harmonized with their environment and were concordant with their life-style.

[. . .]

Of the many different categories of songs, the lullaby and the lament seem to be within the women's province almost universally. The lullaby obviously further musically binds specific child to mother and children to women generally. All the songs identified as lullabies were sung by women except one sung by an old man who was taking care of a baby boy. In this instance, the man (in his sixties) may not have been displaying abnormal behavior, but rather, behavior appropriate for older people, men and women alike who, like children, are permitted to cross back and forth between men's and women's domains.

Hazara functional lullabies are called *lalai* or *lalu*. (See Figure 17.1, Functional Lullaby.) The songs are essentially an expression of love for the child for whom it is sung. Basically, the text of a lullaby is comprised of the sounds "lalai" or "lalu" with the interjection of terms of endearment such as "mother," "father," "my sweet," "my eyes." They are based on short, stylized phrases containing a number of words in Hazaragi, a dialect of Persian. This tendency to use local terminology is reduced in other Hazara song genres. Most of the lullabies are based on a line of text consisting of eight syllables that appear in conjunction with other rhyming lines. The text is obviously the least flexible element of Hazara lullabies, both functional and stylized.

A characteristic of some lullabies is the use of words or sounds for the effect of the sound rather than for the sake of the meaning. The one lullaby in my collection that was sung by an old man involves words deliberately altered to produce mellifluous sounds. It is also common for a singer to produce a sound by flapping the tongue against the lips (see ᗱ in Figures 17.1 and 17.2).

Some lullabies perform a double function; one, to put the baby to sleep, and two, as a message to the singer's (mother's) lover to pay a visit.

> Bobe bacha shikar rafta
> Da kohi marghozar, rafta
> Tanbe darga jaru ya

Fig. 17.1 Functional Lullaby

Fig. 17.2 Stylized Lullaby

Pasi darga khuru ya
Tailone tanbaco biya
Jega bale sako biya
Lalui lalui bobe aya

Baby's father went hunting
He went to the Marghozar Mts.
The door latch is straw
The rooster stands at the door
Come by the tobacco field path
Come to the bed on the platform
Lalui lalui mother's father

There are examples of men singing stylized lullabies, that is, lullaby song-types sung for the sake of performance. (See Figure 17.2, Stylized Lullaby.) Although the stylized lullabies display many of the same musical characteristics heard in functional lullabies, the performance intent and context are clearly different.

The examples of stylized lullabies were sung by men who accompanied themselves on the *dambura*. The lullaby examples indicate that there is a clearly demarcated dichotomy between men's and women's songs.

The women's functional lullabies are based on melodies within a range of a minor third consisting of both minor and major second intervals while the men's stylized lullabies are sung within a range of a major third consisting of major second intervals. Both men and women commonly include phrases with an ascending or descending disjunct fourth interval. This disjunct fourth interval is an important feature of Hazara songs and appears most often in the beginning of phrases.

[. . .]

Three musical features stand out as crucial in determining Hazara melodies: first, the importance and use of the open fourth interval; second, the relatively small melody range of a fifth or less; and third, the downward melodic contour. All three musical features are clearly emphasized in the genres discussed here. The lullaby, the most versatile of all the repertoires because it can be represented as a *chang* melody as well as a men's accompanied song, especially exhibits the intervalic content and other stylistic features so characteristic of prototype melodies. Yet, to the Hazara, it is only the men's stylized, accompanied lullaby that is considered legitimate music [. . .] The Hazara situation seems to follow a common tendency in many societies to ignore the contributions of women and to allow them to go unrecognized because so often the cultural definitions of music and musician focus solely on male traditions.

References

Elphinstone, Mountstuart. (1819) *An Account of the Kingdom of Caubul*, 2 vols, 2nd ed. (London: John Murray).

Hitti, Philip K. (1970) *History of the Arabs from the Earliest Times to the Present*, 10th ed. (New York: St. Martin's Press).

Rosaldo, Michelle Zimbalist. (1974) "Woman, culture, and society: a theoretical overview," in Michelle Zimbalist Rosaldo and Louise Lamphere, eds, *Woman Culture and Society*. (Stanford, CA: Stanford University Press).

Sakata, Hiromi Lorraine. (1968) Music of the Hazarajat. MA thesis, University of Washington, Seattle.

18

Race, class and gender in *Carmen*

Susan McClary

Susan McClary, *Georges Bizet, Carmen* (Cambridge: Cambridge University Press, 1992), pp. 29–43.

McClary's wide-ranging essay on the representation of others in opera focuses on one of the major case studies of *Words and Music*, Carmen – referring to the ill-fated character of the hero Don José as well as Carmen herself and the other major characters Zuniga, Micaëla, and Escamillo – the opera by Georges Bizet, and the novella by Prosper Mérimée on which the opera is based. The Halévy family are significant in two respects here: that Bizet married Geneviève and that her cousin Ludovic co-wrote the libretto to the opera (with Henri Meilhac).

Bizet's *Carmen* has often been understood as a story of ill-fated love between two equal parties whose destinies happen to clash. But to read the opera in this fashion is to ignore the faultlines of social power that organize it, for while the story's subject matter may appear idiosyncratic to us, *Carmen* is actually only one of a large number of fantasies involving race, class and gender that circulated in nineteenth-century French culture. Thus [. . .] we need to reexamine the critical tensions of its original context – the context within which it was written and first received – as well as the polities of representation: who creates representations of whom, with what imagery, towards what ends?

Musicologists have long recognized *Carmen's* exoticism as one of its most salient features, but they usually treat that exoticism as unproblematic. Indeed, until quite recently, most of the exotic images and narratives that proliferate in Western culture were regarded as innocent: the "Orient" (first the Middle East, later East Asia and Africa) seemed to serve merely as a "free zone" for the European imagination. Edward Said, however, has shown that this "free zone" was always circumscribed by political concerns.[1] Some of these were relatively benign. In the eighteenth century, for instance, the "Orient" offered a vantage point from which French writers could criticize their own society. Thus Rousseau addressed the East as a utopian philosopher contemplating alternatives with the West, and Montesquieu adopted the persona of a Persian traveler writing letters home about the odd social practices he encounters in Paris.[2]

But serious "Orientalism" dates from Napoleon's Egyptian campaign of 1798, an invasion that stimulated the growth of academic disciplines investigating Middle Eastern archaeology, religions, linguistics and anthropology. While many Orientalist scholars no doubt believed they were amassing disinterested knowledge, their information was also mobilized for purposes of state and commercial colonization. [. . .]

French artists soon began to manifest a profound fascination with things Middle Eastern. Victor Hugo defined the terrain and agenda of cultural "Orientalism" succinctly in the preface to his collection of poetry *Les Orientales* (1829):

> The Orient, as image or as thought, has become, for the intelligence as well as for the imagination, a sort of general preoccupation which the author of this book has obeyed perhaps without his knowledge. Oriental colors came as of their own accord to imprint themselves on all his thoughts, all his dreams; and his dreams and his thoughts found themselves in turn, and almost without having wished it so, Hebraic, Turkish, Greek, Persian, Arab, even Spanish, because Spain is still the Orient; Spain is half African, Africa is half Asiatic.[3]

Several details in this manifesto are worthy of note. First, Hugo describes (surely somewhat disingenuously) his exploitation of the East not as active volition, but rather as the East's having seduced him into surrendering his Western rationality over to its agendas. He presents himself as a prototype of Don José, lured by the mystery and sensual overload of the "Orient" into deserting the Apollonian poetic tradition of the *ancien régime*: in Hugo's words, "In the age of Louis XIV one was a Hellenist; now one is an Orientalist." The statement above also indicates without apology the radical interchangeability of exotic types for the cultural Orientalist: Persian, Greek, Jewish, Spanish, African – all wash together in an undifferentiated realm of Otherness.

Hugo's discussion of Spain is especially important for our purposes. Whatever the reality of Spain's history or culture, French Orientalists ascribed to it the same inscrutable, luxuriant and barbarous qualities they imagined to be characteristic of the entire Middle East. In his preface, Hugo writes rapturously about Spain, especially the tension – described with lavishly gender-coded language – between the austerity of its gothic Christian remnants and the mystery of its Moorish elements "opened out to the sun like a large flower full of perfumes."

Within his imagined, autonomous realm of "the Orient," Hugo can safely construct his poems of bloodthirsty warriors, pirates, djinn, harem girls. Central to his many verses on exotic women is the veil: that sign of ownership, modesty and intrigue which can be coaxed into lifting for the pleasure of poet and reader alike. While such images of denuded harem girls may seem innocuous enough, in fact they participated in a much larger socio-cultural agenda. In Orientalist texts these women stands for the East itself: veiled in mystery but finally penetrable by the Western desire to know and possess. The East as a whole became "feminized," understood as sensual, static, irrational and nonproductive; though fertile with resources and ripe for plunder. The East's seductiveness seemed even to invite its own ravishment, just as Hugo claims he enters this terrain "perhaps without his knowledge" – and just as Don José, Mérimée's narrator and we, the audience are lured into Carmen's world "almost without having wished it."

[. . .]

[I]f part of the motivation for Orientalism was to criticize the West and its attitudes towards Others (Hugo writes that "ancient Asiatic barbarism was perhaps not so devoid of superior men as our civilization wishes to believe"), that very critique constituted a threat to the belief in Western supremacy that underwrote the colonizing enterprise. The idealization of the East easily and frequently led to a backlash of reimposed Western domination, especially in narratives in which the Westerner surrenders all claims to privilege and "goes primitive," but then tries to reverse the process, reasserting domination all the more insistently for having let it slip. [. . .]

The tension between desire for the exotic and fear of its seductive potency runs through many of the cultural artifacts of Orientalism – including *Carmen*, which was written at a time when France was experiencing particular humiliation with respect to its position as a world power. Nelly Furman writes, "after the 'ignominious' defeat of the French army in the Franco-Prussian War of 1870, during which the Emperor Napoleon III and his armed forces were taken prisoner at Sedan, Bizet's opera shows us a well-meaning but naive soldier beguiled by an enticing foreigner. Napoleon III had married a Spaniard . . . By implying that the woman causes the soldier's downfall, as traditional interpretations of the opera suggest, Bizet and the librettists . . . seem to propose a psychological explanation for a political and military event."[4]

[. . .]

From the seventeenth century on, operas had regularly made use of exotic settings, although the music itself only occasionally was designed to sound "Oriental." Nineteenth-century musical Orientalism began soon after the Egyptian Expedition and became enthusiastically Arabic around 1830 – just after the French conquest of Algiers.[5] The themes that mark literary and artistic Orientalism show up in music as well. Félicien David, for instance, visited the Middle East, and his music reflects both his impressions and French cultural concerns. His *Le Désert* (1844) depicts caravans, muezzins calling the faithful to prayer and the ubiquitous dancing girls.

During the second half of the century, Orientalism saturated opera production in France. In the discussion of "exoticism" in his *Nineteenth-Century Music*, Carl Dahlhaus explains this trend by reproducing uncritically the attitude that ethnic cultures merely provided raw materials to stimulate the exhausted European imagination. He writes, "exoticism offered nineteenth-century opera librettists an *untapped reservoir of material that virtually cried out for exploitation?*" (emphasis added).[6] Some of the operas that resulted from this supposedly solicited exploitation include Gounod's *La Reine de Saba* (1862), Saint-Saëns' *Samson et Dalila* (1877), Delibes' *Lakmé* (1883) and Massenet's *Thaïs* (1894). Even instrumental music indulged in this fashion, as in d'Indy's *Istar* (1912), a set of variations that begins with the most extravagant version and casts off veil after veil until the theme itself – identified as the goddess Istar – is revealed gloriously naked.

Bizet's infatuation with exoticism can be traced as far back as his Symphony in C, a piece completed when he was seventeen, which features Orientalist themes in its inner movements. Such subjects persisted throughout his career. *Djamileh* is a full-fledged Orientalist fantasy, involving a slave girl who begs her master to reenslave her (the dénouement involves her unveiling). Some of his other exotic moments required some connivance: *La Jolie Fille de Perth* is set in Scotland, but features a band of gypsies who suddenly materialize for a ballet; *Carmen* engages with Hugo's Orientalist Spain. The music Bizet wrote to represent the exotic rarely had much to do ethnographically with the purported locales of these operas, but he knew how to invoke with uncanny deftness the French notion of the racial Other.

Carmen differs from many Orientalist texts in that its terrain is not uniformly exotic. The opera involves an encounter between an aristocrat of northern stock, marked as "one of us," and a gypsy, who bears most of the burden of exoticism for the duration of the composition. Thus *Carmen* operates in part as an Orientalist work, but it also participates in another genre prevalent in nineteenth-century France: that of the racial Other who has infiltrated home turf.

For not all "Orientals" were located in imaginary lands. Two principal groups classified as Oriental – gypsies and Jews – circulated in French society. While occupying very different positions within that society, they were often presented in cultural artifacts (which exploited them in part for exotic color) as interchangeable. Thus the gypsy Esmeralda in Hugo's *Notre Dame de Paris* is first taken to be Jewish, as is Mérimée's Carmen. Balzac identifies Esther, the martyred prostitute in his *Splendors and Miseries of a Courtesan*, as a Jew and describes her as Oriental, mysterious, pagan, sexually precocious.

Far more than actual Middle Easterners, gypsies and Jews were regarded as dangerous, for while marked as alien, they lived on native soil. They were too real; they passed through the boundaries between European Self and Other that made classic Orientalism safe for the aesthetic gaze. And both groups were linguistically treacherous: they mastered the languages of their host countries so as to be able to "pass" as indigenous, while retaining fluency in their own archaic tongues – tongues that remained opaque to those around them. Carmen's linguistic versatility is one of her greatest threats in Mérimée, and Bizet constructs her with a similar virtuosity with respect to musical discourses.

The boundaries of race or ethnicity were not the only ones threatened by these groups: issues of class and sexuality were inextricably bound up with popular perceptions of the "Orientals" at home. The label "bohemian," for instance, could refer to the gypsies or to the underclass subculture that became a breeding ground for both avant-garde artists and political unrest.[7] Gypsies performed their exotic songs and dances for the benefit of popular audiences in Paris, and Bizet (along with his collaborator for *L'Arlésienne*, Alphonse Daudet) frequented their haunts of ill-repute for entertainment. "Local color" was available, in other words, as a constant feature of Parisian night-life: the "Orient" had been reconstituted at home, and one could dabble in exotic women and music without ever leaving the city.

Jews would seem to have little in common with migrant gypsies. By the nineteenth century, they had become leaders in France in the arts, the economy and politics. Yet the status of artists such as Meyerbeer or the Halévys did not prevent Jews from being regarded as foreign parasites. The Dreyfus Affair later revealed the virulence of French anti-Semitism, but novels by Balzac and the Goncourts had already depicted Jews as sinister, sexually depraved outsiders. Hitler's genocidal agenda (in which many of the French participated) grouped Jews with gypsies and "sexual deviants" as targets for extermination. *Carmen* becomes far more complicated when lifted from Hugo's "Orient" and resituated within a domestic context that was experiencing tensions between the "pure-blooded" European and the dark, seductive interloper.

Contemporary tensions bound up with class likewise pervade *Carmen*. In the years since the French Revolution, the dominant middle class in

France had advanced through several phases. Initially, universal emancipation was embraced as the proper liberal sentiment. But as the working class began pushing for its own liberation, the contradictions undergirding the French bourgeoisie became increasingly apparent. Since middle-class living standards required a large, malleable labor force, the bourgeoisie was reluctant to extend parity to workers. Revolutions rocked France in 1830, 1848 and 1871, causing many middle-class individuals to perceive the disenfranchized as alien (if necessary) presences. Demands for rights were received as violent threats, the sordid poverty of the underclass seen as a cesspool breeding crime and promiscuity. Bizet introduces Carmen as a common laborer in a cigar factory patroled by Don José's military unit. During Act I, we witness the violence of this working class in Carmen's knife fight with her co-worker, her insubordination with Zuniga, her treachery with José. Later we are treated to scenes of smuggling and prostitution. None of this would have seemed coincidental in 1875, a scant four years after the trauma of the Commune.

Despite its general loathing of the proletariat, some members of the middle class, especially those inclined to be artists, aligned themselves with the underclass through the bohemian subculture. Without question, these dropouts greatly romanticized the conditions of working-class life; yet the factors that drew them to abandon their middle-class comforts resembled those that caused the "Orient" to appear so attractive at this same time: release from a regimented bureaucratic society and rigid sexual mores that demanded the sacrifice of pleasure for duty. Carmen appeals to Don José in part because she offers him freedom from the strictures of his bourgeois life. But the cost of his escape from respectability soon becomes clear. His descent into the underworld is dramatically conveyed through his abdication of the bright public street of Act I for the den of iniquity of Act II and the uninhabited wilderness of Act III. He reemerges into the light of Act IV as a dissolute, common criminal wandering the streets.

Interestingly, Bizet himself was branded a "bohemian" by his in-laws, the Halévy family, who initially resisted his marriage proposal on those grounds. To be sure, Bizet's bohemianism remained rather shallow: it seems to have been limited to his promiscuity and penchant for nighttime slumming. It did not affect his political attitudes, for he – like many affluent bourgeois – fled Paris in disgust during the Commune. Yet both Bizet's flirtation with the underclass and his subsequent recoiling from it might be considered possible factors in his compulsion to set Mérimée's *Carmen*.

But an even more important factor in the appeal of *Carmen* was Mérimée's treatment of sexuality, which engaged so effectively nineteenth-century cultural ambivalences concerning women. As with issues of race and class, the earlier nineteenth century had dealt with women through narratives of benign co-existence, possible so long as an unchallenged hierarchy prevailed. Just as the "Orient" seemed to serve as the passive landscape upon which the Western artist projected his fantasies and the working class appeared to labor voluntarily under the conditions of capitalist industry, so women were thought to thrive in domestic confinement, their energies absorbed by the duties of wife and mother. The assumed dominance of the white, middle-class male guaranteed that all these relationships – whether of race, class or gender – appeared to reflect the natural order of things.

In literature and painting of the mid-century, chaste, domestic female figures abound. This stereotype found one of its most striking realizations in Coventry Patmore's *The Angel in the House* (1863), in which the sexless, selfless wife and mother maintains the spiritual and material comforts of the hearth as compensation for the depersonalized public workplace. On the French stage, her most reliable venue was the Opéra-Comique, which had exalted this figure in operas for several decades; she was one of the defining characteristics of the *opéra-comique* genre and appeared as heroine in Auber, Gounod and in *La Dame blanche*, the opera so detested by Bizet. She resurfaced as Micaëla in *Carmen*, and she even entered Bizet's life in the form of Geneviève Halévy. In 1867 the notorious womanizer reported his infatuation with his wife-to-be thus: "No more *soirées*! No more sprees! No more mistresses! All that is finished! Absolutely finished! I am saying this seriously. I have met an adorable girl whom I love! In two years she will be my wife! . . . I tell you this seriously; I am convinced! I am sure of myself! The good has killed the evil! The victory is won!"[8]

The majority of middle-class women in the nineteenth century complied with hegemonic ideals of femininity: they withdrew from participation in the public sphere, and some even denied themselves sexual expression in conformity with the images proliferating in conduct manuals, novels and operas. But many women rejected the prescribed role of "angel in the house." As Peter Gay writes, "Man's fear of woman is as old as time, but it was only in the bourgeois century that it became a prominent theme in popular novels and medical treatises . . . Men's defensiveness in the bourgeois century was so acute because the advance of women all around them was an attempt to recover ground they had lost."[9]

Accordingly, the images in culture began to shift, from reveries of benevolent submission within a preordained hierarchy to nightmares involving powerfully constituted, monstrous Others threatening to overwhelm the weakened, victimized dominant order. Sexually assertive, self-willed women appeared increasingly in novels and paintings in the last decades of the century. According to Gay, "Woman as vampire, man as victim: that was, if not the general consensus, a strong current of male feeling in nineteenth-century France."[10] Eventually, the *femme fatale* shows up in opera as well – with a vengeance. Bizet himself describes Myrrha, the Carmen-like *femme fatale* in his *La Coupe du Roi de Thulé*, in these words:

> She is an old-style courtesan, sensual as Sappho, ambitious as Aspasia; she is beautiful, quick-witted, alluring ... In her eyes must be that greenish look, the sure sign of sensuality and egoism pushed to the length of cruelty ... Yorick by himself is free; he sings his love with passion and frenzy; he tells it to the clouds and the stars. With Myrrha present he is extinguished ... She comes in (for the first time) slowly, dreamily, absent-mindedly; she turns her glance on all around her, and fixes it almost disdainfully on Yorick.[11]

[. . .]

Bizet's well-documented exploitation of prostitutes has already been mentioned, but one figure in his life in the *demi-monde* deserves special treatment. In 1865 he met a woman who lived near his father's country home. Comtesse Lionel de Chabrillan was born Céleste Vénard, an illegitimate child who fled her abusive family at thirteen. She became a *fille inscrite* – a prostitute registered with the Paris police. By sixteen, she was involved with the poet Alfred de Musset and soon left the brothels to appear as a dancer at the Bal Mabille where she was named "La Mogador," after a Moroccan city recently bombarded by the French. She became a celebrity who traveled in the same circles as prominent figures in French culture. After marrying the Comte de Chabrillan, she was at last removed from the police register. She then turned to writing, and although she had no formal education and notated her works phonetically, she became a prolific and popular author of novels, libretti, plays and memoirs.[12] When Bizet met her, she was a forty-one-year-old widow, writing but still singing at the popular Café-Concert du XIX^ieme Siècle. Since her repertory included songs by Yradier, it is possible she introduced Bizet to the song that became the "Habañera." In any case, she took Bizet under her protection, permitted him to use her house as a retreat in which to compose, and even bought him a piano.

Unlike most such women, Céleste found the means of accounting for her own life in her writing – of representing herself. Her candid views of Bizet (who may or may not have been her lover) describe him as "an aristocratic savage": "I never saw him laugh outright. Georges Bizet was not very gay at this time. He was still living on hope."[13] Critics have suggested that Céleste was a model for Carmen, especially because of her vivid self-characterization:

My character was formed early. I loved passionately or hated furiously
. . . When I hate people, I wish they would die . . . Moderation is no part of
my nature. Joy, sorrow, affection, resentment, laziness, work – I have over-
done them all. My life has been one long excess . . . I feel with a passion that
devours me . . . When I take up a book, I want to understand it so quickly
that the blood rushes to my head. I can't see straight, and I have to stop. Then
I go into a ridiculous rage at myself . . . I beat my brain. When I try to learn
to write and my hand disobeys, I pinch my arm black and blue . . . Two
defects in my character have protected me. I have always been capricious
and proud. No one, among women whose tendency it is to say *yes*, derives
more pleasure than I do from saying *no*. So the men to whom I have given
the most are those who asked least of me.[14]

Carmen clearly belongs to this category of women. She is known to the
men in the community as available – albeit (as she makes clear in the
"Habañera") on her own terms. She tells Don José in the "Seguidilla" that
she often changes lovers and that she frequents Lillas Pastia's, a house of
ill-repute in which she and other women provide entertainment, consort
with patrons and arrange liaisons for after hours. Her gypsy comrades at
Pastia's joke with her about her new-found "love," and José's senior officer
tries to set up a routine assignation. Even though Zuniga and Escamillo
are put off temporarily, they both assume they are simply awaiting their
turns. Bizet's relationship with the benevolent Céleste might account for
much of Carmen's strength of character and her positive attributes. But
this relationship was not by any means his sole model, for the story of
Carmen takes some nasty turns – in keeping with the many other treatments of prostitution in French Culture of the time.

[. . .]

An opera in 1875 that presented the color *and* the filth of the "Orient,"
the insubordination of an indigenous workforce and the lethal contagion
of female sexuality faced the risk of arousing public indignation, as Flau-
bert's *Madame Bovary* or Baudelaire's *Les Fleurs du mal* had twenty years
before. And *Carmen* did just that with its first audiences and critics. But by
engaging nearly all the controversial themes of late nineteenth-century
culture simultaneously, its scandal and eventual success were virtually
assured. [. . .] *Carmen's* "realistic" treatment of race, class and gender
formed the basis of its initial horrified rejection and also set the terms of its
exuberant acceptance the following year.

To be sure, race, ethnicity, class and gender are separate issues, and they
must not be confused. We are concerned here, however, with representa-
tional constructs, with a story from a moment in European history in
which slippage among all varieties of Others informed cultural artifacts.

Sander Gilman and Klaus Theweleit have written extensively about the ways in which Jews, gypsies, women, the working classes and the insane were lumped together in the late nineteenth century as a single bloody tide threatening to overwhelm European social order. In 1895, Edouard Drumont pulled all these threads together when he wrote, "Besotted by the prostitute, robbed by the Jews, menaced by the worker, the Voltairean and masonic bourgeois begins to perceive that he is in a bad way. He has killed off every ideal and all faith within people's souls; he has corrupted everything around him, and all the corruptions he has sown are rising up before him like the avenging furies to push him into the deep."[15]

Drumont's paranoiac hallucination of the victimized middle-class male could stand as a plot summary of *Carmen* – it is even conceivable that Drumont was influenced by Bizet's opera. Just as "the Orient" imprinted itself on Hugo's dreams and thoughts "perhaps without his knowledge," so *Carmen* entered into the common consciousness and has shaped attitudes ever since its premiere. In the opera, Carmen herself represents virtually all available categories of alterity: inscrutable "Oriental," menacing worker, lawless criminal, *femme fatale*. And José, child of the Enlightenment bourgeoisie who surrenders his claims to racial, class and gender privilege because of her, must pay the consequences in the finale. Yet it is ultimately Carmen who pays – with her life – for José's identity crisis and Bizet's fantasies of alterity.

The lurid context from which *Carmen* originally emerged has retreated from us a bit: we may no longer link the opera's exotic elements with the colonized "Orient," insubordination with the Commune or female sexuality with syphilitic infection. And we do not like to remember the enterprises – colonial wars, genocidal purges of European ethnic minorities, massacres of striking laborers, increased regulation of women's bodies – that arose to counter nineteenth-century destabilization. But the opera continues to play along important faultlines of racial, class and gendered Otherness, however they may be construed at any given historical moment. Whatever else it is, *Carmen* is emphatically *not* a story about fate.

Notes

1 See Edward Said, *Orientalism* (New York, 1979).
2 See James Creech, "Others," in *A New History of French Literature*, ed. Denis Hollier (Cambridge, Mass., 1989), pp. 409–15.
3 Victor Hugo, preface to *Les Orientales*, my translation.
4 Nelly Furman, "The languages of love in *Carmen*," in *Reading Opera*, ed. Arthur Groos and Roger Parker (Princeton, 1988), p. 169.

5 See the chart in Danièle Pistone, "Les Conditions historiques de l'exotisme musical français," *Revue internationale de la musique française* 6 (1981), p. 22.

6 Carl Dahlhaus, *Nineteenth-Century Music*, trans. J. Bradford Robinson (Berkeley and Los Angeles, 1989), p. 304.

7 See Jerrold Seigel, *Bohemian Paris: Culture, Politics, and the Boundaries of Bourgeois Life, 1830–1930* (New York, 1986).

8 Letter to Edmond Galabert, October 1867. As quoted in Curtiss, *Bizet and his World*, p. 206.

9 Peter Gay, *The Bourgeois Experience: Victoria to Freud, I: Education of the Senses* (Oxford, 1984), p. 169.

10 *Ibid.*, p. 193.

11 Letter to Edmond Galabert (1868), as quoted in Winton Dean, *Georges Bizet: His Life and Work* (London, 1965), p. 60.

12 See Mina Curtiss, *Bizet and his World* (New York, 1958), pp. 165–71.

13 *Ibid.*, p. 169.

14 *Ibid.*, pp. 170–1.

15 Edouard Drumont, "Le Monde de Murget," *La Libre Parole* (June 26, 1985), as quoted in Jerrold Seigel, *Bohemian Paris: Culture, Politics, and the Boundaries of Bourgeois Life, 1830–1930* (New York, 1986), p. 180.

19

Oh Brother, Where Art Thou? and the blues

Richard Middleton

From Richard Middleton, *Voicing the Popular: On the Subjects of Popular Music* (London: Routledge, 2006), pp. 40–51.

[The blues is] a genre commonly regarded as central to representation of African-American experience but also one with huge significance for whites. Consider three events from the beginning of the twenty-first century:

First, the White Stripes, a guitar-based duo from Detroit, emerge as "the most exciting rock band in the world" *(The Guardian*, March 29, 2003), on a platform of emotional truth, pared-down simplicity, recall to tradition. Their style is centered on musical influences and an aesthetic of authenticity drawn from blues; their first two albums are dedicated to blues singers Son House and Blind Willie McTell, respectively. The White Stripes are only the most prominent of a number of likeminded bands. We seem to have yet another blues revival on our hands.

Second, in 2002 Alan Lomax, arguably the first significant folklorist to look for blues in the field (as distinct from tripping over them among other types of song), dies, and his book, *The Land Where the Blues Began*, which recounts his fieldwork experiences in the 1940s, '50s, and '60s, is republished.

And third, the Coen Brothers' movie, *O Brother, Where Art Thou?*, set in the 1930s and organized around the nostalgic appeal (but also the political potency) of "old timey" music, is an unexpectedly huge hit. Although the focus of the soundtrack is on early hillbilly music – and it triggers another revival, this time of bluegrass – a racial theme, with a blues strand, is crucial. Early in the film, the three white heroes led by Everett Ulysses Grant are joined on their travels (which are part escape from prison, part search for "treasure") by an African-American singer-guitarist modeled on a real bluesman of the time (whose name he carries), Tommy Johnson. Part of the fun is that the initial meeting takes place at a crossroads, where, paying due homage to legend, Tommy has just met the Devil (he was white and had a "mean look") – and, presumably, traded his soul for musical prowess. Tommy is on his way to Tishomingo; the real Johnson would more likely have been on his way to Jackson – but close enough.

Our four heroes miraculously form themselves into a band, and their version of "Man of Constant Sorrow," featured on local radio, is a smash hit, subsequently securing their pardons after they perform it at a political campaign rally in support of Governor Pappy O'Daniel. This song is a "white blues": the standard I-IV-V chord-sequence is truncated into a ten bar verse, with a four-bar refrain after each two-verse segment; the vocal follows familiar melodic shapes and drips with blue notes; Tommy's bluesy, riff-heavy guitar anchors the song "down home." In another important episode in the film, Tommy is rescued from the clutches of the Ku Klux Klan; the KKK's Grand Wizard is revealed to be O'Daniel's racist political opponent, who, appalled, describes our boys as a "miscegenatin' band." (The point is confirmed when, in the performance at the rally, Tommy's guitar fits effortlessly into the marvelously intricate textures of a full blue-grass band sound – a sound which, by the way, did not yet exist, any more than did the label "bluegrass.")

These three events, though distinct in many ways, have several aspects in common. First, "revival:" the past is conjured up, brought into the present, re-configured (reinvented even, as the point about bluegrass dating suggests). At the same time, this past is a "folk" past: what is conjured up is "tradition," a home that has been lost. And finally, these transactions are unavoidably racialized: white rock musicians, white scholars, white filmmakers drawing on black roots – only to find (at least in the movie) a white investment already in place, right back down home.

Much is at stake in this way of picturing the blues past, as we can see if, approaching from a different direction, we take up Charles Keil's scandalous suggestion[1] that, far from fitting the "folk" paradigm, blues in its origins was urban and modern rather than rural and archaic, was circulated and developed on records as much as (perhaps more than) through live performance and oral dissemination, and was from the beginning an interracial phenomenon – that, in a sense, it was even a white invention, with which black musicians then had to come to terms, which they reconfigured. Writing at a time when the claims of African-American identity politics were being shouted from the rooftops, Keil would probably be less than surprised that his speculations have not been widely pursued. Of course we know (e.g., from the work of Tony Russell)[2] that in the vernacular musical practice of the South there was a cross-racial "common stock" of tunes, songs, and vocal and instrumental techniques going back at least to the nineteenth century and including features and songs that we would now associate with blues (hence, for instance, "Man of Constant Sorrow"). But although this is important and relevant (it provides the broader historical backdrop to Keil's more specific point), it is not the same argument. We may quibble with the idea of origin (where in the endless relays of cultural practice does anything begin, and how could such an *ex nihilo* claim justify its authority?), but nevertheless when a genre is *named* and a certain cultural place discursively established, then we identify a moment possessing a particular historical power.

There is no significant historical evidence for the existence of a discrete blues genre before 1902–03, the period when Gertrude "Ma" Rainey, Jelly Roll Morton, and W. C. Handy all claim to have heard (or in Morton's case, made up) blues songs for the first time; all, however, were speaking (and naming the genre) with the benefit of hindsight. During the next few years, several folklorists included verses resembling blues in published collections, but they did not identify them as such nor show any special interest in them. The big moment came in 1912 with the first publications of blues compositions, including Handy's "Memphis Blues." In fact, Handy (a trained, middle-class musician, far from "the folk") had put together his tune in 1909, as "Mr Crump" (as yet without words), for his band to play in a political contest (another!) in Memphis; but he was beaten to publication by the white bandleader, Hart Wand, with his instrumental, "Dallas Blues" – just as he was closely followed in 1913 by Leroy "Lasses" White's "Nigger Blues" (White, who was also associated with Dallas, was, ironically but appropriately, white and a blackface minstrel), which in turn became one of the first blues to be recorded (in 1916). A torrent of publications followed.

From the start, the blues craze set off by these publications involved white bands as well as black, and (preponderantly) white singers – Gilda Gray, Blossom Seeley, Marion Harris – until Mamie Smith's "Crazy Blues" of 1920 (which is as much a torch song as a blues, actually). The female black singers following in Mamie Smith's wake, singing "vaudeville blues," were part of this rich interracial culture of commercial song, including but not limited to blues, and they also, arguably, played the single biggest role in establishing a black performing presence within it, touring the South and disseminating their records there as well as in the Northern cities. But in the 1920s blues were also a key part of the repertoires for many white singers, for dance bands, both black and white, and for theater and jazz musicians. The first significant blues recordings by a male singer came out in 1924, from the banjo-playing, minstrel-show songster, "Papa" Charlie Jackson. No "folk blues" records appeared until Blind Lemon Jefferson's in

1926, and, although his success initiated a down-home blues recording boom during the late twenties and early thirties, the most commercially successful male blues singers at this time were the jazzy Lonnie Johnson, and Leroy Carr – sophisticated in a different way, based in Indianapolis, with a style locating itself far from the cotton fields and levees.

This story is familiar enough. But the inferences that Keil would draw are less so. What had happened, it would seem, is that whites (together with a good number of middle-class and ambitious blacks such as Handy and Perry Bradford, composer of "Crazy Blues"), working in a context defined increasingly by a sequence of black-tinted music fads – coon song, ragtime, jazz – and by conventions of blackface performance, had crystallized a new commercial song genre out of their appropriations of a bundle of African-American vernacular practices. As part of this process, white singers, drawing on images of black style, had created models of blues vocality, which black performers could not evade.

From this point of view, "Nigger Blues," usually dismissed as a wooden travesty, becomes interesting. Recorded by an up-market white "character" singer from Washington, D.C., George O'Connor, its meanings flow when placed where it belongs, in a metropolitan drawing-room. Like many of Handy's compositions, White's song jams together an assortment of lyric clichés, familiar from many other songs, and puts them to a formulaic blues melody over the standard twelve-bar changes. It is O'Connor's delivery that speaks to the regulative norms of the culture within which "blues" would now exist. Whose voice(s) do we hear? Two at least, I would suggest, or even three: the singer's, itself split between that of the white elite, to which he belongs and which he addresses, and that of an imaginary object that he strives to imitate; and second, that of the object itself – or rather, the object wanting to subjectivise itself, to make its own desire heard, conjured up in our imaginations now. Here is the "plantation South" transplanted to the white drawing room (and then to our ears), the exotic reified (in dialect, in rhythm, in melodic gestures): desire, and lack, coursing through the gaps between the voice we actually hear, the voice O'Connor wants us to imagine, and the voice blotted out but that we know is there, somewhere, could we but find it.

The "nigger" has been, precisely, folklorized, a blues revival set in train even before its source has been sufficiently established to copy. (Cecil Sharp, who would shortly make his fieldwork visit to the Appalachians, where he would collect, among many other songs, a version of "Man of Constant Sorrow," would certainly have recognized what was going on.) The full blues folklorization process comes later, however, starting in the 1950s. Thus the historical schema that follows from pursuing Keil's proposal is striking. The blues Golden Age – when black reappropriation gives the music sufficient relative autonomy to produce its moment of condensed historical force – is very short, running from the 1920s to the 1950s. It is preceded by a period when blues as an emergent pop fad covers over, but at the same time provides a hazy refraction of, a no doubt rich, multivalent vernacular practice. It includes two even shorter peaks of down-home assertiveness (Mississippi, late-'20s/early '30s; Chicago, late '40s/early '50s), which would subsequently provide the core sources for the (mostly white) pattern of folklorization and revival that constitutes one pole of the afterglow, the other pole marked by the marginalization of blues for African Americans. The Golden Age coincides with a period of enormous tension, shaped by forces promoting the modernization of the South on the one hand, and explosive racist reactions, centered on such organizations, as the Ku Klux Klan, on the other. *O Brother* sits in the middle of this period, exploring the tensions with a comedy as black as it is hilarious. "Real" blues, it confirms, is a construction always mediated by white desire – which thus also enfolds blacks within this structure. Despite the pressures of identity politics, this position does not rob blacks of the blues: the music's political potential as a cultural resource remains, but inescapably embedded in a larger racial dialogue.

In *O Brother*, Governor O'Daniel, rushing into the radio station to do a show immediately after our heroes have made their record there, declares excitedly for modernity: he is "mass communicatin'," he boasts. Communicatin' what? Well, the past: "culture 'n' heritage," to use a well-worn and rather suspect Southern phrase, also deployed by O'Daniel's KKK opponent, disgustedly describing the "miscegenating band": "This ain't *my* culture 'n' heritage," he asserts. Blues too points both forward and back; it is modern, as we have seen, but from the start also sounds old.

As a genre, blues comes into being with sheet music and records, and registers the social effects of Reconstruction and its failure, followed by the profound economic shifts – industrialization, urbanization – of the late nineteenth- and early twentieth centuries. It speaks of culture shock: mobility, deracination, alienation, freedom – both sexual and more general. Even in the core of down-home territory, the Mississippi Delta, the social and economic geography was the result of quite recent developments – large-scale migration from the surrounding hill-country; drainage projects through levee building, settlement of new land, the coming of the railways, producing "the conditions of an urban ghetto spread out over a rural landscape."[3]

Yet from the beginning blues *sounds old*: "back then" is built into its aesthetic ("Times ain't now nothing like they used to be . . . I done seen better days but I ain't putting up with these . . .": Rabbit Brown's "James Alley Blues" (1927)); and "going back" (to that same old used to be, etc.) is as common as "going to" (Chicago, Kansas City, etc.). As Tommy Johnson puts it, "Crying, Lord, will I ever get back home" ("Cool Water Blues" (1928)), and "Well, I'm going back home, gon' fall down on my knees" ("Lonesome Home Blues" (1930)). The motif is still there – indeed, not surprisingly, intensified – when Muddy Waters records such songs as "I Believe I'll Go Back Home" in Chicago in 1948. At the same time it cannot be entirely separated from a much older trope: the mythological "dear old Southland" of the minstrel-show plantation, still clearly present in many early commercial blues songs (for example, Spencer Williams's "Tishomingo Blues" (1917) and "Basin Street Blues" (1928) and Handy's "Way Down South where the Blues Began" (1932)).

From this point of view, blues, as Houston Baker puts it, is the "always already" of African-American music: "the song is no stranger . . . I been here before", and blues offers an ancestral voice, "an anonymous (nameless) voice issuing from the black (w)hole."[4] In Paul Oliver's words, "Blues had come from way back, but no one knew then, or even knows now, quite where, when or how they sounded."[5] And blues is "always already" revived, bringing back up something already lost. Race record marketing commonly appealed to an "original" authenticity. For example, Paramount advertised Blind Lemon Jefferson's first release as "a real old-fashioned blues by a real old-fashioned blues singer . . . old-time tunes . . . in real southern style," while earlier, in 1924, they had announced the first issues by Ma Rainey in a style that reads like an ethnographer's celebration of finding a lost tribe: "Discovered at Last – 'Ma' Rainey, Mother of the Blues!"[6] A 1923 advertisement in *The Metronome*, probably placed by the music publishers E. B. Marks, states that "Mechanical companies are tumbling over each other in their eagerness to discover 'real blues.' There are bushels of inferior compositions on the market labeled 'blues' but the genuine article by born writers of 'blues' is as scarce as the proverbial 'hen's teeth.' A 'real blues' . . . sways the hearer almost with every note, and underneath it all there is the wail of the aborigine."[7] In his Introduction to W. C. Handy's 1926 anthology of blues music sheets, white enthusiast Abbe Niles, while locating blues as a new genre, insists on its status as folk music, and describes his task as digging out "their folk source" hidden in a range of previous folk genres, from beneath their popular success.[8] Handy himself, in his autobiography, consistently portrays these pre-blues folk materials as "rough diamonds," which he, as a skilled composer, had refined into more rounded and varied pieces; blues, then, is part of his "mother tongue" and writing blues songs "cannot be delegated outside of the blood."[9]

First-generation blues singers interviewed later in life sometimes bring out the moment early in the century when they encountered the new genre. Tommy Johnson's brother, LeDell, recalls family music-making in the early years of the century as based on "love songs" and "jump ups," but "when all these late blues come out, that's all I studied"; similarly a blind Clarksdale songster told Alan Lomax how his repertoire of the early 1900s, jump ups and reels, gave way to blues: "we were entering the jazz age and the old world was being transformed." Just as often, however, they refer to deep, mysterious pre-twentieth century origins: thus, for Memphis Slim, also talking to Lomax, "Blues started from slavery," while for John Lee Hooker, "it's not only what happened to you – it's what happened to your foreparents and other people. And that's what makes the blues."[10] No sooner had blues exploded into popular consciousness, it seems, than it was mythologized as "old time." The interplay of "modernity" and "folk-loric" deeply embedded in blues discourses maps this dialectic of old and new.

The folklorization process assumed the force of a movement in the 1950s and '60s, but this is prefigured by the collecting and publishing work of John Lomax, and especially his son Alan, in the 1930s and '40s, and to some extent, with a rather different sort of focus, by activities associated with the Harlem Renaissance of the later 1920s. There is a clear lineage, constructed through the wider "folk revival", via the Lomaxes, the Seegers, and their associates, leading to young revival singers of the 1960s such as Bob Dylan, along with the British "blues boom" of the same period.

The iconic figure of Leadbelly has an important transitional status. Dis-covered in 1933 by the Lomaxes in Angola state prison, Louisiana, his songs published three years later,[11] promoted as a "folk singer," Leadbelly (Huddie Ledbetter) became a key point of focus within the early white American folk revival. Leadbelly was a songster, but he sang blues and, so he claimed, had worked with Blind Lemon Jefferson; more importantly perhaps, he seemed to carry a disappearing culture (the Lomaxes' aim in 1933 was "to find the Negro who had had the least contact with jazz, the radio, and with the white man").[12] Moreover, he had charisma, not least because of his fearsome reputation for violence, which had led to several imprisonments for assault and murder.

It is hard not to suspect that, for many middle-class whites, here was the body of a noble savage on to which forbidden desires and anxieties could be projected, a suspicion intensified by many of Alan Lomax's later descrip-tions of similar experiences to those on the 1933 trip. His romantic account of a Son House performance at the moment of his "discovery" in deepest Mississippi in 1941 (actually House had made commercial records some ten years earlier) can stand for many:

His voice, guttural and hoarse with passion, ripping apart the surface of the music like his tractor-driven deep plow ripped apart the wet black earth in the springtime, making the sap of the earth song run, while his powerful, work-hard hands snatched strange chords out of the steel strings the way they had snatched so many tons of cotton out of brown thorny cotton bolls in the fall . . . Son's whole body wept, as with eyes closed, the tendons in his powerful neck standing with the violence of his feeling and his brown face flushing, he sang in an awesome voice the *Death Letter Blues*.[13]

Alan's father had described his response to the music at a Texas dance on their 1933 field trip: "I felt carried across to Africa, and I left as if I were listening to the tom-toms of savage blacks."[14] But Leadbelly was no savage, nor a rural simpleton. He actually discovered blues (as distinct from other song genres) in the early 1900s, working in the red-light district of Shreveport; and at the same time he was picking up contemporary vaudeville and Tin Pan Alley songs as well, a process that continued throughout his career: established as a folk singer, he added pop, jazz, and country songs to his repertoire, including Jimmie Rodgers yodels. The Lomaxes tried to dissuade him, arguing that he should stick to "older folk songs." For John Lomax, Leadbelly "was a 'natural,' who had no idea of money, law or ethics and who was possessed of virtually no self-restraint" – which posed both a problem and an opportunity, for "his money value is to be natural and sincere"; unlike contemporary commercial African-American singers, "Leadbelly doesn't burlesque. He plays and sings with absolute sincerity. To me his music is real music. On the occasion of Leadbelly's folkloric debut – at a Modern Languages Association conference in Philadelphia in 1934, at which he was scheduled along with a performance of "Elizabethan Ayres to the virginals" Lomax was complimented on his "talented aborigine" who produced "a treat of uncontaminated 'original' music."[15]

Such primitivism was there from the time of the first surge in white enthusiasm for "authentic" folk blues in the mid-1920s. Carl Van Vechten – critic, writer, socialite, "undisputed downtown authority on [black] uptown night life"[16] and tireless supporter of all forms of African-American culture – begged blacks to pursue the "primitive" blues back to their sources in the South, to value their "wealth of eerie melody, borne along by a savage, recalcitrant rhythm," rather than reject these in the interests of upward cultural mobility; his description of a Bessie Smith concert homes in on her "rich, ripe beauty of southern darkness," "the monotonous African pounding of the drum," "her strange rhythm rites in a . . . wild, rough Ethiopian voice, harsh and volcanic, but seductive and sensuous too."[17]

A litter later, Big Bill Broonzy, though a very different character from Leadbelly, underwent a similar transformation. Mississippi born, Broonzy moved to Chicago as early as 1920, and played a key part in the evolution there, in the 1930s, of a citified, commercially orientated band-based blues style. With his career in decline after the war, he was picked up by the revivalists, toured Europe, and was remade as a "folk" artist. In Lomax's account, based on interviews with Broonzy, his 1930s trajectory was a forced response to the demands of "villainous" and "vulgar" record company bosses demanding "slavish and uncreative imitation," "cheap 'novelty' blues," "drowning the poignant and often profound poesy of the earlier country blues in oceans of superficial swill." Charles Edward Smith's picture in his Foreword for the 1964 edition of Broonzy's memoir is similar, presenting the singer's later career as a *release* into renewal of an earlier rural identity that mentally he had never left. Yet, as Charters points out, this renewal was *also* a response – a response to Broonzy's sense of a new market, and many of his new recordings were transformations of songs that had first been recorded in band formats, or even picked up from records by others or from songbooks.[18] What is interesting here, though, is that in both his Lomax interview and his own memoir Broonzy goes along with the revival narrative. He defends his "old time blues," describing them as "the real blues,"[19] and traces many of his songs back to youthful experiences in the South; it is as if he himself is "inventing" a musical past that would substantiate his folk persona. There is, it appears, a double consciousness at work here – a mask that can always turn but that, from both directions, casts a particular light on the more obvious screen constituted by the blackface cork.

   Black involvement in the folklorization process can be traced back to the early decades of the century. As mentioned previously, at that time folklorists (including a few African Americans as well as whites) paid little attention to blues, despite booming interest in African-American folk song. This is not surprising. Conceptions of folk culture were conventional. Dorothy Scarborough's viewpoint, though perhaps rather cruder than most, gives the drift: she writes of songs with a "rough, primitive charm" which "show us the lighter, happier side of slavery, and recreate for us the rustic merry-making of the slaves"; this results from the fact that the Negro "is closer to nature" – but this will not last, and there is an urgent need to collect these songs "before the material vanishes forever, killed by the Victrola, the radio, the lure of cheap printed music." It was hard to fit blues, "that peculiar, barbaric sort of melody . . . sung in vaudevilles everywhere," into this paradigm.[20] The usual line was that blues were a regrettable commercial product with buried folk origins, but this product could in turn be taken back and folklorized. As Newman White put it, blues, "which were originally folk material but which come back to the Negro, through phonographs, sheet music, and cabaret singers, as a factory product whose dubious glory may be attributed to both white and Negro 'authors,'" have now reached a stage where the "folk blues and the factory product are . . . almost inextricably mixed." White also points out that African Americans, as they emerged from the folk stage (that is, as an aspect of modernization), were starting to appreciate their own folk heritage – but so far their perspective was little different from that of white folklorists.[21]

A shift in educated African-American attitudes only came with the Harlem Renaissance, although it was the subject of fierce dispute. By now, spirituals had been accepted as folk heritage; Roland Hayes and the young Paul Robeson (who was friendly with Van Vechten and his circle, and with many Renaissance figures) were singing them, along with other black folk songs, on the concert stage. As we have seen, W. C. Handy, with Abbe Niles's support, insisted on the folk sources of blues but also on the need for professionals to aestheticize these sources. (George Gershwin was pursuing a parallel policy – Paul Whiteman's celebrated Aeolian Hall concert, which included the premiere of Gershwin's *Rhapsody in Blue*, took place in 1924 – a policy congruent also with the "uplift" approach to folk materials of Renaissance vanguardist, Alain Locke.) Renaissance intellectuals such as Sterling Brown, Waring Cuney, and Langston Hughes began to deploy phraseology, themes, and diction drawn from blues in their poems. B. A. Botkin's *Folk-Say* (1930) included several of these and also Brown's critical study, "The Blues as Folk Poetry," perhaps the first fully worked out scholarly attempt by an African American to assimilate current recorded blues to the criteria of folk song. (Van Vechten had followed a similar line, although in much less detail, in an article published in 1925, and the white scholars, Howard Odum and Guy Johnson, put the same argument in their 1926 book, *Negro Workaday Songs*; much the same turn is apparent in Langston Hughes's poems and supporting critical writings from the same period, although Hughes was more interested in the urban realism of the blues than in any romantic folk origins.)[22]

Brown describes the border between "authentic" blues and "urbanized fake folk things" as vague, the work of Rainey and Bessie Smith as "of the folk," and current blues songs in general, "at their most genuine," as "accurate, imaginative transcripts of folk experience."[23] By the time of the appearance of *The Negro Caravan* (1941), a landmark collection of African-American literature of all kinds, partly edited by Brown, we find not only spirituals, traditional ballads, work songs, and two of Langston Hughes's blues poems, but a whole section devoted to blues which includes examples by Handy and Morton, songs drawn from the Lomaxes' Leadbelly collection, and also transcriptions from records by Ma Rainey, Bessie Smith, Bill

Broonzy, Lonnie Johnson, Memphis Minnie, and Ida Cox. In a move typical of a modernist outlook, blues has been situated as on the one hand, folk culture, on the other, a source for art. Around the same time that *The Negro Caravan* came out, Harry Smith was starting to assemble the interracial repertory for his celebrated *Anthology of American Folk Music*, a collection that would act as a basic archive for the 1950s/1960s folk revival, documenting that "old weird America," as Greil Marcus has called it.[24] In effect, Smith turned earlier entrepreneurs like Ralph Peer into folklorists, for, in an innovative and revealing move, he sourced his anthology from (by then almost forgotten) commercial records of the pre-Depression era.

In fact, this moment (the moment that Smith and *The Negro Caravan* can stand for, running from the late 1930s through the 1940s, roughly speaking) saw a veritable explosion of revivalism (down-home blues, in Chicago; "traditional" jazz; bluegrass; folk-blues and other folk musics), although in a sense the moment simply folds a further phase into an already established recessive pattern. This is also the moment in which *O Brother Where Art Thou?* is set, and, as far as the structure of revival is concerned, the film is exemplary: it enacts through its own success a revival of a culture that is already, in the film narrative, reviving its own past. The story seems to be set around 1937, but O'Daniel's campaign-song, "You Are My Sunshine," written in 1940 by country musician Jimmie Davis, was actually used in Davis's campaign for the Louisiana state governorship in 1944.[25] By contrast, an unknown Tommy Johnson is most likely to have been encountered traveling to Tishomingo (Jackson) during his early period of recording, in the late '20s or early '30s. Like a dream, then, the film diagesis condenses several periods in a historical transition on to a mythical moment, which can then serve as a node within an even longer pattern. The lynchpin song, "Man of Constant Sorrow," is "traditional." It had been first published around 1913, in a pocket songster by the blind (white) Kentucky singer, Richard Burnett, collected in the field in the Appalachians in 1918 by Cecil Sharp, who published it as "In Old Virginny," and first recorded in 1928, by hillbilly singer Emry Arthur (who knew Burnett). It was revived by bluegrass group, the Stanley Brothers, and influentially recorded by them at the Newport Folk Festival in 1959, which led to a spate of revivalist versions in the early 1960s, by Bob Dylan, Peter, Paul & Mary, and others. In the Wake of *O Brother*, it became a hit all over again, together with the elderly Ralph Stanley himself. In this structure, the object of revival forever recedes from view.

Ironically (it might seem), this lost object is disseminated in the film by *modern* technology. However, records, far from destroying what we have lost, are better seen (like photographs) as producing this loss itself – or

rather, as contributing to a momentous reconfiguration of the interrelations of loss, memory, and presence. Records circulate disembodied voices: spectral emanations that at one and the same time seem to come from *beyond* (beyond the grave?) and to be contained *within* an object, reanimating it in a novel form of mimesis. Friedrich Kittler among others has exhaustively explored the associations of the early phonograph and gramophone with figures of death, memorial, and the supernatural – and the striking conjunction of the technological changes with the birth of Freudian psychoanalysis (in which the unconscious is taken to write itself, its losses, memories, and desires, in an equally uncanny way).[26] Ethnographers were quick to take up the new technology, and tales of their subjects' uneasy reactions to its supernatural power are legion.[27] Both Erika Brady and Michael Taussig, though, note that urbanized Westerners were equally likely to fall into a magical interpretation, suggesting a projective/ introjective structure that reflects a strange reciprocity between primitivism and modernity.[28]

But if records refigured otherness – the rush to preserve creating the very gap it recorded, in a move that Lacan's neo-Freudian theory would shortly enable us to interpret in terms of the "object voice," that voice situated uncannily outside any locus of subjectivity – they built on long-established foundations. The link between disembodied voice (as in echo, for example) and supernatural power is an anthropological commonplace; the use of totemic ritual masks designed to enable the actor to represent godlike authority not only visually but also vocally has been widely documented. "Primitive" responses to the new technology from rural African Americans actually seem to be rather rare: Alan Lomax tells of an old farmer who, on hearing the recording of his friend that Lomax has just made, exclaims, "That's a ghost . . . It purely a ghost"; but he is immediately slapped down by the musician as "old-fashioned."[29] Was this acceptance because, even in remote areas of the South, blacks were actually *moderns*? Lomax's anecdote is set in 1942, but even in the late 1920s, when the first blues recordings to be made in the South were produced, people were familiar with technology (railways, steamboats, cotton gins, radio – and phonographs). In Ma Rainey's stage act, she used to emerge from a huge cardboard Victrola, reconnecting the voice to the body and marking this easy acceptance.[30] Or was this acceptance a residue of neo-African superstition – voodoo voices, hauntings, and the familiarity of the doubling strategies offered by masking (not least in the secular parody laid out by blackface performance)? Or a combination of both, perhaps? On this account, Edison's "fugitive sound waves"[31] – always receding from grasp – represent a reconfiguration of an old dynamic, whereby fetishes externalize human powers (at the same time as making nonhuman nature speak). When, in *O Brother*, as the moment for Tommy's lynching approaches, the Grand Wizard mimes Ralph Stanley's spine-chilling song, "Oh Death," through the mask of his (oh-so-white) shroud, the layers of cultural meaning run very deep.

Notes

1 Charles Keil and Steven Feld, "People's Music Comparatively," in *Music Grooves: Essays and Dialogues* (Chicago: University of Chicago Press, 1994), 197–202. Keil's piece had been initially published in 1985 (in *Dialectical Anthropology* 10:119–30).
2 Tony Russell, "Blacks, Whites and Blues," in *Yonder Come the Blues: The Evolution of a Genre*, ed. Paul Oliver, Tony Russell, Robert M. W. Dixon, John Godrich, and Howard Rye (1970, Cambridge, UK: Cambridge University Press, 2001), 143–242.
3 David Evans, quoted in Francis Davis, *The History of the Blues*, (London: Secker and Warburg, 1995), 47 see also Alan Lomax, the *Land Where the Blues Began* (New York: Pantheon, 1993), 64–70; David Evans; *Big Road Blues: Tradition and Creativity in the Folk Blues* (New York: Da Capo, 1987), 169–74.
4 Houston Baker Jr, *Blues, Ideology and Afro-American Literture: A Vernacular Theory* (Chicago: University of Chiaago Press, 1984), 4, 64, 65, 5.
5 Paul Oliver, Tony Russell, Robert M. W. Dixon, John Godrich, and Howard Rye, *Yonder Come the Blues: The Evolution of a Genre* (Cambridge, UK: Cambridge University Press, 2001), 2.
6 Quoted, Samuel B. Charters, *The Country Blues* (1959, New York: Da Capo Press, 1975), 63; Oliver et al., *Yonder Come the Blues*, 2001, 262–3.
7 Quoted, Evans, *Big Road Blues*, 1987, 63.
8 W. C. Handy, *Blues: An Anthology*, ed. Abbe Niles (1926, New York: Da Capo, 1990), 12, 20.
9 W. C. Handy, *Father of the Blues* (New York: Da Capo, 1991), 231; and see 137–51.
10 David Evans, *Tommy Johnson* (London: Studio Vista, 1971), 18, 19; Lomax, *Land Where the Blues Began*, 1933, 55, 460; Oliver et al., *Yonder Come the Blues*, 2001, 203.
11 John A. Lomax and Alan Lomax, *Negro Folk Songs as Sung by Leadbelly* (New York: Macmillan, 1936).
12 John A. Lomax and Alan Lomax, *American Ballads and Folk Songs* (New York: Macmillan, 1934), xxx.
13 Lomax, *Land Where the Blues Began*, 1993, 18.
14 Quoted, Charles K. Wolfe and Kip Lornell, *The Life and Legend of Leadbelly* (New York: Da Capo, 1993), 112.
15 Ibid., 145, 141–2, 2, 130, 135.
16 Nathan Huggins, *Harlem Renaissance* (New York: Oxford University Press, 1971), 199.

17 In Bruce Kellner, ed., *Keep A-Inchin' Along: Selected Writings of Carl Van Vechten about Black Art and Letters* (Westport, CT: Greenwood Press, 1979), 48, 162.

18 Lomax, *Land Where the Blues Began*, 1993, 446, 447; Bill Broonzy (with Yannick Bruynoghe), *Big Bill Blues: Big Bill Broonzy's Story as Told to Yannick Bruynoghe* (1955, New York: Oak Publications), 1964), 11–25; Charters, *Country Blues*, 1975, 177–80.

19 Broonzy, *Big Bill Blues*, 1964, 31.

20 Dorothy Scarborough, *On the Trail of Negro Folk-Songs* (Cambridge MA: Harvard University Press, 1925), 128, 161, 264, 281–2.

21 Newman I. White, *American Negro Folk-Songs* (Cambridge MA: Harvard University Press, 1928), 25, 389, 5.

22 Sterling A. Brown, "The Blues as Folk Potery," In *Folk-Say: A Regional Miscellany*, ed. B. A. Botkin (Norman OK: University of Oklahoma Press, 1930), 324–39; Carl Van Vechten, "The Black Blues," in Kellner, *Keep A-Inchin' Along*, 1979, 43–9 (first published, *Vanity Fair*, August 1925); Howard W. Odum and Guy B. Johnson, *Negro Workaday Songs* (Chapel Hill: University of North Carolina Press, 1926); Langston Hughes, "The Weary Blues," (1926) in *The Negro Caravan*, ed. Sterling A. Brown, Arthur P. Davis and Ulysses Lee (1941, New York: Arno Press, 1970), 367–8; Langston Hughes, "The Negro Artist and the Racial Mountain," *Nation*, June 23, 1926: 692–4.

23 Brown, "Blues as Folk Poetry," 1930, 324, 339.

24 Greil Marcus, *Invisible Republic: Bob Dylan's Basement Tapes* (London: Picador, 1997); *Anthology of American Folk Music*, comp. Harry Smith, Smithsonian, Folkways FP 251, 252, 253 (1997) [1952].

25 Intriguingly, Davis also recorded white blues, was considerably influenced by black music, and even recorded with a black musician, Oscar Woods; see Tony Russell's account, "Blacks, Whites and Blues," 2001, 206–9.

26 Friedrich A. Kittler, *Gramophone, Film, Typewriter* (Stanford, CA: Stanford Univeristy Press, 1999).

27 See Erika Brady, *A Spiral Way: How the Phonograph Changed Ethnography* (Jackson: University of Mississippi Press, 1999).

28 Ibid., 30–2; Taussig, *Mimesis and Alterity*, 1993, 208–11.

29 Lomax, *Land Where the Blues Began*, 1993, 9.

30 Davis, *History of the Blues*, 1995, 72–3.

31 Brady, *A Spiral Way*, 1999, 1.

20

Jùjú live

Christopher Waterman, *Jùjú: A Social History and Ethnography of an African Popular Music* (Chicago: Chicago University Press, 1990), pp. 196–204.

This blow-by-blow account of a live musical performance in Nigeria is extracted from Waterman's ethnographic study of *jùjú*, a popular genre of dance music. An *àríyá* is a kind of celebration, and 'double toy' refers to a set of bongo drums. Acute and grave accents indicate high and low and low tones respectively.

It is Saturday, August 4, 1979, the occasion a Muslim funeral celebration in the town of Ogbomọṣọ, some fifty miles north of Ibadan. The host has hired the Olúmọ Soundmakers, led by Ọlatoye Ajagunjẹun, a.k.a. Uncle Toye Ajagun the "Magbe-Magbe Man," one of the most successful band captains based in Ibadan. [. . .] Uncle Toye's style – the *Máàgbé-Máàgbé ("Don't Carry, Don't Carry") Sound*, [is] a reference to a hold used in wrestling during Muslim festivals [. . .]

[. . .]

It is 11:00 P.M., and the Olúmọ Soundmakers have been playing in front of the host's compound for half an hour. Suddenly, for the second time that evening, the electricity fails, stilling the amplifiers and throwing the celebration into darkness. A great moan arises from the participants: "Oh no!"; "*L'álẹ́ yìí ò da-o!*" ["This evening is not good, oh!"]. "NEPA, lẹpa! [Nigerian Electrical Power Authority, Leper!]". I am seated to one side of the band, and the band manager approaches me and requests that I turn off my tape recorder. After a few moments, the petrol generator is started, and the tape rolls again. Uncle Toye tests his amplifier, arpeggiating a tonic major triad, and signals the band to action (see fig. 20.1). This pattern is gradually picked up by the other guitarists, with the lead and bass guitarists and double toy drummer improvising fills. After nine repetitions of this opening theme, Uncle Toye plays his signature motif on the guitar (see fig. 20.2) and attempts to cool the disgruntled celebrants' feelings by singing:

= strings choked, struck sharply with plectrum

Fig. 20.1 Introdictory theme (Toye Ajagun)

Fig. 20.2 Toye Ajagun's signature motif

Fig. 20.3 Opening vocal line

Ẹ má jẹ́ kó bàjẹ́-o-e
Ẹ má jẹ́ kó bàjẹ́-o, kò bàjẹ́ lọ́wọ́ àgbà
Olúwa árọ́n wá lọ́wọ́-o
    Don't let it spoil, oh
    Don't let it spoil, oh, it does not spoil in the hands of the elders
    God will help us, oh

This phrase, sung to the melody of a hit record by Ajagun's former captain Idowu Animaṣaun (see fig. 20.3), is intended as a pep talk for the host and guests – upon whose mood the night's profits will depend – and for the band itself, which has lost some steam as a result of the repeated interruptions. The celebratory ethos of the àríyá must be rescued. Uncle Toye repeats the line, joined by the five chorus vocalists, who texture and amplify his prayer with three-part harmonies:

Ẹ má jẹ́ kó bàjẹ́-o-e
Ẹ má jẹ́ kó bàjẹ́-o, kò bàjẹ́ lọ́wọ́ àgbà, Olúwa árọ̀n wá lọ́wọ́-o
Don't let it spoil, oh
Don't let it spoil, oh, it does not spoil in the hands of the elders,
God will help us, oh

Samuel, the lead talking drummer, inserts a relevant proverb:

Lọ́wọ́ mi, kò kúkú wùn Elédùmarè, lọ́wọ́ mi
In my hand, it surely does not please God [to see this occasion spoiled],
in my hand

The guitarists continue to make small adjustments, the lead player melodically embellishing the I–V^7 framework established by the tenor guitars using his echo-plex to soar over the dense ensemble texture. Meanwhile, I fend off a celebrant's request that I behave like a normal human being, that is, that I get up and dance rather than sit next to the band taking notes. "Work first, pleasure later!" He shrugs and heads for the dance area. The opening vocal sequence is repeated, first by Toye, and then by the chorus:

Ẹ má jẹ́ kó bàjẹ́-o-e, ẹ má jẹ́ kó bàjẹ́-o, kò bàjẹ́ lọ́wọ́ àgbà, Olúwa árọ̀n wá lọ́wọ́-o
Ẹ má jẹ́ kó bàjẹ́-o-e, ẹ má jẹ́ kó bàjẹ́-o, kò bàjẹ́ lọ́wọ́ àgbà, Olúwa árọ̀n wá lọ́wọ́-o

Samuel, seated at the side of the band, turns toward the bass chorus singer, and drums:

Yísáù!

Yisau responds affirmatively ("Ẹ̀ẹẹẹ"), and Samuel drums him a proverb:

B'ẹ́nìyàn bínú b'Ọlọ́run kò bá ti bínú àbùṣe-bùṣe
If man is angry and God is not, it is finished [i.e., there is no problem].

By three minutes into the performance, the supporting patterns have stabilized, and the tenor guitarists have negotiated an ostinato in parallel thirds (see fig. 20.4). The chorus singers smile and begin moving more fluidly, teasing one another. One of the tenor vocalists, turning a face of mock surprise in my direction, calls out:

Òyìnbó!
White man!

Uncle Toye begins a new prayer sequence, his voice echoing powerfully into the moonlit sky:

Ilàyí Elédùmarè
Elédùmarè, ọba oníbú-ọọrẹ
God in the highest
God, king of a thousand gifts

Fig. 20.4 Supporting instrumental patterns (The Olumo Soundmakers)

The tenor guitars continue to play their cool I–V⁷ pattern, their right hands moving in a steady 16th note pattern. After a short pause, Toye enters again:

> Ọba tí gba aláìlárá
> Ọba tí pèsè fún àwọn aláìní
> Ṣe tèmi níre o, ọba, mímọ́n
> > The King [God] has accepted those with no family
> > The King has provided for the needy
> > Make mine good, holy King

Samuel responds by drumming a fragment from a proverb (see also fig. 20.5):

> Olówó gbo-gbo-gbo tí ny'ọmọ ẹ l'ófin, yọ mí
> > Capable person who frees his child from a trap, free me

and Uncle Toye begins another praise sequence:

o-lọ́-wọ́ gbo - gbo - gbo   tí ny'ọ-mọ   ẹ l'ọ́ - fin   yọ   mí

Fig. 20.5 Talking drum phrase

[upward slide]

Fig. 20.6 Interaction of àdàmọ̀n and guitar

> *Alájì mi-o,*
> *Mólèyájọ́ bàbá ni*
> My Alhaji, oh
> Moleyajọ is the father

In the back row of the band, Samuel teases the lead guitarist. He flashes his eyes at him and beats:

> *Alàó, bàbá ìbejì*
> Alao, father of twins!

Alao laughs, and responds immediately with an upward slide on his guitar, while one of the chorus singers runs to Samuel and pretends to beat him on the head. Uncle Toye praises Alhaji Moleyajọ and his wife, Iyabode, who sway proudly in front of the band, decked out in white and pale blue lace. Iyabode, ornamented with high heels, necklaces, earrings, and imported silk head-tie, clutches an expensive leather purse.

> *Alájì betilayi, àláji humura*
> *Mólèyájọ́, mo ba rò de àtàtà*
> *Adúdúyemi, gbajúmọ̀n mi, ẹni re*
> *Ọkọ àlájà-o, ọkọ àlájà Iyábòdé*
> *Mólèyájọ́, gbajúmọ̀n mi àtàtà*
> *Àràbà ṣá ni bàbá*
> *Ẹni a bá l'ábà ni bàbá*
>> Alhaji betilayi Alhaji humura [Muslim salutations]
>> Moleyajo, I follow you out, important person
>> Black and beautiful ["one whose black suits them well"],
>> popular person, good person
>> Husband of the Alhaja, Husband of Alhaja Iyabode

> Moleyajọ, my popular person, important person
> The silk-cotton tree is certainly the father [of trees]
> The person you meet in front of the farm-hut is the father

This proverb implies, first, that Moleyajọ is a father; second, that his own recently deceased father is worthy of great reverence; and, third, that both of them, like giant *àràbà* trees, tower over other men.

The Olumọ Soundmakers, almost six minutes into their performance, focus their collective attentions on the wealthy host. As Uncle Toye begins another sequence of praise, Moleyajọ glides majestically up to the band. Standing in front of Toye, turned sideways so that all the participants may observe clearly, he pulls a handful of banknotes from the voluminous recesses of his silk gown. Inexorably, bill by bill, he presses the money onto Toye's sweaty forehead. The band captain continues to sing:

> *Àlájì betilayi, Móleyájọ́, gbajúmọ̀n mi àtàtà, ọkọ àlájà Iyábòdé*
> Alhaji betilayi, Moleyajọ, my dear important person, husband of Alhaja Iyabode

The bass vocalist, Yisau, leans behind the other chorus singers, wiggles his eyebrows at me, and emits a sharp-edged, nasalized imitation of American English into the microphone:

> *Òyìnbó!*
> White man!

One singer holds the accumulating money against his captain's forehead, while another periodically gathers it in a clump and drops it into a beer carton in the middle of the band. Toye sings a solo call:

> *Ìwọ àlájì mi-o*
> You, my Alhaji

and, in three-part harmony resounding with electronic reverb, his chorus responds:

> *Àlájì mi ọmọ dára o lẹ́wà*
> *Àṣìkò yíò wu o lè jẹ́, Ọba òkè k'ó fun lá dùn sọ́rọ̀-e*
> My Alhaji, good child, you are beautiful
> It might be anytime now that the King will put sweetness in
> your affairs [your reputation, your story].

One of the chorus singers murmurs "Haj!" (Alhaji) into the microphone and Samuel drums (see also fig. 20.7):

> *Ọlọ́run Ọba kìí bínú*
> The Lord God does not get annoyed

Ọ - ló - run Ọ - ba   kì - í bí - nú

Fig. 20.7 Talking drum phrase

Samuel repeats this phrase every four bars, making it into a dance rhythm, a message pulsing subliminally beneath Toye's continued praise singing:

Mólèyájó, gbajúmòn mi àtàtà, ọkọ àlájà-o, Iyábòdé
Mègídá lojẹ gbajúmòn àyọnfẹ́ lojẹ, adúdúyemí-o tiwa ni
    Moleyajọ, my popular, important person, husband of Alhaja Iyabode
    [Hausa term of respect], you are popular, you are beloved, black
    and beautiful, oh, our own.

Toye pauses, allowing the supporting guitar and drum parts to be heard, and then continues:

Èsò pẹ̀lẹ́ ọmọ olóyè Mólèyájó
To bá mí lọ kírun pè mí dá ní-o
To bá mí lọ kírun pè mí dá ní-o
Afínjú imàle tó ńjẹ àlájì nle
    Gently, son of a chief, Moleyajọ
    If you are going to the mosque call me along
    If you are going to the mosque call me along
    Fastidious Muslim who bears the title Alhaji

As he reaches the end of this ascending melodic phrase, Uncle Toye's voice cracks, and he is forced to play the last word, *nle*, on his guitar. Samuel responds in a split second, drumming the sarcastic observation (see also fig. 20.8):

Óò tó bẹ́ẹ̀!
    It isn't finished like that!!

The band boys laugh, and Toye turns slightly, fixing the guitarists – though not the talking drummer – with a baleful stare. Moleyajọ has finished pasting Naira notes to Toye's forehead, and moved back into the crowd of dancers. The chorus repeats the previous praise sequence:

To bá mí lọ kírun pè mí dá ní-o
To bá mí lọ kírun pè mí dá ní-o
To bá mí lọ kírun pè mí dá ní-o
Afínjú ìmàle tó ńjẹ àlájì nle

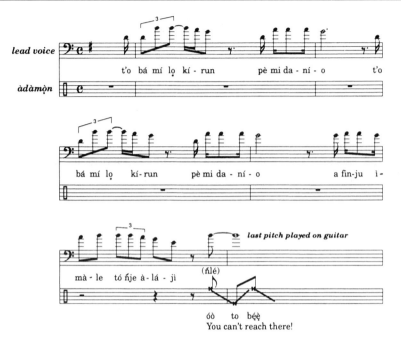

Fig. 20.8 Interaction of captain and àdàmọ̀n

To bá mí lọ kírun pè mí dá ní-o
   If you are going to the mosque call me along
   If you are going to the mosque call me along
   If you are going to the mosque call me along
   Fastidious Muslim who bears the title Alhaji
   If you are going to the mosque call me along

21

Rhythm, rhyme, and rhetoric in the music of Public Enemy

Robert Walser

Robert Walser, 'Rhythm, rhyme, and rhetoric in the music of Public Enemy', *Ethnomusicology*, 39:2 (1995), pp. 193–212.

"My job is to write shocking lyrics that will wake people up," said Chuck D, when asked about his goals as leader of the rap group Public Enemy (Dery 1990:94) In less than fifteen years, rap music has grown from the local performance practices of a Bronx subculture to a multi-billion-dollar industry which mediates a music made and heard around the world. And since 1988, Chuck D's lyrics have been at the center of many of the controversies surrounding hip hop culture, awakening, energizing, and unsettling fans and critics. They have helped to make Public Enemy one of the most successful and influential groups in the history of rap, and Chuck D has been accepted by many people as an important spokesperson for the hip hop community, and even for African Americans more generally.

Chuck D's message exceeds the literal meaning of his lyrics, however; only the musical aspects of rap can invest his words with the affective force that will make people want to wake up or get them upset enough to call for censorship. Yet despite widespread debates over the meanings and significance of rap, its musical elements have largely escaped all but the most superficial discussion. The infamous *Newsweek* travesty of hip hop culture, for example (Adler et al. 1990), took it for granted that rap couldn't be discussed as music and mentioned only the thumping power of the bass and the noisiness of everything else. More sympathetic and sophisticated analysts typically concentrate on demonstrating rap's verbal complexity and the cultural significance of its lyrics (see, for example, Wheeler 1991; Keyes 1984). But the lyrics and reception of rap cannot be detached from the music. Even though many rappers and fans stress the primacy of the message delivered by the lyrics, some, like pioneering rapper Melle Mel, argue that the instrumental parts are actually more important than the rap because they create the mood, set the beat, and prompt the engagement (Keyes 1991:199). Chuck D's words would not have reached millions of people as poetry or political commentary; it is the music of Public Enemy that gains them access to channels of mass distribution and underpins their power and credibility. Yet that music has scarcely been mentioned in critical debates over the meanings and importance of hip hop culture.

[. . .]

"Fight the Power" was one of Public Enemy's biggest hits, especially after it was featured in Spike Lee's film, *Do the Right Thing*, and the hard-hitting indictment of racism offered by its lyrics has been much discussed. Thus it has been easy to overlook the music of Public Enemy – if they don't have melody or harmony, if they don't play musical instruments or sing, what is there to discuss? Even some of rap's defenders would resist close scrutiny of musical details; Bruce Tucker warns that "rap, like so many other black musical genres, suffers at the hands of the deeply held formalist assumption that the notes themselves are meaningful" (Tucker 1992:497). Tucker is right to warn against ahistorical and acultural interpretations of musical discourse. Yet despite the discouraging example of so many formalist analyses of popular music, it is possible to interpret notes as abstractions of performances with social meanings, and the terms and stakes of current debates over rap suggest that there are important reasons for doing so.

I want to turn to a closer reading of "Fight the Power" in order to draw attention to two neglected aspects of rap music: the rhythmic declamation and rhetorical strategies that make up the performative aspect of rapping, and the rhythm track or groove which underpins the delivery of the lyrics. I hope to explain to some extent the power and meanings of this music, but the analysis should also have the more basic effect of demonstrating the coherence and complexity of music which has been so widely dismissed as monotonous and impoverished. This is itself no small accomplishment, given the shape of recent debates over rap music, which have too often seemed mired in what Paul Gilroy calls "the struggle to have blacks perceived as agents with cognitive capacity and historicity" (Gilroy 1992: 187–88; see also Gilroy 1991).

Mapping the groove

Figures 21.1 through 21.6 are excerpts from "Fight the Power," transcribed into standard Western musical notation, a tactic that requires some justification. Many things cannot be represented in such notation, of course; timbre is largely invisible, as are many of the rhetorical nuances that make performances powerful. Yet if notation conceals, it also reveals. Rhythms and certain other kinds of relationships can be sketched with some amount of accuracy, if we keep in mind that we are looking at static representations of dynamic relationships. Transcription is particularly useful in this case because coherence and complexity are precisely what have been denied to hip hop, and those are the qualities that notation is best at illuminating. Moreover, the stacked array of parts in this visual map parallels the hip hop compositional process of laborious assemblage of separate voices through sampling, drum machines, and sequencing.

A few writers have transcribed hip hop music before: Keyes (1991) used notation in order to demonstrate the existence in rap music of certain techniques, such as word stresses, hocket, "trading phrases," and interlocking rhythms, and Costello and Wallace's (1990) transcription of Eric B. and Rakim's "Paid in Full" labels the samples that were used to construct the piece. Here, I will use notation as a means of presenting evidence for interpretations of affect and social meanings – as a beginning, not an end. I see transcription as a way of opening up for discussion the musical details of a style that many people do not think *has* musical details.

Figure 21.1 is my transcription of the two-measure groove that begins "Fight the Power" (actually, a brief introduction, based on a sample of the band Trouble Funk, precedes the establishment of the groove). With a few minor changes, this two-bar unit underpins the entire song, except for the choruses, which switch to a different tonal center and use a somewhat different beat, and a few sections at the end that strip down and chop up the fundamental groove. Composed wholly of samples, the music is based on a combination of drum patterns taken from songs by Funkadelic, Sly Stone, and the Jacksons (Dery 1990:92). On top of this Hank Shocklee and the Bomb Squad have layered additional sounds from a drum machine, along with sampled vocals, guitar, bass, and synthesizer. The resulting groove, then, for all its complexity, provides a stable platform for the rapping.

The line labelled "kick" at the bottom of my transcription, the bass drum, is in itself a good introduction to how the producers use rhythm to construct an affect of urgency for this tune. The eighth-notes at the beginning of each measure clearly define the beat, and the pickup to the second bar helps articulate the two-bar pattern. But in the middle of each measure, what might have been a literal repetition of the eighth-note pattern is set with the first note placed one sixteenth-note notch ahead of the beat. Within every bar, the metric pattern is established and then pushed against, creating a dynamic tension even within the line of a single instrument.

Fig. 21.1 "Fight the Power," opening groove

The snare drum appears to provide a standard backbeat on beats two and four; however, there are several different snare drum sounds being utilized, and they vary in pitch, placement, and position in the stereo field. On beat two of each measure we hear a strong, stereo-centered backbeat. On four of the first measure, we hear a lower-pitched drum off to the right; on four of the second measure, the same drum along with another, even lower drum, panned to the left. Beat four is prepared in each measure by a different snare's pickup, and a higher-pitched snare in the center answers each backbeat on four, one sixteenth-note later. Timbres, volumes, and placements vary, so that this line too has its own dynamic pattern of interaction, even as these backbeats serve to anchor the entire rhythm track. The cymbals and shaker sounds also steady the groove at the eighth-note level, with additional accents that result from the layering of several drum samples.

The bass plays a repeated pattern that can be heard either as syncopated – it pushes against the metric framework just as the kick drum does – or as polyrhythmic, a layering on of the 3-3-2 pulse (here, in eighth notes) that is known as one version of the "standard pattern" of African and African American music (see Johnson and Chernoff 1991:67; Kauffman 1980). The bass defines a tonal center on D; its drop to the lower octave on beat four sets the stage for a more emphatic articulation of the downbeat of each measure, grounding the start of each rhythmic cycle regardless of the tensions and ambiguities enacted within the groove. Some sort of sampled noise or scratching (the next line on the score) answers each utterance of the bass in the first measure of the pattern, providing a grungy counterpoint. The synthesizer note is one of only two sustaining, nonpercussive sounds in the groove, and its drawn-out B clashes with the D established by the bass. It can be heard as pulling at the tonal orientation, redefining the D as its own third degree, but its fade in each measure weakens this tendency, and the B ends up perched uneasily above, as the unresolved sixth of D.

The guitar sample is so scratchy and percussive that its exact pitches are difficult to discern. Moreover, funk guitar players often lift their fretting fingers just enough to dampen the strings while continuing to pick, creating a bright scratch, an additional sound between pitch and silence; I have notated these moments with x's in place of the note heads. The guitar's pitches are typical of funk harmony, sustaining the minor third of D while playing with the alternation of major sixth and minor seventh degrees; this is a favorite riff because it confirms the mode but creates and releases the tension of the tritone. Rhythmically, the guitar adds to the polyrhythmic mix with a 3-3-3-3-4 pattern at the sixteenth-note level. We begin to see that a variety of musical lines operates at different rhythmic levels, remaining within the overall organization of the meter and the two-measure unit, but filling the groove with complex tensions.

The vocal samples drop out when the rapping begins, but during the opening vamp they add further layers of rhythmic direction. The top line marked "voice" articulates nearly the same pattern as the guitar, but placed one eighth-note out of phase. Fragments of the phrase "give it" add urgency to the first measure of each cycle. The second voice answers the first with the syncopated imperative "come on, and get down." And just after the downbeat of the second bar, the third voice's rising line contradicts its text ("down") and anticipates the end of the second voice's phrase. The last line of vocal samples, marked "J.B.," shows the placement of two different samples of James Brown's trademark percussive grunt. One, higher pitched, anchors the downbeat of each two-measure cycle, while the lower-pitched one punctuates the last eight note of each measure, pushing against metric balance. (There is no better demonstration of the poverty of transcription than the reduction of this famous sound to "uh!")

Careful attention to the music of even these two measures of "Fight the Power" reveals a solid but richly conflicted polyrhythmic environment in which the rappers operate. If the analytical category of melody seems peripheral, and that of harmony is represented by the sort of static vamp often found in James Brown's music and some earlier blues, the complex interrelationships of rhythm and timbre are paramount. I will return to further discussion of the significance of this musical complexity after discussing the rhythmic performances of the rappers, Chuck D and Flavor Flav.

Mapping the Rapping

In his rapping, Chuck D creates the same kind of polyrhythmic flexibility that energizes the rhythm track. Although he is supported by the groove, he refuses to be constrained by it. His phrasing signifies on its regular repetition as he spills over its boundaries, imposes his own patterns over it, or pulls up short to confirm it. In Figure 21.2 the last eight measures of the first verse, he begins with a repeated pattern marked by rhyme and alliteration. James Snead (1984:70) has analyzed the rhetorical figures most commonly used in black preaching; he would call this "epanalepsis," repetition at the beginning and the end of a clause ("Listen if you're missin', swingin' while I'm singin'"). But just as important, the rhythmic placement of the phrases creates polyrhythmic tension up against the groove. The repeated pattern takes up three beats, while the meter measures out a four-beat framework: 1 2 (rest) 4 | 1 (rest) 3 4. Chuck's rapping not only overlays a conflicting rhythm at the quarter-note level, but because the pattern internally accents eighth-notes in alternating groups of three articulated and three silent, he creates another layer of rhythmic tension at the same time, a superimposed triple meter: 1&2 (&3&) 4&1 (&2&) 3&4 (&). Similarly, in the chorus of the song (Figure 21.3) Public Enemy avoids

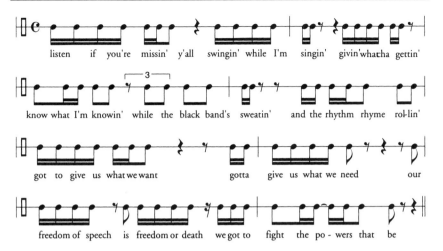

Fig. 21.2 "Fight the Power," verse 1, mm. 5–12

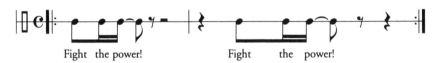

Fig. 21.3 "Fight the Power," chorus, mm. 1–6

flat repetition by displacing every other "Fight the power!" by one beat. The emphatic repetition of the title serves as a rallying cry for collective struggle, but even here there is flexibility and rhythmic clash, as a different part of the phrase is energized each time: *Fight* the power! Fight the *power*! *Fight* the power!

This is what makes rap so different from predecessors such as Gil-Scott Heron or the Last Poets. The music is not an accompaniment to textual delivery; rather, voice and instrumental tracks are placed in a more dynamic relationship in hip hop, as the rapper interacts with the rest of the music. Without the framework of the groove, Chuck D's phrases would simply be parallel utterances. But his rhythmic engagement produces a dialectic of shifting tensions. Because the groove itself is non-teleological, it situates the listener in a complex present, one containing enough energy and richness that progress seems moot. Form and direction are imposed on the song by the rapper through rhetorical fiat, by means of rhythmic patterns, rhyme schemes, the ideas and exhortations of the lyrics, and the verse/chorus alternation.

The second verse begins with more polyrhythms (Figure 21.4), this time triple patterns at the sixteenth-note level. Rhyme, assonance, and precise rhythmic placement keep Chuck D sounding smooth and coherent, even as the rhythms of his speech are in constant tension with the beat. After the first measure, he moves beyond this strict sixteenth-note pattern into a more complicated rhythmic virtuosity, deftly shifting among syncopation, triplets, and alignment with the meter. In the last two measures of this example, he sticks more closely to the beat, first presenting an idea, "People, people, all the same," then rejecting it: "no, we're not the same cause we don't know the game." The emphasis on the beat in these measures helps portray the first idea as a simplistic platitude and makes Chuck's dismissal seem inevitable. The rhythms thus support his textual argument: pretending that difference doesn't exist won't make injustice go away.

In the third verse (Figure 21.5) Chuck D works less with the intricacies of each beat or with polyrhythmic tensions, and more with larger-scale rhetorical flow. In measures seven and eight, he directs each phrase toward a landing on beat four, intensifying the eighth measure by shifting to duple rhythms and including more syllables. Black pride and energy in the first phrase parallel critique of the politics of public representation in the second ("most of my heroes don't appear on no stamps"). Having established a sequence and led us to expect arrivals on beat four, Chuck D then raps

Fig. 21.4 "Fight the Power," verse 2, mm. 1–8

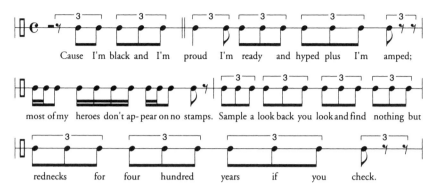

Fig. 21.5 "Fight the Power," verse 3, mm. 6–10

straight through measure nine, not cadencing until the fourth beat of measure ten. His precise, undeviating triplets – "Sample a look back you look and find nothing but rednecks for four hundred years if you check" – articulate an anger that draws upon the power of every beat but relentlessly clashes with every subdivision of the groove. Exploiting the rhetorical power of parallelisms, he rolls past the stopping point he had implied in order to deliver a longer, weightier line of text; an indictment of four hundred years of racism.

At the very beginning of his rap (Figure 21.6), Chuck had already been playing with such rhetorical patterns. In the first measure of the first verse, accent, rhythmic pattern, and overlapping rhymes combine to emphasize the backbeats, beats two and four (*"number," "summer"*). But in the next measure, Chuck skips beat two, hitting three hard (*"sound* of the funky drummer") and accelerating into a sixteenth-note sequence that lands on the downbeat of measure four. He establishes a pattern through repetition, drops in a surprising gap, and then comes upside your head with the answer. By playing with expectations and shifting among rhythmic subdivisions, Chuck presents himself as a wilfull virtuoso, negotiating the complex groove with ease.

Repetition also creates the horizons of expectation that enable dialogue and participation (see Snead 1984). The interaction of Chuck D and Flavor Flav makes the rapping dialogic at strategic places in the song, and in this excerpt their exchanges are supplemented by a third voice, which confirms Chuck's downbeat while leaving Flavor Flav free to make his interjection, "brothers and sisters." The end of Flav's comment is overlapped by Chuck's "hey!," which is itself answered by the third voice's "hey!" at the end of the measure. Chuck then goes on to solo for a while, but Flavor contributes both collective affirmation and dialogic counterpoint throughout the

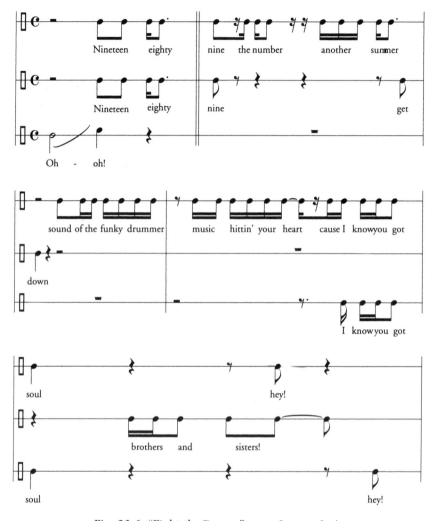

Fig. 21.6 "Fight the Power," verse 1, mm. 1–4

song. His interjections support and amplify Chuck's line of thought, but they also constitute a diegetic representation of a broader communal endorsement.

Dialogue and other aspects of rhythmic rhetoric demand social explanations, for notes produce meaning only as they unfold in communities. [. . .] For as Christopher Small has pointed out, an analytical focus on internal relationships too often displaces attention from external (social) relationships; the closer we analyze, the more impoverished our sense of what it all means (1987:289). It is difficult indeed to put "Fight the Power" back together after having so dissected it; it is not easy to account for its coherence and cumulative effect after having isolated its components, for the interactions of groove, rapping, lyrics, and formal trajectory all happen at once, in a real time upon which verbal commentary necessarily drags. But our scrutiny of the musical details of "Fight the Power" does prepare us to ask: What is the attraction of these musical strategies? Upon what sorts of values and experiences does their efficacy depend?

[. . .]

To be sure, the intensity of the music may provide some listeners with an avenue for reasserting male power or for energizing the defense or claim of some other privilege. That is, for some fans, "Fight the Power" might not mean much more than "Annoy Your Parents." But differences in reception cannot simply be drawn along racial lines. Declining expectations, the injuries of deindustrialization, the growing disparity of wealth, the disruption of communities, and the dismantling of social support programs are not limited to black communities, although they have been hit hardest; Public Enemy's lyrics articulate anger and protest that many other people find resonant with their own experiences. Rap has both achieved widespread popularity among white fans and "Africanized" many white musical traditions because the values it embodies have been found so attractive by so many. In this respect it participates in an ongoing process: Amiri Baraka recently criticized his own book *Blues People* because it insufficiently registered the fact that African American culture has been so influential that it is not neatly separable from American culture (Baraka 1991:109). And as George Lipsitz points out, in a world where more and more people feel dislocated and disenfranchised, the culture of people who have historically lived with the contradictions of being outsiders becomes increasingly relevant to everyone (1990). While the pro-black rhetoric of rap is often perceived as promoting separatism, in fact many white youth develop black friends and reject their parents' racism because of the respect they have developed for black rappers (Tate 1990).

The music of Public Enemy enacts survival in a complex, dangerous world; however oppressive and dissonant that world, it is made to seem negotiable through dialogue and rhythmic virtuosity. The dancing or gesturing body seems able to seize and rearticulate the power of the music, in contexts of reception that are communal even when they depend upon mass mediation. Many fans seem to be attracted to the flexibility and multiple perspectives of hip hop, to its embrace of contradictory values, such as an emphasis on building community which coexists in tension with individualism. In the groove and the rhythmic virtuosity of the rapping, perhaps even more than in the lyrics, they find experiences that are available nowhere else yet seem highly relevant to the lives they lead. Although the importance of Public Enemy's verbal critiques and other messages should not be minimized, their success with black and white audiences depends just as much upon the kinds of musical experiences they offer their fans.

In the 1931 movie *Public Enemy*, James Cagney starred as a young gangster for whom music and verse are perfect symbols of social impotence. No one succeeds in the greed-driven world of *Public Enemy* – the women are utterly dependent on the men, and the men are either criminals, who end up dead, or menial workers, who end up in dead ends. But involvement with poetry (Cagney's older brother) or music (the ill-fated "Putty-nose") is an especially sure sign of weakness. Rappers are often accused of articulating a similarly bleak social vision, and their music has figured in the "culture of poverty" discourse that conservatives have used to shape debates about the lives and problems of urban black people. But as heirs to a cultural tradition that prizes verbal eloquence and rhythmic rhetoric, rappers' means and ends clash with this model of dispair and rebellion, even when they adopt a "gansta" image. Despite the history of injustice that fuels their anger – as Naughty By Nature puts it, "Say something positive? Well, positive ain't where I live" (1991) – what rappers create is more important than what they critique. Public Enemy 1989 = *Public Enemy* 1931 + affirmation, celebration, political critique, and a call to arms, evoking the "double consciousness" of the blues and other minority culture.

Public Enemy's lyrics became the subject of so much controversy in part because some listeners find Public Enemy's music assaultive and alien, the figuration of experiences they do not want to have or understand. They hear complexity as chaos, noise and power as the signs of a nihilistic threat; for them, polyrhythms are disturbing because they inscribe multiple patterns that refuse the discipline of an overriding rhythmic hierarchy. Others hear such rhythms as their own, as part of a cultural history they value or as a social model to which they are attracted, particularly since the samples hip hop musicians use are overwhelmingly drawn from previous African American music and thus bring a sedimented history into their new contexts. But at the same time that such grooves offer a dialogic, polyphonic environment, they also present these possibilities in noisy, technological, urban terms, making this social ideal seem relevant to the specific historical situation of many fans. In the terms of Tricia Rose's analysis (1994), the polyphonic layering and repetitive flow create continuity, while rhythmic ruptures teach participants to find pleasure in and develop creative responses to social ruptures.

Music, as Christopher Small has argued eloquently (1987:46), is one of the most important media through which social relationships are explored, affirmed, and celebrated, through which identities and subjectivities can be altered, shored up, or tried on for size. Hip hop contains many raps, many grooves, and many meanings. Its musicians compose rich, complex music that makes rap more than protest – makes it, as Cornel West says, a "paradoxical cry of desperation and celebration" (West 1988:186). If we are to understand why rap is so important to millions of people and why it stands at the center of debates over culture and affects struggles over resources, analyzing lyrics is not enough – any more than is formalist musical analysis, or sociological analysis that accepts the music industry's dehumanizing assumptions about its "product." We need to begin to hear not only what these rappers are saying, but also what these musicians are composing – how they are using rhythm, rhyme, and rhetoric to enact survival and celebration, clamor and community.

References

Adler, Jerry, et al. (1990) 'The Rap Attitude,' *Newsweek*, March 19, 56–59.

Baraka, Amiri (1991) "The 'blues aesthetic' and the 'black aesthetic': aesthetics as the continuing political history of a culture," *Black Music Research Journal*, 11:2, 101–9.

Costello, Mark, and David Foster Wallace (1990) *Sighifying Rappers: Rap and Race in the Urban Present* (New York; Ecco).

Dery, Mark (1988) "Rap," *Keyboard* (November), 32–56.

Gilroy, Paul (1991) *There Ain't No Black in the Union Jack; The Cultural Politics of Race and Nation* (Chicago: University of Chicago Press).

—— (1992) "Cultural studies and ethnic absolutism," in Lawrence Grossberg, Cary Nelson, and Paula Treichler (eds), *Cultural Studies*. New York: Routledge, pp. 187–98.

Johnson, Hafiz Shabazz Farel, and John M. Chernoff (1991) "Basic conga drum rhythms in African-American musical styles," *Black Music Research Journal*, 11:1, 55–73.

Kauffman, Robert (1980) "African rhythm: a reassessment," *Ethnomustcology*, 24:3, 393–415.

Keyes, Cheryl L. (1984) "Verbal art performance in rap music: the conversation of the 80's," *Folklore Forum* 17:2, 143–52.

—— (1991), "Rappin to the Beat: Rap Music as Street Culture Among African Americans, Ph.D. diss., Indiana University.

Lipsitz, George (1990) *Time Passages; Collective Memory and American Popular Culture* (Minneapolis; University of Minnesota Press).

Naughty by Nature (1991) "Ghetto Bastard," *Naughty by Nature* (Tommy Boy, TBCD 1044).

Public Enemy (1989) "Fight the Power," extended version (Motown MOT-4647).

Rose, Tricia (1994) *Black Noise* (Hanover, NH: Wesleyan University Press).

Small, Christopher (1987) *Music of the Common Tongue: Survival and Celebration in Afro-American Music* (New York: Riverrun).

Snead, James (1984) "Repetition as a figure of black culture," in Henry Louis Gates, Jr. (ed.), *Black Literature and Literary Theory* (New York: Methuen), pp. 59–79.

Tate, Greg (1990). "Manchild at large," *Village Voice* (September 11), 77.

Tucker, Bruce (1992) "Review of Public Enemy, *It takes a Nation of Millions to Hold Us Back* and De La Soul, 3 *Feet High and Rising*," *American Music*, 10:4, 496–99.

West, Cornel (1988), *Prophetic Fragments* (Grand Rapids, MI: William B. Eerdmans).

Wheeler, Elizabeth A. (1991) "'Most of my heroes don't appear on no stamps': the dialogics of rap music," *Black Music Research Journal*, 11:2, 193–216.

22

The Maori *haka*

Jan Bolwell and Keri Kaa

Jan Bolwell and Keri Kaa, 'Maori dance: an indigenous view', in Adrienne L. Kaeppler and J. W. Love (eds), *Garland Encyclopedia of World Music*, vol. 9 (New York and London: Garland, 1998), pp. 948–51.

Keri Kaa is a Maori artist and educator: the following interview with Jan Bolwell of Wellington College of Education was recorded in 1986.

KERI. We do *haka* to tell stories and score political points. It's actually social comment; and for the men, the most powerful *haka* is political comment. Often they're political protests; they're vehicles for the protest. In the actual words, some quite vicious things are said. I remember my father being appointed the interpreter when the Commissioner of Lands came to the East Coast in the forties, and my father was thrilled to be the interpreter and to escort this minister. It wasn't until halfway through the ceremonies that he realized his cousins had appointed him as the translator because the whole *haka* was actually a protest against the government, and our poor father had to sit there and give this gracious translation, when in fact they called the Parliament things like: "Barking dogs are here to grind away at us in the form of taxes." They saw a whole lot of governmental decisions as financial punishments, and they called the Commissioner of Lands bluntly: "Welcome, you bloody bugger; you've come here to eat our lands."

JAN. So are you saying that the way the *language* works is more important than the *gesture* or the *form* of the dance?

KERI. A lot of the language is hard-hitting. Some of the gestures are graphic, and if you were just looking at them as gestures, they would be obscene. For instance, if you ever see an action where the fist is made, that's usually to do with the phallus. When you wave that at people, you're making a statement about the anger and the bitterness you feel. In many dances where people are making this angry kind of statement, they frequently gesture, talking about the males to the genital area, and you know, the pelvis sort of does a rotation, and they hoist their hips up.

JAN. So are you saying that Māori dance can serve as a cathartic release?

KERI. Oh, it is! If people watching the dance are applauding the exciting movement, I have a chuckle, because if they really knew what was said, some of the dances would not be permitted to be done in public, but it's the people's way of expressing how they're feeling. Probably the most contemporary composer of *haka* who can do that and do it effectively is Bub Wehi, and he does it with words and gestures. Tīmoti Kāretu in some of his *haka* does it with the words, but you have to be a skilled linguist to appreciate what's actually happening. There are gestures where all the lines get down on the ground, and they make a fist and they pound the ground before they rise again.

And *haka* can also be celebratory, where you can have fun *haka*. We have got a hilarious one that we learned as children, all about eating fermented corn. It's still danced in our valley, and the little kids at the last tribal festival, they got up and did the *kanga kopu haka*, and of course those of us who had learned it as children stood up in the audience and did it with these little kids, and the leader was a six-year-old!

And we've got dances where one tribe belittles another tribe; and the belittling might have taken place fifty years ago, but the dance is retained, and now they're done for fun. My people, from my valley, went to see the people from Kuini Moehau's valley. (She's a Māori woman, probably the best one we've got of contemporary *haka*.) And something went wrong with the food. The people from my village came back saying that her people weren't hospitable because they gave my people little eels and what people now call hearts of palm, but they were cabbage-tree shoots. It was probably all the poor things had in their food pits. It wasn't considered a good lunch to have given to visitors, so my lot have this *haka*. Whenever they see the people from that valley, they get up and they welcome them and they say, "Welcome you people from your side of the river who eat little weenie *kūmena* [sweet potatoes], and can only afford to cook up cabbage-tree shoots." And one of the people who loves to do the *haka* is my father's last surviving brother, who's in his eighties, and whenever he spies this family from there, that's how he greets them, with this little dance.

JAN. Is there a history in those relationships between the tribes?

KERI. Oh yes, it's a wonderful way to do it, but my fear is that the knowledge about such matters is really held in only a few people's heads.

JAN. Is there a releasing of that knowledge, or is it still contained within a tribal context?

KERI. Oh, people make assumptions that they actually all know this stuff, and they don't. Not everybody knows it because only some families talk about such incidents and recreate all those dances. So you see, the *haka* for us is quite significant, because it contains a whole lot of stories. There's one, probably the most famous one, that everybody else does and most people do badly, a *haka* called "*Kura Tīwaka.*" The *Kura Tīwaka* was a sacred canoe, which had all these people on board, brothers or cousins, and there was rivalry amongst them. A lot of it had to do with who was the most important person on the *waka* [canoe], and it's a *haka* which has up to thirteen changes of rhythm. It's a real masterpiece to do, and that's why it's so difficult to perform. There's this flood that comes up at sea, and huge swells, and one of them manages to get back to shore because he summons up help from the depths of the ocean. It's a famous dance, and it's a myth really. It's a myth that people still dance in town, but it also serves as a warning to tribes about what happens when you don't have unity in good working relationships within a group.

JAN. Are you saying that the dances are tribally specific?

KERI. Oh yes! "*Rūahuka,*" the one that everyone says is about the earthquake god, for instance, is really nothing to do with earthquakes. "*Rūaumoko*" was written by a woman, and so that bit is never acknowledged, because "*Rūaumoko*" is about the phallus in action. I was about thirty before I clicked at what the *haka* was really saying. The explanation is that only a woman could describe what the penis was doing, because she was the recipient of it. So, it's about the penis in motion, and it's graphically expressed in the actions. But of course for public viewing and for public consumption, there's another story attached to it, partly to make it palatable for audiences.

JAN. So a lot of *haka* were sexually explicit?

KERI. Oh yes, a lot of them were, and a lot were explicit about the activity of eating people, killing them. There's one that says, "*Homai kia whiti-whiti,*" and you illustrate when you do it, you're actually disemboweling somebody – literally, "Give me your guts, and I'll tear them apart for you." And you realize there's been an incident where somebody has actually been killed in battle and accordingly disemboweled. So in a lot of the *haka*, the lyrics are ferocious. To have an appreciation of *haka*, you have to have a good understanding of the language. A lot of *haka* have been watered down to make them palatable for audiences.

JAN. Is this the influence of Christianity?

KERI. Yes, then you have got to thank missionaries for that – and because people turned away from warfare, and turned to singing together and praying together.

JAN. Well, what's your view of this? I mean, when we think about Māori dance, if we use the word *traditional* as opposed to *contemporary*, what meaning does that have for you?

KERI. I think when you're watching *haka* today, sometimes I think we're watching only the surface of it. But the real guts of it sometimes cannot be readily understood except by a learned few, and I think that's beginning to change with the *haka* schools that are developing round the country, where young men who are qualified in the *reo* [language], who are good speakers of it, are starting to ask probing questions, starting to unearth information they feel they need. Irirangi, for instance, one of the great storehouses of knowledge, would tell so much information to his classes and then stop, because he felt that some of the knowledge was probably knowledge that they wouldn't have been able to handle.

JAN. Are you saying that some of that knowledge will never be passed down?

KERI. Yes. Because he probably felt it was unsafe. Irirangi was the last person I know of who fought a duel. He was challenged to this fight, and said to this man, "Choose your weapons." I don't know what the man chose, but Inirangi chose his *patu*, his short fighting club. It was a fight to the death, but Irirangi stopped short of the killer blow, with his *patu* raised for the killer strike. He stopped when he got that far. Now he has done the same thing to his pupils: he stopped short of the killer strike. That's why it was a sad time when he died. There were things he could never discuss with anybody except men as learned as he was, so some of that knowledge has gone to his grave with him.

JAN. So where does that leave young people today?

KERI. Some of them learn the material. They learn the words, the actions, how to coordinate it; and they learn how to perform it. But I think some of them need to go a step further and start reading, and talking, and going to workshops to talk things through, because to me there's a gap in the learning. They don't understand about movements, which, when you're teaching them to new students, are physically quite dangerous, and can wreck people's ankles and feet if people's bodies aren't properly prepared.

I'll be interested to see where people take *haka* in the next century, whether it'll reshape and recreate itself. What I see the groups doing, and what I see them as signaling, is the development of a new kind of dance, a dance that's telling the stories of now. We've got dances about drugs, about AIDS, and one of the dances I find most entertaining is about space people. In the thirties and forties, people were creating dances about things they saw happening, about airplanes.

JAN. Well, look at the music they took from that age. You could call it appropriation, but they were taking from everything that was happening around them in popular culture.

KERI. Rarotonga is a wonderful example. They've got a dance for men where the men have their arms out like airplane wings. It was clear to me what that was the minute I saw it, because they would have been miming what they saw coming down from the sky. They've got a really entertaining dance about a man on a horse, and you can tell because the dancer actually raises one leg and mounts his imaginary horse, and then rides it about. And of course you and I have seen their entertaining butt-dance, so people are being presented with these new things and then creating what they have seen. And, hey, presto! you get a new dance.

JAN. But still rooted in the traditional form?

KERI. Yes, And a *haka* that diverts from that gets itself into difficulties rhythmically, because if you don't have that solid, basic beat going, the rest of the dance goes haywire. I've seen some *haka* where people have tried to fly through the air, and they've not quite managed it because they haven't come back to the basic rhythm. But I always think, well, that's great, because people are experimenting with an idea. I've seen *haka* movements used in aerobic sessions – which my father would have been frowning heavily at.

A lot of tutors need to go back to school, because there's a need for good, solid teaching. You should tell people why they're doing what they're doing. Many tutors don't even tell their performers why they stand in lines. I heard one say because it's neat and tidy! People need to have an understanding of where this has come from. We have to get up off our chuffs and do it ourselves, because we're coming from inside the dance.

Part IV

Song and ritual

23

Wassailing in Somerset

Kingsley Palmer and Robert W. Patten

Kingsley Palmer and Robert W. Patten, 'Some notes on
wassailing and ashen faggots in south and west Somerset',
Folklore, 82:4 (Winter 1971), pp. 281–91.

In this part of Somerset wassailing fall into two classes – wassailing apple trees and wassailing the important inhabitants of the village. The vast majority of the wassail songs also falls into two classes – one which contains the line 'Hatsful, capsful, and three bushel bagsful' and is generally called, *The Apple Tree Wassail*, and the other which frequently begins 'Wassail, wassail all over the town' and has verses addressed to 'Master and Missus' and can be termed, *The Visiting Wassail*. Unfortunately the division of the songs does not correspond exactly to the division of the customs, so that 'Wassail, wassail all over the town' was sometimes sung to apple trees and *The Visiting Wassail* sometimes contained the 'Hatsful, capsful' lines. This causes problems where [Cecil] Sharp recorded only the tune and words and no details of the actual custom.

Apple tree wassailing is in fact a visiting custom in that each orchard in the village should be visited. It must be an apple tree that is wassailed and it is said that the custom ceased at Dunster when it was found that a pear tree had been wassailed due to the men having had too much cider. After such a *faux pas* they did not have the nerve to go out the next year.

Wassailing apple trees still survives in a modified form at the village of Carhampton. One tree in the orchard behind the Butchers Arms Inn is wassailed and the landlord alone sings the song although most of the people present join in the shouting and about half a dozen shotguns are usually in evidence. This wassail takes place on January 17th – Old Twelfth Night on the Folk Calendar. Soon after 8 p.m. everybody gathers in the orchard and the landlord, Mr Eric Tarr, sings the Wassail Song which is very similar to the song Sharp collected at Bratton, a couple of miles away, and published in *Folk Songs from Somerset* Vol. V. During the shouting at the end of the song the guns are fired into the tree, 'to scare off the evil spirits', a bonfire is lit, there is more firing of guns and singing starts. Hot spiced cider is passed around, some in the silver, three-handled Wassail Bowl which is inscribed;

INTERNATIONAL
WASSAIL
BOWL
1960
Yakima-Carhampton
USA   England

When things have quietened down somewhat, Mr Tarr calls everyone over and places some toast soaked in the hot cider in the branches of the tree, 'for the robins'. Then all return to the Inn for more refreshments.

The custom has had two revivals at Carhampton – one about fifty years ago by Mr Tarr's father when attendance had dropped to a low level, and another about twelve years ago. A visiting American saw the wassail and took the idea back to Yakima which is in a large apple growing area, where it was used as publicity. Each year a young lady from Yakima attends Carhampton Wassail to act as an ambassador.

Apart from the recent additions the wassail is essentially what happened in each orchard. There were local variations – the landlord of the King William IV Inn at Curry Rivel has a Wassail Lamp which originally came from the Ilchester area; the oil lamp is in a square brass and glass case which is about eighteen inches high and about twelve inches square. The case is inscribed;

APPLE TREE
I LIGHT WITH GLEE
WHILE BELL AN CANDLE
WASSAIL THEE

An informant at Wootton Courtney on Exmoor can recall his grand-mother wassailing her apple trees on her own before 1914. She sang an abbreviated version of *The Apple Tree Wassail* in her cracked voice and then put some dry toast in the tree. She had no gun and no cider to soak the toast but obviously, for her, wassailing the trees was an important part of growing apples.

At Sea, near Ilminster, cider was poured around the roots of the tree, in this case it was the tree that gave the most apples and made the best cider that was wassailed. At Crowcombe there was a further piece of ceremony, a boy was lifted up to put the toast in the branches of the tree and after all had had a drink of the cider the remainder was poured around the roots of the tree. The tree chosen was either the oldest or the best. Then all ran back to the farmhouse where the women, who had been left behind, had locked the doors. The women tried to keep the men out and when they finally got in they would sit and drink more cider.

In *F.S.S.* V, Sharp quotes from *Devonshire Notes and Queries* that at Wiveliscombe the wassailers danced in a circle around the tree and after the firing of the guns and noise making they stooped down and raised themselves up three times and shouted the end of their song.

According to local tradition the noise and the gun firing is to scare off the evil spirits and the toast is for the robins. It would seem, however, that the custom contains elements of fertility charms, now long forgotten.

After wassailing the apple trees it was sometimes the custom to go round the village and wassail the chief inhabitants. In some cases it would appear that the apple tree wassailing was dropped and the visiting custom alone has survived. At any rate, only the visiting custom has survived to the present in the neighbouring villages of Curry Rivel and Drayton, near Langport.

[. . .]

The Curry Rivel song was collected from the wassailers outside of a house in the village on 5.1.71. This song has altered considerably from that Sharp collected in 1909 – it has lost three verses and gained another, though it may be that the 'gained' verse was one that Sharp's informant omitted. Sharp published the song much as he had collected it.

The Drayton song was collected from Mr Charles Showers, one of the wassailers, on 31.12.70. There are only one or two minor differences between the version collected in 1970 and the version Sharp collected in 1903. However when Sharp published this song he altered it considerably.

Comparing the tunes is more difficult because transcribing a tape of half a dozen singers in varying keys and not completely sober presents its own problems; suffice to say they are closely related.

Both wassails are held on January 5th – Old Christmas Eve on the Folk Calendar and both start from an inn – the Crown at Drayton and the King William IV at Curry Rivel – at about 6 p.m. At Curry Rivel there are about five or six wassailers but at Drayton the number varies a great deal; as few as three and as many as ten have been known in recent years. There is no set route, the wassailers call at the bigger houses where they feel sure of a welcome and the time of the visit can be arranged beforehand. On arrival at a house the song is sung and the toast said but knocking on the door is forbidden. This last point is strictly adhered to, presumably because knocking would reduce wassailing to a begging custom, which the last verse of the Drayton song so strongly denies. In return for the song and the toast the wassailers are generally invited in for a drink and a bite to eat or are given a tip. The Drayton wassailers have no set finishing place and this year their last call was at a house where they had been invited for supper. At Curry Rivel they try to be back at the inn in time for the ashen faggot burning.

The custom at Drayton does not seem to have changed a great deal since Sharp saw it except that then there were twelve to fifteen wassailers and they started at the vicarage.

According to tradition January 5th is Old Christmas Eve, probably more significant is that it is Twelfth Night Eve, thereby connecting it by date to the January 17th wassails.

The Visiting-Wassail songs of this area contain a number of interesting verses – the cup, 'of the good old ashen tree', may be a straightforward reference to wooden utensils or there may be some deeper significance due to the magical properties of the ash tree. The maid with the silver headed pin frequently occurs and in the Curry Rivel song that Sharp published she also had a glove and a mace. In his notes 'mace' looks more like 'mask', but this does not rhyme with 'face' and 'place'. Possibly these references are all that remain of a piece of lost ritual or pantomime. There are a number of nonsense verses like that of the old man and the cow which only seem to be included as an excuse to ask for more drink.

[. . .]

The Apple Tree Wassail; Carhampton,

Collected from Mr Eric Tarr, Carhampton, 16.1.71.

Old Apple Tree we wassail thee,
And hoping thou would bear,
For the Lord doth know where we shall be
Till apples come another year,
For to bear well and to bloom well,
So merry let us be,
Let every man take off his hat
And shout at the old apple tree,
Old Apple Tree we wassail thee,
And hoping thou would bear,
Hatsfuls, capsfuls, three bushel bagfuls
And a little heap under the stairs.
Hip hip hooray.

[. . .]

The Visiting Wassail; Curry Rivel,

Collected Curry Rivel, 5.1.71.

Wassail, oh wassail all over the town,
The cup it is white and the ale it is brown,
The cup it is made of the good old ashen tree,
And so's the beer from the best barley.
  To you our wassail,
  I am joy come to our jolly wassail.

CURRY RIVEL WASSAIL

Fig. 23.1 Curry Rivel Wassail

Oh, here we take this door held fast by the ring,
Hoping Master and Missus will let us all walk in,
And for to fill our wassail bowl and sail away again,
    To you our wassail,
    I am joy come to our jolly wassail.

Oh Master and Missus have we done you any harm?
Pray hold fast this door and let us pass along,
And give us hearty thanks for the singing of our song.
    To you our wassail,
    I am joy come to our jolly wassail.

Spoken: God bless Master and Missus and all the family,
        Hoping they've had a merry Christmas and wishing them a happy
        New Year
        And many.

The Visiting Wassail; Drayton,

Collected Drayton 31.12.70.

Wassail, oh wassail all over the town,
The cup it is white and the ale it is brown,
The cup it is made of the good old ashen tree
And so is the beer of the best barley.
    For it's your wassail
    And it's our, our wassail,
    And I'm jolly come to our jolly wassail.

There was an old man and be had an old cow,
And how for to keep it he could not tell how,
He built up a barn to keep his cow warm,
    For no harm, boys, harm,
    No harm, boys, harm,
    And a cup of good liquor will do us no harm.

Oh maid, maid, maid, with your silver headed pin,
Pray open the door and let us all in,
And then you shall see how merry we shall be,
    For it's your wassail, etc.,

The Missus and the Master were sitting by the fire,
Not thinking we poor travellers were travelling in the mire,
Come fill up our bowls and we'll be gone from here.
    For it's your wassail, etc.,

We're not come here for to eat or to drink,
But to keep up the custom until another year.
    For it's your wassail, etc.,

Spoken: God bless Missus and Master and all the family.
        Wishing you a happy Christmas and a bright and prosperous
        New Year,
        And many of them.

DRAYTON WASSAIL

Verse 1

Wassail, oh was-sa - il all over the town, The cup it is white and the

ale it is brown, The cup it is made of the good old ashen tree,

And so is the beer of the best ba - rley. For it's your wassail,

And it's our, our wassail, And I'm jol - ly come to our jol - ly wa - ssail.

Verse 2

There was an old man and he had an old cow, And how for to keep it he

could not tell how, He built up a barn to keep his cow warm,

For no barm, boys, harm, No harm, boys, harm, And a cup of good liq - uor will do us no harm.

Verses 3 and 4 as 2 above

Verse 5

We're not come here for to eat or to drink, But to keep up the cus - tom until another year.

For it's your wassail, And it's our, our wassail, And I'm jol-ly come to our jol-ly wa-ssail.

Fig. 23.2 Drayton Wassail

24

The carol revival

Frank Howes

Frank Howes, *The English Musical Renaissance* (London: Secker & Warburg, 1966), pp. 73–5, 81–3.

In Howes' chapter on the English revival he credits for the revival of carols, both the folk-song collectors (particularly Cecil Sharp) and the nineteenth-century Anglo-Catholic 'Oxford Movement' which influenced worship in the Anglican church.

Folk-music is the music created by the common people, and in practice this means by peasants not by townsmen. Popular music is music addressed to the people and this generally is a town product addressed to urban people. There is thus a wide difference between them; folk-music grows, popular music is composed. But the history of the carol shows that the two kinds of plebeian music are in contact with each other. Carols were written mainly in the late Middle Ages by clerical authors who wanted to preach the Glad Tidings to the common people, such as knew no more Latin than a few tags like *Gloria in excelsis.* To ensure popular adoption they included elements drawn from common speech, common experience, and common knowledge. Individual and communal authorship were thus mingled. Such a carol as the now universally known "The Holly and the Ivy", a true folk carol, still shows half a dozen different strains. Its doctrinal teaching is plainly clerical in origin, its refrain of jumbled images:

> The rising of the sun,
> The running of the deer,
> The playing of the merry organ,
> Sweet singing in the choir.

is witness to its origin in the round dance (a carol is by definition a dance-song); its tune has been handed down not only in print, but by an independent oral tradition which was picked up by Cecil Sharp in Gloucestershire nearly two hundred years after it was printed on a broadside.

But though the traditions are mixed – the professionals have had a hand in many a traditional ballad – the distinction is quite clear, and can be even more clearly discerned in the tunes than in the poems of traditional songs and ballads. After all the scholarly warfare of the last century on the origins of this traditional and anonymous art – fought mainly by literary men and philologists – it has become clear that folk-song owes its distinctive character to its communal and not to its individual element. It is no longer claimed that "das Volk dichtet". Committees cannot write letters, still less could they compose lyrical ballads. "First of all one man sings a song, and then others sing it after him, changing what they do not like" (or do not remember, which comes to much the same thing). This was the formula for explaining the origin of folk-song which Cecil Sharp, with his immense first-hand experience of the material, took over from Böhme and adopted as the explanation of the problem of origins, and he adds: "The solution of the mystery of the origin of the folk-song is not to be found by seeking an original – that is a vain quest – but by examining the method by which it has been preserved and handed down from one generation to another. In other words, the method of oral transmission is not merely one by which the folk-song lives; it is a process by which it grows and by which it is created."

This does not contain the whole of the matter, since carols, as already indicated, show how a more professional element is often gathered up in the communal process, and the folk-songs of the Celtic peoples in this country show a similar professional influence of bards and harpers; experience of American negroes also shows that something not far from spontaneous communal composition is possible, given the currency of certain stock phrases and a certain emotional temperature to provide the flash point at which the diverse elements will fuse into a new folk-song. But Sharp's theory is basically sound and contains the root of the matter in it. The distinctive character of folk-song, which is so marked that those who deal in it soon learn to recognize the genuine article almost by the smell, arises from its continuous evolution by oral tradition as it passes from the lips of one singer to the ear of another and so on to his lips and thence down the generations without ever a note of it or a line of verse being put to paper. The song, then, is actually fashioned by its oral transmission; by passage through many minds whatever of individuality it once had is transformed into a communal product. And it is this representative quality, so acquired, winning the assent of unnumbered singers, who may each reject it in whole or in part or in detail but who in fact love it enough to transmit it, that gives to the folk-song its national character. And because no song has a chance of survival which does not bear repetition by generations of singers and which does not conform in the last resort to national taste and character, the folk-singer is in the happy position of being able to declare that his best is also his most typical. It was, however, the quality of the tunes, not their national character, which first caught the attention of the early collectors in England.

[. . .]

There was another revival of traditional melody proceeding simultaneously and producing the unmathematical phenomenon of two parallel lines which met. This was of the carol, which was fostered by the Oxford Movement and ultimately joined the folk-song revival, in that folk-carols were discovered and were presented to the world by Vaughan Williams in his *Fantasia on Christmas Carols* (1912). The carol is by definition a seasonal song with a burden which was derived from the dance. It flourished in the late middle ages along with the mystery play – the Coventry Carol is representative of the way in which an originally pagan and secular song was christianized and attached to the Nativity. The Christmas carol therefore had a clerical element in its origin and was transmitted in manuscript and print as well as by oral tradition. Early in the nineteenth century it was in decline or tending to go underground as the folk-songs did, and conscious attempts to preserve it were made by two antiquarians, Davies Gilbert and William Sandys, who published in 1822 and 1833 respectively two small collections containing those carols best known in Victorian times, such as "God rest you merry", "The First Nowell" and "The Cherry Tree Carol". But the Christmas spirit as revealed in Dickens's short novel, *A Christmas Carol*, consisted of heavy eating and general benevolence – the only actual carol mentioned being "God rest you merry" piped through Scrooge's keyhole. The next collection to be published marked the change of attitude which gradually brought back the more religious aspect of the festival, its mysticism and the tenderness of the mediaeval lullabies. This was *Carols for Christmastide*, published in 1853 by the Rev. T. Helmore and the Rev. J. M. Neale, both high-churchmen. They had been given a copy of *Piae Cantiones*, printed in Finland in 1582, which had been brought from Stockholm by Her Majesty's Envoy to that capital and from which the tunes of "Good King Wenceslas" and "Good Christian men rejoice" (*In dulci jubilo*) were taken. The Oxford Movement encouraged the practice of singing carols in church rather than leaving them to street performance, and to meet the growing taste for this ancient music Bramley and Stainer published their famous collection, *Christmas Carols, New and Old*, in 1865, which restored to currency a number of traditional carols. In 1900 *The Cowley Carol Book* proceeded farther in the same direction and added still more carols from abroad. Other tributaries that swelled the now vigorous carol tradition were the discovery by the folk-song collectors of ballads of the Nativity and mummers' carols (e.g. "O mortal man remember well"), pagan wassail songs and a true folk-carol like "The Holly and the Ivy". The macaronic carol, in which Latin and the vernacular alternate (e.g. *In dulci jubilo*), French noëls (e.g. *Quittez pasteurs*), Christmas hymns (e.g. *Adeste fideles*), German lullabies (e.g. *Joseph lieber, Joseph mein*) were further additions to carol literature, for which a largely agnostic twentieth century has shown an insatiable appetite. Musically the carol, now largely confined to Christmas, has united scholars, ecclesiastics, musicians and the great public, including the unmusical, into a fellowship unparalleled in the realm of music. By 1930 the new liturgy of Nine Lessons and Nine Carols, devised by Archbishop Benson after ancient precedent when he was Bishop of Truro as far back as 1880, and adopted by King's College, Cambridge, for Christmas Eve, had become a national institution, to which millions attend through its broadcast by radio.

Though terminologically carols should more properly be called popular than folk, both folk-song and carols can rightly be called traditional and their revivals have coalesced.

25

Papal legislation on sacred music

Robert F. Hayburn

Robert F. Hayburn, *Papal Legislation on Sacred Music 95 A.D. to 1977 A.D.* (Collegeville, MN: The Liturgical Press, 1979), pp. 17–23.

This item concerns a famous papal bull of 1324–35 on the subject of sacred music, setting out which compositional procedures would be permitted in which contexts. It is not necessary to know the contemporary music theory in detail in order to grasp the essence of the argument: *hocquetus* or *hocheti* (hocket), *discanti* (discant or descant), *tripla* and *motectus* refer to particular techniques of polyphony (i.e. of ways of combining more than one voice) or to specific kinds of vocal line in polyphonic textures current in the fourteenth century; *cantilenae* is the Latin for chant. The Antiphonal and Gradual are books containing the chants intended for specific liturgical occasions. The Goliards were wandering scholars, poets and composers of the period.

In the thirteenth century particularly, secular texts were often inserted into the music of the Church, many times in vernacular, rather than in Latin words. Occasionally the tenor was taken from a secular tune. At times the texts were both secular and French. At other instances, one was religious and in Latin (or Greek), while the other was secular and in French.

[...]

These musical innovations, and their effect on contemporary writers, are discussed in the writings of churchmen, pious souls, theorists, and Church councils. Here Jacob of Liege inveighs against tasteless and ill-trained singers:

> There are some who although they contrive to sing a little in the modern manner, nevertheless, they have no regard for quality; they sing too lasciviously, they multiply voices superfluously; some of them employ the *hocquetus* too much, breaking, cutting and dividing their voices into too many conso-

nants; in the most inopportune places they dance, whirl and jump about on notes, howling like dogs. They bay and like madmen nourished by disorderly and twisted abberations, they use a harmony alien to nature herself.[1]

[. . .]

The dissatisfaction aroused in the clergy by the contrapuntal writing of many composers would seem to have reached a climax in the early fourteenth century. When remonstrances and admonitions had already been attempted in vain, a grave step was taken by Pope John XXII (1316–1334), ruling at Avignon. [. . .]

The document itself comprises three main sections. The first brings to mind secular teaching and the practice of the Church. The second denounces infractions of the established laws of Church music. The last section treats of polyphony and points out that it may be used in certain services of the Church.

[. . .]

The competent authority of the Fathers has decreed that, in singing the offices of divine praise through which we express the homage due to God, we must be careful to avoid doing violence to the words, but must sing with modesty and gravity, melodies of a calm and peaceful character. For it is written, "from their lips came sweet sounds." (First responsory in the Office of the Dedication of a Church.) Now, sounds are truly sweet when the singer, while speaking to God in words, speaks to Him also with his heart, and thus, through his song, arouses the devotion of others. It is for this purpose, namely, to arouse the devotion of the faithful, that the singing of psalms is prescribed in the Church of God; and for this same reason, the day and night offices, as well as the celebration of the Mass, are sung by the clergy and by the people to melodies which are grave yet varied, and thus, while we are pleased by such diversity, we are charmed by their gravity.

But certain exponents of a new school, who think only of the laws of measured time, are composing new melodies of their own creation with a new system of notes, and these they prefer to the ancient, traditional music [. . .] By some, their melodies are broken up by *hocheti* or robbed of their virility by *discanti* (two parts), *tripla* (three parts), *motectus,* with a dangerous element produced by certain parts sung on texts in the vernacular; all these abuses have brought into disrepute the basic melodies of the Antiphonal and Gradual; these composers, knowing nothing of the true foundation upon which they must build, are ignorant of the Modes, incapable of distinguishing between them, and cause great confusion. The mere number of the notes, in these compositions, conceal from us the plain-chant melody, with its simple, well-regulated rises and falls which indicate the character of the Mode. These musicians run without pausing, they intoxicate the ear without satisfying it, they dramatize the text with gestures and, instead of promoting devotion, they prevent it by creating a sensuous and innocent atmosphere. Thus it was

not without good reason that Boethius said: "A person who is intrinsically sensuous will delight in hearing these indecent melodies, and one who listens to them frequently will be weakened thereby and lose his virility of soul."

Consequently We and Our Brethren (the cardinals) have realized for a long time that this state of things required correction. And now We are prepared to take effective action to prohibit, cast out, and banish such things from the Church of God.

Therefore, after consultation with these same brethren (the cardinals), We prohibit absolutely, for the future that anyone should do such things, or others of like nature, during the Divine Office or during the Holy Sacrifice of the Mass. Should anyone disobey, by the authority of this law he will be punished by suspension from his office during eight days, [. . .]

However, We do not intend to forbid the occasional use – principally on solemn feasts at Mass and at Divine Office – of certain consonant intervals superposed upon the simple ecclesiastical chant, provided these harmonies are in the spirit and character of the melodies themselves, as, for instance, the consonance of the octave, the fifth, the fourth, and others of this nature; but always on condition that the melodies themselves remain intact in the pure integrity of their form, and that no innovation take place against true musical discipline; for such consonances are pleasing to the ear and arouse devotion, and they prevent torpor among those who sing in honor of God.

Made and promulgated at Avignon in the Ninth Year of Our Pontificate. (1324–1325).[2]

The significance of this document for the musical practice of that time can be seen in its toleration of the use of polyphony in the services of the Church. It is true that this was not a general permission, but it did allow the use of the new art on the greater feasts of the Church and at both the Mass and the Divine Office. However, a condition was laid down, namely, that the chant must have priority and be employed as in the past. Pope John XXII was principally occupied with the fate of the ancient plainsong of the Church. Therefore his bull was aimed at preserving the music of the Church in accord with the liturgical usage of the time. However, musical development at this period was taking place according to living musical practice. If these practices were to be introduced into the liturgy, they should be fitting accompaniment for acts of sacred worship. The Pope, in the third section of the bull, made plain that polyphonic devices were to be allowed on the greater feasts and by means of octaves, fourths, and fifths. Thus he did not exclude from the liturgy these practices but rather regulated them in accord with liturgical propriety.

An important effect of this bull of Pope John XXII concerned the Goliards and wandering singers, who sang in the market place and in church. In many places these individuals had gained a monopoly over new compositions, into which, under the pretext of singing motets of better quality, they introduced in favor of polyphony a thousand declamations injurious to the clergy, prelates, and papacy. The sections of the papal bull which concerned vernacular and non-liturgical texts was aimed at these problems. It was by means of the addition of new texts that these criticisms were made by the Goliards. This carping spirit penetrated, on great liturgical feasts, into the very churches and created ceremonies there not always conformable to a religious spirit. Where the bull was enforced, therefore, this problem was eliminated, since the liturgical texts, according to the wording of the bull, were to be sung without alteration.

It is difficult to evaluate the complete effect of this bull of Pope John XXII. It is probable that many of the musical abuses continued in provincial areas and states, as the bull was not well promulgated because of the political and religious events of the time. Since John XXII was an Avignon pope and lived on French soil, the enemies of the French would be hostile to decrees coming from a pope whom they considered as being under the undue influence of the French king. These events during the Avignon papacy (1305–1376) did not favor and facilitate the diffusion of this bull. [. . .]

It is probably safe to say, however, that the bull did have disciplinary effects in particular localities. The choir records of the cathedral of Paris would seem partially to confirm this assumption. The School of Notre Dame was the home of the first and greatest school of discant. Yet in the year 1408, eighty-six years after Pope John XXII had published his edict, discant was still restricted there by the rules for music then in force at that institution. The constitution of the Maitrise, or choir school of Notre Dame, was written in the year 1408 by Jean Charliet. Concerning the discant, the rules read:

> Furthermore, let a master, at appointed hours, teach the children singing, plainsong chiefly, but also counterpoint and certain seemingly discants, not dissolute and immodest *cantilenae*, nor let him dwell upon these musical matters, to the hindrance of their progress in grammar. And let him be very specially attentive to this, inasmuch as in our own church discant is not in use, being prohibited by statutes, at least as regards the voices called mutatae. [*Voces mutatae* refers to changed voices, rather than those of boys who sang soprano.]

This seems to imply that the voices of the boys might be employed in singing a counterpoint upon the chant melody. The legislation thus must have referred to the men rather than to the boys.

Some writers see in the bull of John XXII a cause for the decline in religious composition in the fourteenth century. They claim that the composers turned to secular works where they could use the new devices of musical composition then in vogue. Although the evidence for any notable alteration of musical practice which might be traced to Pope John XXII is not conclusive, nevertheless this bull is a significant historical document and an important act of legislation on Church music.

Notes

1 "Speculum musicae," *Scriptorum de musica medii aevi novam seriem a Gerbertina alteram collegit nuncque,* ed. Charles Coussemaker, 4 vols. (Paris: A. Durand, 1864–1875), 2:394.
2 *Corpus juris canonici, ed. a. 1582 cum glossa (in aedibus populi Romani, iussu Gregorii XIII)* (Leipzig: Ed. Aem. Friedberg, 1879–1881), 1:1256–1257.

26

Jungle paths and spirit songs

Marina Roseman

Marina Roseman, *Healing Sounds from the Malaysian Rainforest: Temiar Music and Medicine* (Berkeley: University of California Press, 1991), pp. 3–10.

In her ethnographic study of the Temiar people of Malaysia, their music and its relationship to healing rituals, Roseman represents some sounds of the Temiar language using IPA characters: [ε] pronounced as the e in bed, [ɔ] as oa in board, and [ŋ] as ng in bang.

Traveling through the Malaysian rainforest, one first senses the presence of a Temiar settlement through a change in the density of jungle foliage: primary forest gives way in patches to secondary forest. These once-tended fields, now overgrown with brush and young trees, might indicate that one has only reached a former settlement site. Such plots are left behind to be reclaimed by jungle growth when the semisedentary Temiar move on after fertile garden sites surrounding a village have been used up, every three to five years. But when the shaded path the traveler has been following through the jungle opens out onto currently tended plots of tapioca plants, their leaves shoulder-height and open to the sun, or onto a field of hill rice farmed in the slash-and-burn, nonirrigated manner of the rainforest peoples, the presence of a current settlement is firmly announced.

Even before one sees the sun upon the tapioca leaves, the sounds of birds unique to lower brush and thickets at the fields' edge hint of an approaching settlement. The path becomes more clearly worn; dogs sensing the traveler's scent begin to bark. Voices of people calling from one house to another, or children playing outside, can now be heard. This mixture of human voices, dogs barking, and birds of the settlement edge replaces the calls of forest canopy birds and mammals which had earlier accompanied the traveler's journey through tall, dense trees. The path ceases to be a narrow trail for single-file travelers, and joins the firmly packed earth of the village, where brush around dwellings has been cleared.

If approached instead by boat or bamboo raft along the river, a footpath winding down to the riverbank announces a village's presence. In the absence of sandy beach or flat river stones, a floating bamboo platform might be attached to the shore here. Women washing clothing and fetching water, or men preparing to set off on river travel, call to people further up along the path, who in turn announce the travelers' arrival to inhabitants inside their dwellings: "Stoke the fire, put some water on to boil, your child's father has returned."

About 12,000 Temiar live in small settlements of 25 to 150 inhabitants along five major rivers and their tributaries flowing down from the mountainous divide that runs through the center of the Malay peninsula. The watersheds spread east into the state of Kelantan and west into Perak. Temiar settlements, from ten minutes to several days' journey apart, range across 2,500 acres of rainforest. Temiar horticulturalists grow tapioca, hill rice, maize, millet, and other crops. They also hunt, fish, and gather jungle products for their own use and for exchange. [. . .]

Temiars are relatively egalitarian, with village leaders and headmen who use influence and persuasion rather than coercion to coordinate community tasks. Village leaders are usually elder males of the core sibling group, some of whom received additional sanction as headman from traditional Malay authorities, a process continued today by the Department of Orang Asli [aboriginal] Affairs. Relationships between the sexes [. . .] reveal a complementarity in everyday tasks that tends toward incipient stratification. While most mediums are male, potential gender inequities are counterbalanced by the structure of ceremonial participation and theories of dream-song composition.

[. . .]

Following a jungle path or a path from the riverbank as it opens out into a Temiar settlement, one realizes that the "settlement" (*deek*) is distinguished from, and yet intimately connected with the "jungle" (*bɛɛk*). Temiar house construction further emphasizes the interpenetrability of jungle and settlement. Thatched houses, raised about 8 feet off the ground, have walls made from bamboo tubes laid horizontally one above the other, similar to the horizontal wooden logs of a North American log cabin. But in Temiar walls, about an inch of space is left between each tube. Similarly, floors are constructed of bamboo slats lashed together with about an inch of space between each slat. Clearly these spaces between wall tubes and between floor slats have utilitarian value: smoke from hearth fires escapes through the space between the tubes; excess bits of food fall through the space between the slats to the chickens below, while young children's feces fall through to the dogs. But when the cold night wind whistles through the spaces between the tubes, and uncomfortable sleepers awaken to huddle for a while around hearth fires, one realizes that this mode of construction has not survived merely for its pragmatic value. Rather, Temiar speak of the need to see out into the jungle, the desire to be sheltered but not enclosed. Neighboring nomadic Semang groups build shelters on the ground completely open on one side to uncleared forest; down-river, the Malays split the bamboo tubes and weave opaque walls. Seminomadic Temiar hunter-horticulturalists, midway between these groups in their relationship to the rainforest, build permeable houses in clearings that mark limits, yet express the intimate interpenetrability of settlement and forest.

The entities that form and inhabit these interpenetrable domains are conceived of as having similar structures and modes of action. Temiars posit a homologous division of potentially detachable souls among humans (who have head and heart souls), plants (which have leaf and root souls), animals (which have upper and lower souls), and landforms (such as summit and underground souls of mountains). Bounded souls can be liberated as unbounded spirit during dreams, trance, and illness (see Benjamin 1979). The shared properties of upper:lower and bound:unbound souls make interaction and the flow of information possible between human and nonhuman entities. In Temiar ideology, this relationship of resemblance enables dream and trance encounters, promoting song composition and precipitating illness. When unbound as spirit, entities of both jungle and settlement are capable of engaging humans in benevolent interactions as spiritguides, or malevolent ones as illness agents. Jungle is not opposed to settlement as the realm of danger versus the realm of safety, as is sometimes found among Malays; rather, both domains exhibit positive and negative dimensions.

During dreams, the detachable, unbound head soul of the dreamer meets with detached upper- or lower-portion souls of entities (such as trees, river rapids, tigers, houses) who express their desire to become the dreamer's spiritguide. The relationship is confirmed through bestowal of a song from spiritguide to the dreamer. Later, singing that song during ceremonial performance, the person becomes imbued with the voice, vision, and knowledge of the spiritguide. Singing the song links person and spiritguide; thus transformed into a medium for the spirits, a person can diagnose and treat illness.

When I first heard mediums sing during ceremonial performances, I was told what they were singing: "*nɔŋ*." *Nɔŋ*, I wrote in my notebook, must mean "song." When I asked what the female chorus, vocally responding to each line sung by the medium, was doing, they responded with the word: "*wɛdwad*." That must be "choral response," I thought. One day, as I was walking with Temiars through the forest on the way to the rice fields, someone pointed out a path between the trees and commanded: "*Wɛdwad nɔŋ-na'*." What are these people doing talking about songs and choral responses out here, I wondered in surprise. What I had been told, they explained, was to "follow that path." I realized, then, that songs were paths, and choruses were following the path. The spiritguide shows a path, a way, a route; the medium sings of the route traversed by the spiritguide, describing the visions and vistas seen by the spiritguide during its travels. The path links spiritguide, medium, and other ceremonial participants.

My experience on the path points toward a fundamental method in the study of ritual performance: if you want to understand the building blocks of ritual, the movements, the music, the colors, the shapes, you cannot spend all your time taping rituals and playing them back for transcription and analysis. Even moving from documentation to performance and singing with the chorus or dancing with dancers gives but a partial picture. You must live the life of a people, follow their paths, dig in the dirt, gut a fish, ford a stream, and always be alert for the links between daily life and ritual activity. These links, which Gregory Bateson called "the pattern that connects," are the threads that give coherency to culture.

[. . .]

For Temiars, the symbolic power of the image of the path arises from their daily travel along land and river routes running through the jungle and settlement. The pervasive sensate experience of the path is given symbolic expression in the root metaphor *nɔŋ*. Negotiating the path, knowing the way through the jungle, constitutes essential knowledge in Temiar life. Getting lost, losing the path, can be fatal in the jungle. Consequently, in Temiar etiology, illness often results when a person's detached head soul gets lost or waylaid; treatment then involves singing a "way," finding the head soul, and leading it back home. If the chorus fumbles when repeating the medium's initial phrase, their mistake is also spoken of as "losing the path." The foot path or *nɔŋ* links jungle and settlement; the path of the river links one settlement and another. As a song describing the path of the spirits, this gift from the dream-time sung during ceremonial performance conjoins human and nonhuman realms; as a metaphor, it links domains of traveling, knowledge, singing, and healing.

[. . .]

Temiar mediums sing when they cure. A major technique of healing involves singing/trance-dancing ceremonies in which mediums sing tunes and texts given to them during dreams by spiritguides. Songs are paths that link mediums, female chorus members, trance-dancers, and patients with spirits of the jungle and settlement. Even treatment of less serious cases, which occurs outside the ceremonial context, involves singing by the medium.

[. . .]

These ritual singing and trance-dancing performances are embedded in a network of social life that extends far beyond the parameters of the ceremonies themselves. Commenting on the difficulties of delimiting the range of inquiry, Margaret Mead jokingly bemoaned how anthropological residence involves attending to a village full of "people whose every word, grunt, scratch, stomachache, change of wearing apparel, snatch of song sung on the road or jest flung over someone else's wall is *relevant*" (1977:200). Never content to limit the range of my inquiry before I knew how far I must trace the network of associations, I observed and documented the range of Temiar daily and seasonal life – from hunting among the men to gathering tubers with the women, from clearing swidden fields to collecting fruits. During my stay among the Temiar, minute details of social interaction among women walking to the river, chance observations out amidst the jungle foliage, and laborious translations of song texts would suddenly combine to reveal the meaning of a ritual gesture recorded months earlier. To understand the ritual form of bending, swaying dance movements precipitating trance, for example, I traced an aesthetic value that led from the supple swaying of a woman's walk, to rainforest foliage waving in the breeze.

The way Temiars pattern their daily actions in relation both to one another and to the rainforest reveals as much about the ordering of their cosmos as time- and house-bound ceremonies do. When the order of daily life is disrupted by a promise broken, for example, or when a food is incorrectly prepared, consumed, or named, then illness might occur. To study that moment of articulation between medical and musical domains exemplified by healing ceremonies, I traced the fabric of meanings leading through settlement and jungle, person and cosmos, dreams and performance, ritual and everyday life.

References

Benjamin, Geoffrey (1979) 'Indigenous religious systems of the Malay Peninsula', in A. L. Becker and Aram Yengoyan (eds), *The Imagination of Reality: Essays in Southeast Asian Coherence Systems.* (Norwood, NJ: Ablex), pp. 9–27.

Mead, Margaret (1977) *Letters from the Field 1925–1979* (New York: Harper & Row).

27

The Karelian lament

Elizabeth Tolbert

Elizabeth Tolbert, 'Women cry with words: symbolization of affect in the Karelian lament', *Yearbook of Traditional Music*, 22 (1990), pp. 80–8.

Tolbert's study of lamenting draws on ethnographic research in the Karelian community in eastern Finland: her informants were refugees from Russian (then Soviet) Karelia who were unable to return to their homes on the other side of the international border. A couple of other references deserve explanation: 'separation, transition, reincorporation' (paragraphs 3 and 5) refer to the three stages of ritual according to the anthropologist Arnold van Gennep (1873–1957); the phrase 'icons of crying' (see also Hughes, Item 7) refers to semiotic theory, in which an icon is a sign that *resembles* the thing to which it refers. Tolbert's references to specific field recordings have been removed.

The Karelian lament, or *itkuvirsi*, is an extraordinary expressive form found in eastern Finland and [Russian] Karelia that uses music, language, gesture, and the icons of crying to communicate affect and power. It has its roots in the ancestor worship of the ancient Karelian folk religion, and contains vestiges of classical Eurasian shamanism in its ecstatic, trance-like manner of performance. The lament is performed only by women, usually within the ritual context of funerals or weddings; however, it is also performed at non-ritual occasions with strong overtones of affect, such as when old friends meet after a long absence or as a complaint about the hardships of life. The lament is now only barely remembered by a handful of Karelian women, most of them refugees from World War II now living in Finland. The ritual contexts have completely died out in Finland, although the funeral context still partially survives in [Russian] Karelia. The primary source material for this paper is drawn from my fieldwork with Karelian refugees in 1984–85, who had learned laments prior to World War II in traditional village settings.

Laments survive most strongly in Eastern Europe, stretching from the Balkans to eastern Finland, although they have also been documented in other European areas. Honko (1974:56) postulates that the relative leniency of the Orthodox Church towards pagan traditions in Russia aided the survival of the Karelian lament; this may also help explain why the lament survived longer in Eastern Europe than in other European areas. The Karelian lament has many parallels with other European lament traditions, although its closest affinities are with the Baltic and Russian traditions (Honko 1974:14).

In Karelia, the extensive funeral and wedding ritual complexes contained as many as fifty specific obligatory laments. Laments were sung to accompany all stages of separation, transition and reincorporation phases of the rite of passage, easing the transition from deceased to ancestor, or bride to wife. They acted simultaneously as a commentary on the intricate ritual complexes and as a necessary efficacious force. In the funeral ceremonies, the expertise of the lamenter was needed to guide the soul of the dead to *Tuonela*, the Finnish-Karelian land of the dead, and to restore social and individual equilibrium by relaying messages between this world and the other one, acting as a "bridge between worlds" (Caraveli-Chaves 1980). Laments accompanied the many funeral preparations such as washing and dressing the body and making the coffin, and were an essential part of the remembrance feasts for the dead that continued for years after death at specified intervals.

Wedding rituals were similarly centered around transition. During the engagement period, which lasted between two and three weeks, a lamenter, either an older female relative or a professional, was in constant attendance at the bride's home. The first lament was at the betrothal ceremony, where the ancestors were informed that the bride was leaving her birth family to undergo a ritual "death" and "rebirth" into her husband's family. Subsequent laments were sung during preparations of food, beer, and gifts, and as a farewell to the bride's relatives and friends.

Semi-ritual contexts involving separation, transition and/or strong emotion were also lamented; examples include the christening of a radio station, a bear killing, soldiers leaving for war, or friends or relatives meeting after a long period of time. Non-ritual contexts included singing privately to oneself about the hardships of everyday life, or private communion with the ancestors in the graveyard or in the icon corner of the home.

Crying with words

In Karelia, women who lament are said to "cry with words", as opposed to men who merely "cry with the eyes", i.e. cry in the ordinary sense. In this paper I will address the expressive means of the Karelian lament, the process by which "crying with words" becomes the ritualized crying of the lament. I will be concerned with how emotion is communicated in performance, and in particular, how the lament becomes a "sign vehicle" for affect (Urban 1988:387).

The lament is a central processual cultural metaphor in the Karelian world view, and its sounds and structures are part of a symbolic system that embodies the essence of the cosmology of the Karelian folk religion. This is demonstrated not only in the specific cultural context of the lament and in the surrounding concepts of the Karelian folk religion, but in the musical sound itself, which in its structures is expressive of and instrumental to engendering the trance-like state necessary to make a successful journey to *Tuonela* (Tolbert 1987; 1988). In this paper I will show that the heart of meaning in the Karelian lament is found in the relationship between its ecstatic manner of performance, extraordinary text and improvisatory musical form. In addition, I will investigate how these parameters interact to move the lament from spontaneous expression of emotion to symbol of affect.

The Karelian lament is a particularly striking example of the interplay between language, music and emotional expression, occurring as a fluid mix of speech, song and weeping. This description is not exclusive to the Karelian lament, and is reminiscent of descriptions in the anthropological literature of "tuneful weeping" (Tiwary 1978), "sung/texted/weeping" (Feld 1982), or "ritual wailing" (Urban 1988).

Laments are at the center of an intriguing nexus of issues relating to affect and performance, and there is presently an increased interest in this moving and beautiful musico-poetic genre in several disciplines. They are known throughout the world, and despite wide cultural variation show striking similarities in structure and context, often exhibiting a manner of performance characterized by the icons of crying. One of the most important reasons to study laments is that they provide a case study of the symbolic processes by which musical forms become invested with emotion, and therefore meaning. Insight into the lament process may also help illuminate related theoretical issues such as the place of music within ritual, gender roles and expressive behavior (laments are usually sung by women), the relationship between psychobiological and culturally acquired means of expression, and the interrelationship of various expressive systems within culture.

Poetic means of sorrow

Lönnrot, who collected the earliest surviving Karelian laments, noted that they "have terrible words in them, that one cannot understand after only one or two hearings. And if one asks what this or that word means then the lamenter as well as the transcriber is likely to forget the half of it, and it will never become clear" (Haavio 1934:5; translation mine). This is not only because the lament is an improvised genre which changes with every rendition, but also because the lament language requires a strong familiarity with the tradition to fully comprehend. Even a fluent speaker of Karelian cannot readily understand laments upon first hearing. No native speakers of Finnish (which is for the most part mutually intelligible with Karelian) could understand my recordings of the laments or even accurately transcribe the words. Among the lamenters that I consulted in 1985, they themselves did not appear to understand all of the lament words, and would admit that they could not say exactly what a certain lament meant. Konkka (1985:15) has documented similar cases in [Russian] Karelia.

If laments were so hard to understand, what, then, was their effect on the audience? Although the ability to reproduce laments belonged to the women's world, their meaning in a general sense was meant to be understood, or at least felt, by the entire community. It seems that people understood the emotional tone of the metaphorical language, if not its exact meaning, and that one of the functions of lament performance was to move all those present into a collective expression of sorrow. It was often intimated to me by women that men did not understand lament language, yet the one man that I consulted remembered especially poignant lament phrases from his grandmother's laments, and talked to me at length about how men wept in response to women's lamenting. All of the lamenters that I worked with stressed that the lamenter could make even the most hardhearted person weep. However, the most crucial audience, the dead, were expected to understand the laments exactly, and it was for their sake especially that the lament was sung in the proper manner and with the proper language, as emotionally and efficaciously as possible.

The laments that I recorded in 1985 are rather poor examples compared with the elaborate texts documented in the last century, and even those collected more recently in [Russian] Karelia. The laments that were sung to me were more autobiographical than ritual in nature, even when ostensibly sung as if for a ritual occasion, and were less intricate and developed than earlier laments. However, they do represent essential linguistic and poetic features of the lament which I will draw on to illustrate key aspects of nature and structure of lament language. Because of the difficulty of the lament language, the translations are only approximate.

The content of the lament, although improvised, included a certain number of core episodes that were specific to the ritual context being lamented.

According to analyses of text structure by Nenola-Kallio (1982) and Honko (1974), there is dramatic structure in the lament. For example, in a death lament, expressions of denial are followed by concern, and finally by resignation. Laments also have references to the specific rituals being performed, whether it be washing or dressing the corpse in a death context, or for the bridal sauna, receiving gifts, or undoing the bride's hair in a wedding context. [. . .] In non-ritual autobiographical laments a looser structure prevails, usually with copious references to the lamenter's unhappy life.

In the following lament for a dead husband, the close relationship between the living and deceased is clearly evident. The lamenter addresses her loved one directly. The deceased were often buried in a graveyard on an island, which accounts for the "white waters" in this lament, and may also be a reference to the cosmology of the land of the dead, *Tuonela*, which lies across a river in the north. The lament also refers to the belief that the dead, or at least one of his/her souls, lived in the cemetery. According to tradition, one should not bury the dead too deeply so that they can rise in the spring and look out of the windows of their grave houses. Here, Olga Saavinen hopes that her husband can listen to the spring cuckoos, a bird that is often associated with spirits in Karelian folk belief.

Why did you, my dear life companion, leave me here to wander alone?
We could have wandered the rest of our lives together.
But now we escort you over these white waters
There to the beautiful grave house.
But I won't place heavy earth clods.
Very light earth I'll scatter,
So that you could rise during spring to listen to the cuckooing of the beautiful
    golden cuckoos.

One of the most striking features of the lament, in Karelia and elsewhere, are the rhetorical mourning questions, which sometimes take the form of wondering questions. Death is not accepted stoically. In the face of the irrevocability of death, the first questions express bewilderment and grief that the dead person has departed. Olga Saavinen asks her dead husband "Why did you, my dear life companion, leave me here to wander alone?" Often the living try to ascertain if they themselves are to blame, and because the dead are to be feared, as well as be mourned, they take particular care not to insult him. Feudosia Savinainen placates her deceased husband by asking "How has a mistake been made through speech? How have words offended?"

Similar lack of acceptance of the inevitability of the situation is seen in the wedding laments. A lamenter asks on behalf of the bride, "Why did you give me away for so cheap, for such old cheap copper coins? Why are you giving your own child to strangers?" Another complaint refers to the wedding clothes, which are like mourning clothes, and which are unexpectedly and inexplicably being made. "Why have the white clothes been prepared before their time?"

Because the laments were sung by refugees, they often contained autobiographical elements about the dire circumstances of the Karelian evacuation. The same kinds of mourning questions used in ritual laments are found here. When Alina Repo thinks about her deceased mother, she reflects upon the past by saying "My mother, my dear bearer. I wonder how you were able to get through the bad days. The times had all kinds of sadness and crying." She guiltily wonders about her sister-in-law that she left behind during the war, asking "Could it be that you had enough to eat all the time? Could it be that your shoeless feet were without shoes?"

Not only were the Karelians forced to leave their homes, but also the dead members of their extended families, the ancestors who lived in the graveyard in a world inverse to this one (Holmberg 1964:72). Feudosia Savinainen grieves to her dead parents buried in a graveyard in Karelia that "we are not allowed to come, to compose words (laments) for the cherished ones (the children), because I can't go to my own beautiful cemetery." She also mourns for the time when her parents took care of her. She complains that "We haven't been able to be together like baby birds in a nest for many years, I can't sleep under the protection of wings." Alina Repo also refers to the bird nest analogy for children and parents. "Protect the small ones of Sinisokola, covered with wings in the nest."

The lamenter often refers to her difficult life, and refers to herself as extremely wretched and poor. Alina Repo complains that "I have been given a terrible winter for my own life circumstances." In other contexts she refers to herself repeatedly as "wretched woman".

At the end of the lament, there may be a reconciliation that the inevitable has taken place. In a wedding lament Feudosia Savinainen asks for blessings for her daughter, saying "May the saints give you a happy fate. Better than I myself had. May the saints give you a husband with whom you live in harmony. May the saints give him a happy life." In a wedding lament Alina Repo gives advice along with a blessing. "Try to live in the new place in harmony. Try to listen to women, to women (the mother-in-law and the other older women). May you have much happiness now in your new life circumstances."

The means of expression used in the lament texts are in stark opposition to ordinary speech, and as such are especially suited to the inverse world of the dead. The expressive language serves as ritual protection; Honko (1974) comments that the "lament favour(s) 'obscure' metaphors" (56) due to "the delicacy and sacral ritual of the occasion" (57).

The lament language is highly systematized, with intricate grammatical forms, rhetorical mourning questions, and a complicated system of metaphorical names motivated by a name taboo on the deceased. The exact choice of metaphor is based not only on local poetic tradition, but is governed by a sensitivity to alliteration, parallelism, and a proliferation of verbal nouns with possessive suffixes (Leino 1974). Furthermore, laments are characterized by a complete absence of regular meter and rhyme, in contrast to the steady meter of other Karelian folk traditions, such as the Kalevala epic poetry.

Nenola-Kallio (1982:51) notes that the metaphorical names serve to redefine the social order through use of matrilineal kinship terms. The metaphors are most often names which are calculated matrilineally, either as someone's child or mother. For example, a mother may be addressed as "my dear little bearer", "my dear little rocker", or "my dear little nurser". A father might be a "grandmother's soothed one", a daughter "my nursed one" or "my dear little berry", a son "my dear little apple" (Nenola-Kallio 1982:36–37).

The names are improvised from a stock body of phrases, with content appropriate to the occasion. The phonetic features of the lament are sometimes more important than the semantic ones, and words may be chosen for their sound rather than for their meaning. The names are formed by adding suffixes to verb stems, following procedures that are used in the ordinary spoken language yet to such an exaggerated degree and in such proliferation that the original words are obfuscated both morphologically and semantically. The result is clearly distinct from the ordinary spoken language. A relatively small number of verb stems are used to create a large number of metaphorical names by using a stock body of suffixes. Often, rare or strange verb stems are used; for example, Virtaranta (1973:485) has noted the use of Russian or other uncommon stems.

Long chains of names that end with similar suffixes, such as *jai-ze-ni* (my little one who does *x*), create repetitive sonic patterns within and between lines. For example, the names *kallis kandajaizeni* (my dear little bearer), is derived from the verb stem *kantaa* (to carry), with the suffix *jai-ze-ni*. The name *kallet kandomuoni*, meaning my dear borne ones, referring to children, also uses the verb stem *kantaa*, which now appears with the sufix *ma*. The passive participle *ttu*, *tty* may also be used, in addition to names derived from the frequentative *lla*, *llä* verb stems. In this way a relatively small number of verb stems are used to create a large number of metaphorical names, which are both poetic and expressive of the relationship of various people to the central female figure, the mother. The use of an extraordinary lexicon is not unique to the Karelian laments; it has been noted in other unrelated lament traditions, for example among the Bororo of Amerindian Brazil (Urban 1988:391).

Alliteration is consciously utilized and prized in laments. Alliterative names typically were put together in long phrases, as can be seen in this death lament, *hyvin kepeet multaset ripottelemma jotta voisit noussa kevätil-masina kaunehien kultasien käkösien kukuntoja kuuntelomaa*, where Olga Saa-vinen assures her husband that she will "put light clods of earth on his grave so that he can rise during the spring to listen to the cuckooing of beautiful golden cuckoos". Parallelism, where a similar idea is repeated with varied wording, is also characteristic of lament phrases. Feudosia Savinainen addresses the *suured sukukundu, helie heimokundu* (the big family, the bright tribe), in other words, the ancestors, with alliteration and parallelism, and Alina Repo cries about the absence of children in the deserted homes in Karelia after the evacuation; "Because no dear steppers stepped, no little ones puttered in the yard." (*Kui jo ei ollu armahien askelu-izieni astujaizi, eigö allu pienoizi pihamuahuizil (i) pepettelemä.*)

The musical means of sorrow

Urban (1988:386), who describes lament performance in Amerindian Brazil, identifies three different domains which highlight the semiotic func-tion of the lament: the presence of characteristic musical line with cultur-ally specific stylistic norms; the presence of cross-culturally intelligible icons of crying; and the presence of a dialogic form without the presence of an actual addressee. All three of these semiotic indicators are present in the Karelian lament. The musical line in the Karelian lament demonstrates the attributes of a Finno-Ugric tune type with specific stylistic norms. The icons of crying are present in the form of phrases consisting of descending sigh motifs sung in cry-like exhalations, along with stylized sobbings and other crying icons. The dialogic I/thou form of address, which is often cross-culturally present in the form of rhetorical questions, is also present here. As seen above, the lamenter talks directly to the deceased, asking, for example, why he left, what offense had been committed to warrant his departure, if he needs anything, and other placating questions.

However, the crux of the Karelian lament's semiotic effectiveness is the manner in which linguistic and musical parameters interact to create "words" that are maximally effective: words that provoke the appropriate sense of grief in the community and promote solidarity in the face of death;

that offer crucial ritual protection during the dangerous liminal periods of rites of passage; and, most importantly, that successfully enable the lamenter to complete her journey to *Tuonela*. The symbolization of affect in lament performance is based not only on the icons of crying, but also on the relationship of formalistic structures in the linguistic and musical domains to the crying icons.

The musical meaning of the Karelian lament is dependent on the semiotic indicators outlined by Urban and the contextual background of the lament; its sacred nature, the traditional role of the lamenter and the intricate lamenting contexts, the oblique lament language and the powerful manner of performing lament "words". [. . .]

Even upon first hearing, and without the requisite cultural information, one of the most striking observations is that the musical parameters of the Karelian lament exhibit a very flexible, unstable, almost tenuous structure, and that ambiguous formal relationships abound. The pitches, mode, range, and the phrase structure are not fixed and are continually changing within the course of the lament. It is difficult to establish the identity of any of the above parameters on the basis of the first few phrases, and I have heard cases where the mode and range outline coherent structures only after several minutes.

I propose that the instability and ambiguity of these parameters is crucial and necessary for the successful rendition of ritual, part of the extraordinary measures that must be taken for protection during the dangerous liminal period of a rite of passage. As is true of the lament texts, the musical means of expression in the lament must not be too accessible to outside influences, and furthermore, must be a form of communication that is acceptable to the spirit world.

Because *Tuonela* is a mirror of this world, ritual actions must be performed in an inverted manner, in a way that illustrates their direct opposition to the profane acts of everyday life. The unstable and unclear musical elements in the laments are an expression of its sacred nature, a result of a musical performance style that is in striking opposition to the straightforward performing style of other Karelian musical genres. The efficacy of the performance is therefore determined by adherence to symbolic principles. Oblique, obfuscated expression of meaning is accomplished musically, analogous to the use of metaphor, alliteration, parallelism, and addition of vocables and filler words in the texts.

On the most general level of form the lament phrase is iconic for a sigh. [. . .] The sigh determines the melodic shape, which is descending, and its general manner of performance, which is a sobbing recitative-like melody that borders on speech, weeping and song. Within the general structure

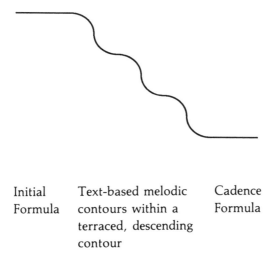

Initial   Text-based melodic   Cadence
Formula   contours within a   Formula
             terraced, descending
             contour

Fig. 27.1 Idealized Melodic Contour of the Karelian Lament Phrase

of the sigh motif, the most usual structure of the Karelian lament is a descending step-wise melodic phrase within the range of a 4th or 5th which is repeated and endlessly embellished. The melodic contour is most often terraced. The mode may be close to minor, although its pitch materials are not derived from the well-tempered scale, but rather utilize pitches that might be categorized as a "neutral" third, a "raised" tonic, or a "raised" fourth. Furthermore, the pitches are not fixed; they fluctuate during the course of a performance and could best be described as pitch areas. The Karelian lament tune type, as characterized by this descending melodic formula is found among other Finno-Ugric people. Its idealized melodic form can be illustrated in the pitch graph (Figure 27.1).

References

Caraveli-Chaves, Anna (1980) "Bridge between worlds: the Greek women's laments as communicative event," *Journal of American Folklore*, 93, 129–57.

Feld, Steven (1982) *Sound and Sentiment: Birds, Weeping, Poetics, and Song in Kaluli Expression*. (Philadelphia: University of Pennsylvania Press).

Haavio, Martti (1934) Über die finnish-karelischen Klagelieder. *Suomalais-ugrilaisen Seuran Toimituksia* 47 (Helsinki: Suomalais-ugrilainen Seura).

Holmberg (Harva), Uno (1964) *Finno-Ugric, Siberian Mythology. The Mythology of All Races*, ed. Canon John Arnott MacCulloch (New York: Cooper Square).

Honko, Lauri (1974) "Balto-Finnic lament poetry," *Studia Fennica*, 17, 9–61.

Konkka, Unelma (1985) *Ikuinen ikävä*. Suomalaisen Kirjallisuuden Seuran Toimituksai 428 (Helsinki: Suomalaisen Kirjallisuuden Seura).

Leino, Pentti (1974) "The language of laments: the role of phonological and semantic features in the word choice," *Studia Fennica*, 17, 92–131.

Nenola-Kallio, Aili (1982) *Studies in Ingrain Laments*. Folklore Fellows Communication 234 (Helsinki: Suomalainen Tiedeakatemia).

Tiwary, K. M. (1978) "Tuneful weeping: a mode of communication," *Frontiers*, 3, 24–7.

Tolbert, Elizabeth (1987) "On beyond zebra: some theoretical considerations of emotion and meaning in music," *Pacific Review of Ethnomusicology*, 4, 75–97.

—— (1988) The Musical Means of Sorrow: The Karelian Lament Tradition. Unpublished dissertation, Department of Music, University of California, Los Angeles.

Urban, Greg (1988) "Ritual wailing in Amerindian Brazil," *American Anthropologist*, 90, 385–400.

Virtaranta, Pertt (1973) Paatenen itkuvirsistä. *Suomalais-ugrilaisen Toimituksai* 150 (Helsinki: Suomalais-ugrilainen Seura), pp. 467–88.

28

Russian wedding rituals and Stravinsky

Richard Taruskin

Richard Taruskin, *Stravinsky and the Russian Traditions: A Biography of the Works through Mavra* (2 vols., Berkeley and Los Angeles: University of California Press, 1996), pp. 1324–30.

This item and Item 29 (van den Toorn) both concern another of the case studies in *Words and Music*, namely Stravinsky's *Les Noces* (*Svadebka*). Here, Taruskin outlines the sources on which the composer drew in his representation of a traditional Russian wedding ritual; in the following extract van den Toorn considers, amongst other things, whether any remnant of the 'source' ritual practice can be identified in Stravinsky's piece.

Every Russian knows by heart the lines in which nurse Filippyevna tells Pushkin's lovesick Tatyana how she came to be wedded:

> . . . For two weeks or so
> a woman matchmaker kept visiting
> my kinsfolk, and at last
> my father blessed me. Bitterly
> I cried for fear; and, crying [*s plachem*],
> they unbraided my tress and, chanting [*s peniyem*],
> they led me to the church.
> And so I entered a strange family . . .[1]

With merciless concision, the passage succeeds in suggesting – at least from the bride's point of view – the full range of the Russian peasant wedding ritual (*svadebnïy obryad*). It is a highly formalized performance (*igra*, lit., game or play); to perform a wedding in "peasant" Russian is quite literally to "play" one – *igrat' svad'bu*. The rite lasts weeks from beginning to end, has an elaborate cast of characters, and is at every turn accompanied by liturgical incantations of every sort, drawn from a vast, regionally diverse repertoire whose collected specimens, out of which Stravinsky fashioned the text for his "choreographic scenes," in his day already numbered in the thousands.

Pushkin's passage adumbrates the specific contents of Stravinsky's first and third tableaux, which suggests it may actually have helped guide the composer's imagination as he threaded his way among the songs in Kireyevsky's, Tereshchenko's, and Sakharov's immense argosies of wedding lore. A preliminary exposition of the traditional *svadebnïy obryad*, drawn from these three sources plus Dahl's dictionary, will help us comprehend the *Svadebka* [*Les Noces*] text and its "starting point in reality."

The most extended, systematic, and comprehensive description of the wedding ritual to be found in the literature Stravinsky is known to have consulted is the eighth chapter of the second volume of Tereshchenko's *Bït russkogo naroda*: a "Survey of Present-day Wedding Rites" ("*Obzor nïneshnikh svadebnïkh obryadov*") – present-day, that is, as of the 1840s.[2] The survey is a kind of summary abstraction of the many individual accounts of local wedding customs in a dozen Great Russian guberniyas, as well as in Byelorussia, "Little Russia" [Ukraine], and among the Don and Ural Cossacks, that are presented later in the book. Stravinsky's song selections show his method likewise to have been eclectic and schematic. In the *Svadebka* text, songs from many different localities and in a multitude of regional dialects combine to produce a synthetic impression that may not be "authentic" with respect to any particular existing wedding rite, but that seeks to transmit, and to transform into art, something of the universal core of symbolically rendered experience in which all the various individual rites participate.

Tereshchenko begins by observing that the irreducible roster of dramatis personae in any Russian peasant wedding includes the bride (*nevesta*) and groom (*zhenikh*), their parents (or stand-ins for the latter, known as *posazhonïye*), and their friends, who form themselves into entourages and choruses for various purposes. In addition there are three essential players: two matchmakers – male (*svat*) and female (*svakha*) – and the *druzhko*, often called the best man in English, but whose multifarious functions go well beyond those of an ordinary best man. As Dahl defines him, the *druzhko* is "a young married man, the chief master-of-ceremonies, a wit, who knows the whole ritual, a glib talker, the general organizer of the entertainment, and a comedian in his own right; it is also he who leads the bridal couple off and stands watch over them during the night."[3] It is not difficult to recognize in this description a survival of the shamanistic agrarian folk religion that preceded Christianity in the Russian countryside, with the *druzhko* – sometimes called the "wedding jester" – taking the place of the skomorokh of old. As Tereshchenko notes, the two matchmakers and the *druzhko* form the essential trio that is responsible for the whole *dobroye delo*, the "good deed" of arranging and accomplishing the marriage from first to last.

The first stage in the *svadebnaya igra* is that of *svatan'ye*, the making of the match. A *svat* or *svakha* is sent by the groom's parents to those of the bride. They go through an elaborate preliminary ritual of small talk, the hosts repeatedly asking the matchmaker to sit down, the latter steadfastly declining. When the subject is at last broached and the proposal provisionally accepted, a toast is drunk. The parents must now appoint a *svat* or *svakha* of their own for further negotiations. This second matchmaker comes dressed up in conspicuous finery, but is nonetheless received by the household that initiated the proposal as a complete stranger whose purpose is unknown, the matchmaker meanwhile pretending to have gotten lost on the road and to have happened on the house of the wedding party by chance. On being asked his occupation, the matchmaker declares himself a merchant and proceeds to describe his "wares." Both sides having thus obliquely made their intentions known, the matter now proceeds to the *smotrinï* (or *glyadinï*), the ritual inspection of the bride, who is led out to be viewed by the matchmaker (or, on a special occasion, by the assembled family of the groom). She being approved, the bargain is sealed with a *rukobit'ye*, a striking of hands.

According to Tereshchenko, the *smotrinï* is the first stage of the *svadebnaya igra* at which prescribed ritual "music" is heard, in the form of a *plach*, a formal lament in which the bride pleads with her father not to send her away. The word *plach*, in common parlance, simply means crying or weeping, as in Nabokov's translation from *Eugene Onegin* quoted above. Most modern scholars (as well as Stravinsky) agree that, as it functions in the wedding ritual, the *plach* is not the spontaneous expression of feeling, but the fulfillment of a prescribed liturgical requirement, performed to a prescribed liturgical text, and sung in a prescribed liturgical manner to a prescribed liturgical formula. Pushkin, a better folklorist than his translator, used the word in this sense, and in canny apposition with *peniye*, which means something more closely resembling that which is denoted by our rougher English word *singing*. In English, both *plach* and *peniye* would be termed varieties of singing, but the Russian peasant usage distinguishes them sharply.

Stravinsky knew this well; his text notebook for *Svadebka* contains a note to himself to look up *plach* in Dahl. When he did so, this is what he found:

a ritual of lamenting for a bride which lasts from the time of the marriage contract to that of the bridal shower, about two weeks [cf. *Eugene Onegin*]; a song of complaint, sung at bridal showers; the bride does not sing, but *wails* [*ne poyot, a plachot*], lamenting her maiden beauty, her raven tresses, her freedom, pleading for her mother's intercession, and so on. Afterward the bride's girlfriends lament for her, cursing the matchmaker, the wedding party, even the groom. *We wailed*, or *We wailed a wail* [means] "we sang such a song." For such laments there are countless tunes or motives, but for the *plach* that laments the deceased, which is performed particularly at dawn, practically throughout Russia there is a single monotonous motive [*napev*], the repetition of three tones, the last being stretched out.[4]

This is a completely accurate and detailed description of the opening of the first tableau of *Svadebka*, even down to the bride's melody (Stravinsky having chosen to ignore Dahl's distinction between nuptial and funerary laments).

To return to our narrative: the preliminary assent, signified by the *rukobit'ye*, leads to the *sgovor* or actual betrothal. Visits and exchanges of gifts by the bride and groom and their families are followed by a ceremony in which the *svat* and *svakha* sit both families down to a formal celebration. The bride and groom are placed side by side and gaze at each other while toasts are made and special toasting songs, known as *velichal'nïye* (lit., songs of praise), are sung to the couple, to their wedding, their dowry, their fertility, and to the bride's father. *Velichal'nïye* are often recognizable by the insertion of the names and patronymics of their addressees. The *sgovor* marks the beginning of the *svad'ba* as such.

The next stage is the appointment of *poyezzhane* (sing., *poyezzhanin*), the members of the wedding procession or train (*poyezd*). The bride and the groom are each provided with a suite or entourage. The suites will eventually accompany the wedding couple into the church and mingle after the ceremony, but they have important individual duties to perform during the two-week period initiated by the *sgovor*. The *poyezzhane* are strictly ordered by rank. The designations of these ranks are hand-me-downs from the nomenclature of the feudal aristocracy. The wedding couple themselves are the *knyaz'* and *knyazhna* (prince and princess), the bride's title being that of an unmarried princess. As soon as the wedding ceremony is completed she assumes the title *knyaginya*, a married princess, by which she will be addressed or referred to during the wedding feast. The groom's *poyezzhane* are known as *boyare* (sing., *boyarin*), lords. Pride of place in the groom's party, after the groom himself goes to a senior member of his family who is known as the *tïsyatskiy*, the Old Russian word for a division commander (*tïsyacha* being Russian for one thousand). Next, another honored male is designated the *bol'shoy barin* (great baron), followed by lesser barons, the matchmakers, the *druzhko*, and so on.[5]

In the Ukraine and neighboring territories, the first task of the *poyez-zhane* is to go from door to door inviting the villagers to the wedding. It is they who will hire musicians (Tereshchenko mentions both regular violinists [*skripachi*] and *gudochniki*, players of the *gudok*, the three-stringed Russian folk fiddle, as well as bagpipers, flute-tooters, kettledrummers and tambourine men [*litavrshchiki s bubnami*]). The bride's *poyezd* helps her pack her trousseau, for which ceremony there is a special category of accompanying choral song.

We come now to the last and most elaborate of the prenuptial ceremonies within the *svadebnaya igra*, the *devichnik*, or bridal shower, which takes place shortly before the wedding itself, usually on the very eve. It is a purely female occasion: once again the bride performs her *plach*, more shrilly and tearfully than ever; her girlfriends divert her with songs of solace and affection. Candles are lit and the *korovai*, the huge and lavishly decorated wedding loaf, is displayed. The bride is seated on a high place, the maidens forming a circle around her. A chosen matron, known as the *prichital'shchitsa*, covers the bride's head with a veil and leads the singing of another form of lament, the *prichot* or *prichitaniye*, in which the maidens bewail the loss of a member of their carefree circle to marriage. Stravinsky looked up *prichot* in Dahl, too, and found it defined as being sung "in a wild monotone."[6] This definition, too, made a strong imprint on his music, and especially on that of the first tableau, which depicts the *devichnik*.

The main business of the *devichnik* is the unplaiting of the bride's braid (*kosa*), the combing out of her tress, and its redoing in two plaits (which will be wound round the head and hidden under a kerchief or headdress for the duration of her married life). A special repertoire of *plach* (for the bride) and song (for the girls) pertains to this ceremony. Her parents bless the bride, and she is led off by the matchmakers to the bath. The girls accompany each action with appropriate songs.

The next morning the girls reassemble to prepare the bride for the altar (*venets*; lit., crown or wreath). She is dressed in special finery, all the while pretending not to know why and giving vent to her biggest bout of *plach*. The *poyezzhane* gather in the courtyard. The groom's *druzhko* arrives to announce the departure of the bridal train for the church. The parents do not attend (the *posazhonïye* go in their place). The departure of the *poyezd* is the signal for the mother of the bride to perform her major set piece, a formal *plach* of leavetaking.

The wedding ceremony itself is called the *venchaniye*, because while the vows and rings are exchanged the "prince" and "princess" wear symbolic crowns. If the crowns should fall off disaster is foretold, so they are held in place by members of the bridal party. Each member of the company holds a candle, which is closely watched for omens. At the conclusion of the church ceremony the priest gives the bride and groom three sips apiece of red wine, after which the groom throws the wine cup to the ground and stamps on it. The priest bids the couple kiss in the presence of the assembled company, and they are wed.

From this point on, *plach* gives way to revelry (*vesel'ye*). The company now repairs to the groom's home, where the couple is blessed by the *posazhoniye*, their church godparents. The bride and groom must fall to their knees three times before the *posazhoniye*, after which they are seated at the head of the "beautiful table" (*krasnïy stol*, also known as the *knyazhenetskiy stol*, the "princely table") and the wedding feast begins. At the conclusion of the meal the *korovai* is cut. The first piece goes to the bride and groom; the second is placed under the pillow of the marriage bed and will serve the couple as their wedding breakfast on the morrow. This ceremony is accompanied by a huge commotion of beating on dishes and glasses with spoons.

Now the *druzhko* comes into his own, leading the revels with all manner of songs, toasts (*velichal'nïye*), jokes, and jingles (*pribautki*). The musicians hold forth to accompany strenuous, competitive male dancing (the so-called *russkaya plyaska*, familiar from *Petrushka*), which soon degenerates into girl-chasing. The merrymaking continues past midnight, often until dawn.

While the festivities are still in full swing, the newlyweds are led off by the *svat* and *svakha* to the bedchamber, which is lit by the same candles that had been held during the *venchaniye*. The couple is bedded down on a hay mattress (*sennik*). Outside, the *druzhko* circles the house on horseback for the rest of the night, saber drawn. In the morning the *svat*, *svakha*, and *druzhko* come to greet the couple. The bride and groom are sent to the bath, after which they consume the piece of the *korovai* that had been set aside the night before. Later in the day they visit the bride's parents, where they are received as guests, for the bride is now considered part of the groom's family, where she assumes the lowest position in the domestic pecking order, after her mother-in-law and sisters-in-law.

Notes

1 A. S. Pushkin, *Eugene Onegin*, trans. V. Nabokov (Princeton, NJ: Princeton University Press, 1991), 2:162.

2 A. V. Tereshchenko, *Bït russkogo naroda* (Moscow: Russkaia Kniga, 1999) 2:116–42. All information not credited to another source in the following discussion comes from this one.
3 V. Dahl, *Tolkovïy slovar* (Moscow, 1978), s.v. *"drug."*
4 Ibid., s.v. *"plakat'."*
5 Ibid., s.v. *"poyezdit'."*
6 Ibid., s.v. *"prichislyat'."*

29

Lamenting in Stravinsky's *Les Noces*

Pieter C. van den Toorn

Pieter C. van den Toorn, 'Stravinsky, *Les Noces* (*Svadebka*), and the prohibition against expressive timing', *Journal of Musicology*, 20:2 (2003), pp. 302–3.

As noted above, this item should be read side by side with Taruskin's (Item 28). (The present extract is taken from a paper critiquing the German philosopher Theodor W. Adorno, although the details of that argument need not concern us here.)

[R]itual and the ritualistic need not be confined to the primitive, unthinking, or herd-like. The archaic wedding rituals that underlie the scenario and music of *Les Noces* are a specific case in point. From what is known of the early performing practices of these rituals, the separation between character and character type, and between genuine feeling and play-acting were by no means hard and fast.[1] One of the aims of these rituals, even when enacted by hired professionals, was to awaken within both the bride and the other participants something of the "specific thoughts and emotions" to which reference was made.[2] Genuine feeling and the feelings demanded by the ceremonial traditions were supposed to overlap. This is what ritual is, of course, not public exercise alone but public exercise mixed with the personal. It involves the expression, by means necessarily public or communal, of what are presumed to be an individual's "thoughts and emotions."[3] Communication with the outside world is guaranteed, while a buffer is afforded against the perils of an individual's isolation. The emphasis falls on commiseration and bonding, but this comes not wholly at the expense of the concerns of the individual. Ritual acts as a go-between in this regard, a way of easing the public strain of personal remorse as well as the community's difficulty in relating to that remorse. The proxy performances associated with the wedding rituals were not entirely formulaic or stereotypical. From the evidence it may be gathered that the formulas were mixed with improvisation, and that the latter was intended as a more immediate reflection the bride's true feelings.[4] By such means, the stock in trade merged with the personal. And successful performances were not only "emotionally infectious" (beckoning the participants in the appropriate way),[5] but designed as a combination of the tradition and the individual.

Inflecting the opening pages of *Les Noces* is the grace note F#. This hint of a sob proves integral not only to the idea of a lament, but to the composer's musical conception as well. The repetition is incantatory and ritualistic in character, imitating the highly stylized vocalizations that informed the early laments themselves. So too, in the first line of the text, is the stutter in the setting of the Russian word *kosal*, meaning "braid." The isolated repetition of the first syllable of this word produces an effect similar to that of the grace note F#, namely that of a gasp or sob, and this is likewise integral. The motivation is not only poetic in the sense of a ritual lament, but musical as well, an aspect of structure and musical understanding.

And yet the effect is spontaneous and unrehearsed as well. Even in the strictest, most exacting performance of *Les Noces*, with the rigidities of the construction in full view, as it were, the experience of the single bride is apt not to be lost. The grace notes and stutter motives are still likely to he heard and understood as those of the single bride. Their effect is still likely to be that of an uncontrollable weeping, spontaneous and hence true to the individual, immediate and reflective of a personal anguish or anxiety – one that is shared and collective in one way or another, but not therefore "impersonal."

What we as participants sense and feel is thus likely to be derived from the experience of the bride. And the more stiff and intransigent the aspects of the construction seem, the more emphatically they succeed in setting off the circumstances of the individual bride. Much of this has been overlooked by the detractors of Stravinsky's music who would equate the repetitious, percussive, and metronomic features of pieces such as *Les Noces* (i.e. the "mechanical") not only with ritual and ritual action, but with a collective voice as well, one that is primitive, autocratic, and "anti-humanistic" in its opposition to the interests of the individual person. "Stravinsky's music identifies not with the victims," T. W. Adorno argued in one of his most extravagant summations, "but with the agents of destruction."[6]

Given the many rules governing repetition in the opening pages of *Les Noces*, the character of this music can indeed seem implacable. Yet the rigidities are balanced by counteraction. [. . .] The stiffness of the construction is countered by fluidity in matters of rhythm, timing, and alignment.

Detail of this kind should not be ignored in studies of the philosophical and socio-political implications of Stravinsky's music, studies that seek a broadened context from which to apprehend the specific nature of the music's appeal.

Notes

1 See the discussion of this in Margarita Mazo, "Stravinsky's *Les Noces* and Russian Village Wedding Ritual," *Journal of the American Musicological Society*, 43 (1990), 99–142, 119–22.
2 Y. M. Sokolov, *Russian Folklore*, trans. Catharine Ruth Smith (New York: Macmillan, 1950), 211–12.
3 Ibid.
4 See Mazo, "Stravinsky's *Les Noces*," 121–2.
5 Sokolov, *Russian Folklore*, 213.
6 Theodor W. Adorno, "Stravinsky: A Dialectical Portrait" (1962), in Theodor W. Adorno, *Quasi una Fantasia: Essays on Modern Music*, trans. Rodney Livingstone (London: Verso, 1998), 145–75.

Part V

Words, music and narrative

30

The Sicilian *cantastorie*

Mauro Geraci

New for this volume.

Mauro Geraci has a unique perspective on the art of the Sicilian *cantastorie* (pl. *cantastorie*), or storyteller, being both a performer himself and an anthropologist and ethnomusicologist. The Italian terms used here are *storia* (pl. *storie*) and *ballata* (pl. *ballate*), the two principal genres he sings; *cartellone*, which is a large poster used as a backdrop to his performance depicting scenes from his tales; and *piazza*, referring both literally to a town square in which he might perform, and by extension to his audience in general. He also refers to another *cantastorie* by the name of Orazio Strano. This item is an edited version of an interview conducted by Laura Leante for *Words and Music*.

Cantastorie are first of all poets, composers of verses who are inspired by all aspects of history, both distant and recent. These compositions, whether *storie* or *ballate*, are then put to music and sung in the *piazza* in front of a large and heterogeneous audience. Often storytellers also produce their own records which are then sold during the shows. A storyteller is not only a writer of *storie* and *ballate*, a singer and musician, he is also a painter. The stories he creates and sings about are inspired by events and portrayed in posters, providing the show's visual background. It could be said that a *cantastorie* is a multimedia artist. This is, briefly, the definition.

This art form has one main objective: to make the audience think about our, and other people's history. I might sing, for example, a *ballata* about the energy crisis or labour problems, so that people listening to my *ballate* can relate them to their own lives and the dilemmas suffered by the rest of society.

Cantastorie do not perform only in Sicily, especially nowadays. It is a show created to be performed outside Sicily, to inform the listener and encourage historical debate beyond the shores of Sicily and beyond the rest of Europe, finding their audiences, for example, among emigrants' cultural circles. Every year storytellers take part in the festivals of Italian culture organized by emigrants in places like Argentina or the United States. Also, thanks to their recordings, their repertoire can be appreciated and recognised beyond the Sicilian borders. This is why the literature of storytellers is not written exclusively using Sicilian dialect. Some storytellers write not only in Sicilian, but also in Italian and even in English. Of course they are Sicilians, but it is also true that it is a kind of Sicilian art form which aims to reach a *piazza* beyond local borders, as vast and as diverse as possible, so that history can be analysed from different perspectives and people with their own personal stories can give their own contributions in constantly redefining that historical perspective.

A storyteller is also a businessman, not an itinerant musician begging for money. If a storyteller is performing and somebody comes up offering say a thousand lire, a euro or a pound, that money is promptly rejected. He would rather promote his own craft selling his records, his tapes and CDs, or even the printed lyrics of the ballads in his poetic and musical repertoire.

A storyteller's main objective is to bring to the fore history's contradictions. A story is never fixed once and for all: it has its own contradictions and ambivalence. Whether Mr Bush is the best US president or not is not a given – some agree, some don't. Let's see how the *piazza* responds. The relationship with the audience is very important in the way the *cantastorie* communicates his knowledge. He needs to try and establish the kind of audience he is addressing, needs to observe people's reactions, and how they mutter to each other. If a member of the audience disagrees with my opinions and says something, in that case I may stop my performance and discuss with him his point of view. I ask if they want to come on stage, if they want the microphone. Very often they do, and they say what they think. With the audience there is an exchange of ideas, which is the most important aspect of a storyteller's performance.

We have talked about the storyteller as a multimedia artist. We haven't talked about the storyteller as a cultural mediator, as someone who acts as an intermediary between the story depicted on the poster and the audience. The storyteller's detachment is a crucial aspect of his poetics. By detachment I mean to distance oneself from the story: 'Ladies and gentlemen, what I'm about to tell you is a version of the story depicted here. I'm just presenting it to you so that you have the chance to form a different opinion from what is normally accepted.' I distance myself from the story so that people can somehow look at the facts with a more critical approach.

Another aspect of a storyteller's role is that of positioning himself between the story and the audience. But he also positions himself between the *presentation* of the story and its *representation.* Presentation of the story is, for example, when the storyteller says: 'Ladies and gentlemen, if you look at the first frame you'll see what is happening. In the second frame you can see what is about to happen. Did you see what has happened in London . . . in Cambridge? This or that has happened.' In this case I'm not representing but rather presenting a story that I narrate in the lyrics, a story depicted in the posters which I am also showing. Then, when I begin to sing, I'll have to start doing the representation. As an actor I have to be able to play the officer, the woman, the child, and all the characters involved in the events. Eventually I will have to be able to go back to the level of the presentation. Therefore a storyteller also mediates between the portrayed events and people's ideas, notions, and versions of those events.

The *cartellone* is a semi-objective source. Very often it is painted by the storyteller himself. Sometimes it is painted by artists who specialise in this work. The *cartellone* provides a starting point to rethink history. It is a device that enables us to reconsider, to reset our judgement: let's reset our own judgements by going back to the poster, let's look at the events again and see whether we reach the same moral conclusions. The storyteller questions the *cartellone*, as it has an explicative function. It summarises within a single picture the sequence of the events. The poster's function is not only to explain. It also invites questioning. I'll direct my questions to it. The storyteller may stop while singing and ask (of a character in the story): 'What did you do, why did you have to shoot?' The *cartellone* helps one to keep the thread of thoughts.

Both the poetic and the visual texts provide a starting point. Storytellers do not belong to the so-called oral tradition. They narrate and write *ballate.* They write *storie.* With regard to the specifications of a storyteller's text, a *storia* may be a very long composition. It can last as long as an hour and a half. It may portray the life and adventures of a character. Or it may be inspired by real-life events, such as the sinking of the Titanic. The *ballata* differs from the *storia* as it does not have the same descriptive connotations. A *ballata* belongs to a more sentimental realm. It dwells on certain aspects of the event and tries to identify its symbolic and sentimental contrasts. It dwells on a more thoughtful perspective of a single facet. The two forms are two different ways to look at the same reality.

Storie are normally structured in octects. These stanzas are made of eight hendecasyllabic lines. Often small *ballate* can be inserted within the structure of a *storia.* That has different poetical and musical features. For each stanza of the *storia* there is a corresponding music module. This music module is normally divided into two parts. The first four and the last four lines are sung using two different melodies. These modules are repeated from the beginning to the end of the story. They have to engage the audience while preserving the story's consistency. This is a fascinating aspect of the storyteller's music: it's repetitive, yet it never tires. This music structure allows variations and interruptions, also leaving room for speech. It's quite a flexible structure. It's a linear structure with very simple melodies, with intervals – like the third or the fifth – which all fall within a tonal framework. There aren't any significant modulations in a storyteller's harmonic and melodic structures. In this way music helps to achieve that moral detachment from history previously mentioned. If I were to add any kind of frills and embellishments to the music these might infer a moral judgement in regard to specific facts. Music must reset the story.

The guitar defines the rhythmic and harmonic framework of the *ballata* and the *storia*. The guitar accompaniment should also be always uniform. There is a special relationship between the storyteller and his guitar. The shows' leaflets normally indicate the storyteller's name 'and his guitar'. It's as if it were one of his physical parts, or his second voice. One of Orazio Strano's five children, Vito, who teaches guitar at the conservatory in Sydney, had tried to follow his father's footsteps before becoming a guitar professor. He wanted to be a storyteller like Orazio. But Vito was a guitar virtuoso, and he knew of harmonisations, embellishments and ornaments. He decided to reinterpret the story of *Pope John XXIII* written by his father. He added his own personal touch with the use of more elaborate guitar melodies. The result was a huge flop. Music should not overlap with or set limitations to the other aspects in the *cantastorie's* performance. A storyteller's performance is not centred on the musical aspect: music serves a wider narrative.

The musical repertoire is not very large. Diego Carpitella, one of the fathers of Italian ethnomusicology, defined a storyteller's musical dimension as being 'indifferent'. According to Carpitella, they are indifferent to music. He was right, which is not to say that music has no value in the economy of the performance, but rather, music is there to sustain the thinking process.

The poetical text may become a record, a tape or a CD, all of which are normally self-produced. It may also be printed on booklets and sheets and sold during the shows. That poetic composition becomes at that point an object, because I'm selling the story. The *cantastorie* sells his story to the *piazza* as an object, whether printed or recorded. The moment that text is presented again in the performance, it loses its objectivity as it returns to the *cantastorie's* performance techniques. A storyteller's singing technique often resorts to oral improvisation. If I want to voice a thought then I stop after the first stanza and do so. If I want to articulate a given stanza rather than sing it, I could use speech. A storyteller's way of communicating implies a constant change of register, moving from singing to acting to improvising without interruption, continuously exploring different modalities to re-present the finite written text.

There are two key words in the *cantastorie's* realm of knowledge: poetry and reality. The reality of everyday life becomes a source of inspiration for *storie*, *ballate*, and therefore poems. Conversely, a *cantastorie's* poetry is a kind of poetry that refers back to reality. Therefore we come full circle. And we always end up talking about the *cantastorie's* performance. I find all this extremely fascinating. For *cantastorie*, reality can only be uttered through poetry, and poetry is not poetry if, to quote Wittgenstein, it does not start from the ground, from the minimal level of knowledge.

31

Song and performance

Edward Cone

Edward Cone, *The Composer's Voice* (Berkeley: University of California Press, 1974), pp. 57–66, 69–72, 76–80.

Cone's argument in *The Composer's Voice* depends on his distinction between different kinds of 'personas' implicit in music: he kicks off this chapter with the distinction already made between the 'vocal persona' – the character implicit in the vocal line – and the 'musical persona' – that implied by the totality of the music.

In order to explain the distinction between different personas he refers to Browning's Caliban – that is, the character Caliban lifted from Shakespeare's *The Tempest* and turned into the protagonist of Browning's poem 'Caliban upon Setibos': behind the voice of Caliban apparently narrating the poem we can also detect that of Browning the poet; similarly, behind the singer's voice lies the character portrayed (the 'vocal protagonist'), and behind him the voice of the composer.

When a song lacks accompaniment, the musical and the vocal personas coincide. In a sense they become identical; yet for purposes of analysis we can still usually distinguish between them, for we can look at the single persona from two points of view. The typical protagonist, we remember, is assumed to be actually unconscious of singing. Not so the implicit musical persona, which is always aware of both words and music; the musical persona is an intelligence in the act of thinking through words and music alike. The distinction becomes clear if we realize that, in the absence of an accompanist, the *singer*, who is, or ought to be, completely aware of every aspect of the song, can be thought of as representing the implicit musical persona; the *persona portrayed by the singer within the song* is the vocal protagonist. Or, to return to two old friends, the protagonist is the voice of Caliban in Browning's poem; the implicit persona is Browning's voice, speaking through Caliban.

There are other cases where, for all practical purposes, musical and vocal personas coincide, even in the presence of an accompaniment. The instrumental part may consist of a single line doubling the voice. The troubadours may well have accompanied themselves, or had themselves accompanied, in this way. Hardly more independent is the instrumental part that, while consisting of simple chords rather than pure melodic doubling, is essentially nothing more than an amplification of the vocal line, as in the accompaniments devised by balladeers for performance on lute, guitar harp, or the like.

All these are examples of what I call *simple song*: song with no accompaniment at all or with "simple" accompaniment – that is, accompaniment that has no individuality. Such an instrumental part, lacking the independence to claim a component persona of its own, should ideally be performed by the singer himself, as an extension of his own part. If he must relegate it to a second person, this accompanist, if sensitive, will do his best to minimize his own presence and to create the effect of the single, "simple" performer.

Many otherwise simple accompaniments contain brief preludes, interludes, and postludes. So long as these are primarily functional, helping the singer to find his pitch and allowing him to rest after each stanza, they can be considered further natural extensions of the voice part. But if these passages take on a life of their own, the accompaniment ceases to be simple and assumes its own persona. If the singer persists in accompanying himself under such circumstances, he is trying to force the protagonist's psyche to envelop and take over that persona. Sometimes this can be successfully accomplished, especially if the accompaniment is not assertively independent; for, after all, one of its functions is to reveal aspects of the protagonist's subconscious, On the other hand, the result is often a severe dramatic strain that parallels the technical strain to which the singer must inevitably subject himself in carrying out the double task.

The fact that simple song projects a single person – a protagonist who in fact or in theory produces his own accompaniment – allows it on occasion to convey the impression that the singer is improvising both words and music, whether or not this is really the case. Thus not only is simple song the obvious medium for natural song of all kinds, but it is also ideal for producing a simulation of natural song. In natural song the concepts of poet and composer are hardly relevant: there is only a musician singing on an occasion calling for musical expression. The simulation of natural song attempts to portray such an occasion.

Another category of simple song, the true ballad, reflects a different situation: the narration of a traditional tale by a storyteller, presumably in response to the demands of an audience, formal or informal, large or small. But our present-day balladeers, in contradistinction to those of old, are actors – though not in the manner of lieder singers who perform Schubert's or Loewe's dramatic "ballads." To be sure, an accomplished balladeer will not fail to do justice to the dramatic aspects of the traditional ballads, but his primary impersonation is not to be found *within* the texts of these songs at all. His is a second-level portrayal: he enacts the storyteller, not the persona of the story told. The sophisticated modern ballad singer is playing the part of a true ballad singer.

Occasionally he may go further. Simple song, in the absence of an independent accompaniment, is often able to absorb a good deal of elaboration and variation in performance. In the presentation of a ballad, such modifications, especially if improvised on the spot, lend a convincing verisimilitude to the fiction that the song is being composed for the occasion. In this case the balladeer impersonates, not a mere storyteller, but a poet-composer in the act of casting his story into a uniquely memorable form.

Some types of fully accompanied song, notably the baroque aria, likewise permit improvisation, mostly in the form of additional ornaments and cadenzas. From an operatic point of view the desired effect ought to be that the character, not the singer, is "composing" the aria, producing a subconscious musical response to a specific dramatic situation. In historical practice the singer often took over, seizing every opportunity for vocal display. The resulting excesses produced what Gluck and others considered an undramatic degeneration of the opera seria that called for a thoroughgoing reform.

Not all musical styles can stand even judicious elaboration on the part of the performer, and it is often difficult to decide just where, and to what extent, it is permissible. These problems, however, are only an exaggerated form of those inherent in all arts of performance. A singer, like an actor, is both a dramatic character and a real person. As a character, he must move in accordance with the prescriptions of the musico-dramatic situation – that is, he must be faithful to the text. But as a person, he must insist on his own freedom of action – that is, he must produce his own interpretation of that text. The tension between these two aspects of the singer's role thus curiously parallels the one we have already noted within the dramatic character he portrays: the tension between his tendencies toward freedom as a "person" and the restrictions upon him as an artistic motif. Whenever we see a play, whenever we hear an opera, and indeed, whenever we listen to a song, we are, or should be, aware of the force of these tensions. Presenting as they do analogues of the tension between freedom and determinism that most of us feel operative in our own lives, they may explain the peculiar appeal of the arts of performance.

The tension can break down, however, as the result of an illegitimate but all too common type of performance: that in which the singer displays an inappropriate awareness of his audience. For just as an operatic character, for example, must appear to be unaware of his accompaniment, or of the very act of singing, so the dramatic situation normally requires him to seem unaware of the presence of an audience. Sometimes [. . .] this rule is deliberately violated, as in the Prologue to [Leoncavallo's opera] *Pagliacci*, and there are occasions when convention allows or requires the characters to sing directly to the audience, as in the finale of [Stravinsky's] *The Rake's Progress*. Indiscriminate indulgence in this kind of behavior, however, has been common in the history of opera, and it inevitably destroys the dramatic illusion by calling attention to the person of the performer at the expense of the character he is enacting.

Although such destruction of the dramatic illusion is perhaps most egregious in a theatrical setting, it is by no means restricted to opera. Similar unfortunate results can obtain even when a concert singer or a balladeer properly directs his performance toward the audience. There is a subtle but clear distinction between the legitimate inclusion of the listeners in the dramatic ambiance of a song and the exploitation of their relation to the singer in order to enhance his personal glory.

The legitimate interpretation, the "faithful" performance for which every singer should strive, is the one in which the two aspects of person and persona fuse. The physical presence and the vitality of the singer turn the persona of the poetic-musical text into an actual, immediate, living being: the *person* of the singer invests the *persona* of the song with *personality*. If the impersonation is successful, if the illusion is complete, we hear this embodied persona as "composing" his part – as living through the experience of the song. The vocal persona may be of various kinds – protagonist, character, etc., but, barring the unlikely possibility that we now ever witness the actual creation of natural song by its composer-performer, the persona is never identical with the singer.

The illegitimate interpretation is the one in which not the vocal persona but the singer – Mr. X or Miss Y there on the stage – becomes the "composer," the experiencing subject of the song. [. . .] The faithful performance, like Shakespeare's Caliban, allows us to hear the persona, and hence the composer's voice behind the persona, speak for itself. The illegitimate interpretation, like Browning's Caliban, forces us to hear the singer speaking through the persona and hence converting the composer's voice into a medium for his own self-expression. (This misappropriation can occur even when a singer performs songs of his own composition, if – as is often the case with pop singers – the emphasis is entirely on the immediate performance. I do not mean to imply that there is anything morally, or even esthetically, wrong about this practice. I merely insist that what one is listening to in such cases – as in many virtuoso performances of "serious" music – is not the piece being performed, but the performance itself.)

The independent instrumental accompaniment is the medium through which the musical persona speaks directly, without the intervention of the vocal component. By the same token, its successful performance produces the impression that its music is being composed, or thought, not so much *by* as *through* the accompanist. For, unlike the singer, he is not enacting the role of a "real" persona; he is symbolically conveying the presence of a virtual persona. Thus he should never assert his own personality in the way that a singer can and must; yet it is through his individual vitality that the virtual persona comes to life. If he is successful, he will produce the effect of a spontaneity that seems to inhere, not in his own activity, but in that of the music itself. The music will then appear to live its own life, so to speak – to compose or to think through itself.

In opera, and in other forms that combine voices with an elaborate orchestral accompaniment, the presence of the conductor adds yet another level of complexity. He is, so to speak, the surrogate of the implicit persona – or ought to be, for he, too, is subject to a tension between person and persona that is sometimes resolved in favor of his own personality. Ideally, however, he turns the persona's demands on behalf of a unified construct into actual commands. The singers must obey; yet neither they nor the characters they impersonate must appear to give up their freedom. (The extent to which an analogous rule applies to the instrumentalists will be discussed in connection with purely orchestral music.) The most satisfactory solution is found when the singers do not give up their freedom but freely do what the conductor enjoins, thus affording a visible and audible symbol of the relationship between the characters and the musical persona that controls them. (The singer's attitude may be compared to that of the believer who strives to will freely the Will of God.) It is just as well, perhaps, that the conductor's position in the pit allows us most of the time to overlook his presence and to forget his insistent beat. The more visible he is, the less individualized the characters can be, and the less we can submit to the dramatic illusion. I suspect that this is one reason why most concert performances of opera are so unsatisfying.

On the concert stage the dramatic illusion is often under attack from another quarter. If a lieder singer impersonates a protagonist, if an accompanist tries to create an effect of spontaneity, how can we tolerate – as we often must – their use of scores? Isn't the illusion bound to fail under these circumstances? Oddly enough, the illusion does not fail, even under apparently more difficult conditions. "Readings" of plays, in which the characters openly read their parts from script, are often effective, and oratorio performances, with no semblance of staging or acting, can be dramatically convincing. To a certain extent such success is due to the familiarity of the convention: we accept these modes of performance and in a sense overlook them. But I think there is a deeper reason for our acquiescence. The physical presence of the score (or of its parts) is a constant reminder – for both performers and audience – of the control of the complete musical persona. In this respect the visible score is not unlike the figure of the conductor. The use of the score threatens the illusion of spontaneity, but at the same time it inhibits the excessive liberty that turns a composition into a vehicle for the performer's self-expression or virtuosity. When we attend a play reading, we are probably more interested in the construction of the whole, and in the author's message, than in the specific portrayals. In the same way, concert performances of operas with highly individualized characters are less likely to be tolerable than those of oratorios, or oratoriolike operas, in which the emphasis is on narrative continuity and abstract musical structures. In these instances it is less important to maintain the fiction of individual freedom than to assert the primacy of the all-inclusive persona.

In the performance of solo song, it is common practice for a pianist, reading the score, to accompany a singer who performs from memory. Aside from matters of practical convenience, this arrangement offers the advantage of visually emphasizing the two differing roles: the actual vocal persona of the singer and the virtual instrumental persona of the accompanist. Indeed, no one who keeps in mind the symbolic nature of instrumental performance in general need ever be disturbed by a player's use of notes. If they inhibit spontaneity, it is the personal spontaneity of the player, not the inherent spontaneity of the music, that suffers. And since the two often come into conflict, it is sometimes fortunate that the presence of the score can remind the performer where his primary loyalty should reside.

If singing and playing from score need not destroy the dramatic illusion, this is especially true in cases where the characterization requires no high degree of personal specificity, as in choral singing. Here again the score, in addition to offering obvious conveniences, can serve advantageously as a continual reminder to each member of the choir of his duties to his vocal section, and of the relation of that section to the whole. The freedom of every choral singer is severely limited, and the score – again like the conductor – is a visible symbol of this circumscription.

At the same time a chorus has a dramatic role to play; and so, accordingly, does every member of it. Each of them, however, should be thought of not as a persona (that is, a protagonist or character) in his own right, but rather as one member of what might be called a multiple persona: a group in which each member foregoes his individuality to take part in a common enterprise. In unison singing, plainsong for example, the entire choir constitutes one multiple persona, representing the body of worshippers. The same is probably true of simple choral part singing, in which each part can still be heard as a component of one persona. More complicated polyphonic settings, however, divide the chorus into what must be perceived as two or more multiple personas, often in dramatic dialogue or even conflict with one another.

[. . .]

It must be admitted that there are many examples in which the composer has apparently not yielded to the demands of dramatic propriety – compositions, say, in which a soloist may stand for a multitude of people, or in which a chorus may represent an individual. Sometimes even this practice may make a dramatic point, as when Schoenberg, in *Moses und Aron,* symbolizes the superpersonality of God by assigning His voice to a complex combination of solos and chorus, of singing and *Sprechstimme,* or when Stravinsky, in *The Flood,* gives it to two solo basses. But what dramatic point could Schütz have intended in his *Auferstehung* when he set as duets the voice, not only of Jesus, who might thus be distinguished from mere mortals, but also of Mary Magdalen?

One possible answer appears if we consider the nature of liturgies and other sacred texts. Insofar as we understand and accept these as received texts, we do not expect one speaking or singing them to assume a dramatic role. If he assumes a role at all, it is a ritual one, as when a priest becomes a celebrant. We imagine the singer of a received text not as "composing" new words but as reading or reciting traditional ones.

If the ritual is complete, we accept the music as equally traditional. That brings us back to functional song, which can be concisely defined as completely ritual song, of which both words and music are "given," that is, determined by some rite, religious or secular. From this point of view, "Happy Birthday to You" and Gregorian chant are equally "sacred" and equally functional. Only when we listen to Gregorian chant as music, not merely accepting it as part of the liturgy, do its esthetic values become important. In this case, even though we still assume that the text is ritually prescribed, we are listening to the music as if it were the (subconscious) expression of a vocal persona. But the persona is to be imagined as *repeating* or *reading* the text, not as living through it.

This way of hearing Gregorian chant is one model for the esthetic apprehension, as opposed to the ritual acceptance, of any music composed for liturgical or other sacred texts. We hear the music as expressive, and hence as embodying the subconscious attitudes of a protagonist, but the protagonist is the devout Bible reader, or worshipper, or celebrant. Thus we can hear Josquin's "Absalon, fili mi," not as a dramatic representation of David's despair, but as the reaction of a reader, or group of readers, to the Bible story. Hence the multiple persona of its choral setting, while dramatically improper, is not inappropriate. In the same way, Schütz's double Magdalen and double Christ might reflect the inclination of the devout reader to view those characters in a special light, to dwell on their words with a special attention symbolized by the relatively elaborate musical realization. Figures of this sort, set off from the musical context yet not fully realized as actual characters, might be thought of as quasi-dramatic: imagined so vividly by the vocal persona that they take on a life of their own. Late versions of the Requiem, such as those of Berlioz and Verdi, contain many movements that might best be thought of in this way. But it is neither easy nor necessary to decide just where this kind of "reading" stops and true drama begins. Does the soprano solo of Verdi's "Libera me" represent a vivid figure imagined by an impressionable worshipper, or is it the anguished cry of a dying soul? Has the liturgical text become for Verdi another opera libretto? Probably the truth is that Verdi could not help turning ritual into drama. The protagonist who presumably began by reading, or reciting, or contemplating the Requiem Mass surrendered to the power of his (her) own imagination (as symbolized by Verdi's overwhelming music) and actually assumed the role of the soul about to face its judgment. Verdi has often been criticized for his theatricality in this work, for his confusion of liturgy with opera. But what he achieved, after all – granted the distance between the styles – is not so different from Josquin's intense realization of David's lament or from Bach's dramatization of the Passion. For "Absalon" may be thought of as representing a group of readers, each of whom not only sympathetically repeats the words of David, but, going one step further, imaginatively identifies himself with the biblical figure. And Bach, through his chorales on the one hand and his arias on the other, suggests the constant presence of the devout reader who, both as a member of the congregation (in the chorales) and as an individual (in the arias), imagines the biblical scenes so vividly that they come to life before his eyes.

Bach's use of the chorale, not only here but in the cantatas as well, musically symbolizes the intermingling of ritual and drama underlying his most powerful conceptions. Like a Gregorian cantus firmus in a

Renaissance motet or mass, the chorale melody, together with its text, is a ritual element because both its words and its music are traditional. But Bach's settings, like the polyphonic elaborations of the Renaissance cantus firmus, are original. In both, the multiple protagonist is a body of worshippers who, while accepting the traditional form (chorale or cantus firmus), think about it, comment on it, modify it. Bach's elaborate harmonizations and the independent instrumental parts that are often an integral part of his settings can be taken as referring to the subconscious attitudes of his multiple protagonist. Thus a chorale as performed in a cantata was not a real but a simulated hymn, taking its place as a component movement in a composition that, although an integral part of the church service, nevertheless produced its effect as a work of musico-dramatic art. At the same time, the ritual nature of its origin was not forgotten – at least by those members of the congregation who joined in the singing of the chorale melody. Provided they did so discreetly, without doing violence to the specific setting devised for the cantata in question, they did not deprive the chorale of its newly won artistic status, but rather added a dimension of true functionality to its simulated functionality, for they were the actual believers whom the choir represented. The chorale thus served in a double capacity: as an artistic motif within the cantata for the congregation to listen to, and as a ritually defined hymn for them to sing. (In this connection Berlioz's explanation of the presence of a third choir in addition to the double chorus of his *Te Deum* is interesting: this choir "represents the people adding their voice from time to time to the great ceremony of sacred music."[1] So do Bach's chorales.)

[. . .]

In Mozart's "Ave verum corpus," the strings (and organ) essentially double the vocal parts, yet they are more active than the voices, surrounding them with an introduction, interlude, and finale, and occasionally elaborating their melodic lines. Here we have an analogue of the "simple" accompaniment of solo song, in this case accompanying a multiple persona. Insufficiently independent to embody a persona of its own, it is heard as an amplification of the chorus. Evidence in favor of this interpretation is the fact that the hymn is occasionally sung *a cappella*. In this form it still makes perfect sense; it is still heard as the same composition, although diminished in size and incomplete.

One could also play "Ave verum" as an instrumental piece simply by omitting the voice parts. But such is the primacy we naturally accord the vocal persona that we do not accept a performance from which it has been banished as entirely authentic. Even though every note of the instrumental version would be Mozart's own, even though it would be more nearly complete than the purely vocal version, we should tend to consider it a transcription: the work of some arranger who made the decision to suppress the vocal parts. As our habit of indicating their authorship by hyphenating two names implies, we consider transcriptions as hybrids, not as the exclusive expression of the original composer's voice. They are comparable to translations: they offer a similar range of possibilities – and they are similarly unreliable.

A faithful transcription, such as Brahms's left-hand piano version of the Bach Chaconne, subordinates the transcriber's voice to the composer's. Indeed, in transcriptions made for purely practical purposes (like four-hand versions of symphonies), the transcriber's voice is negligible; the performers and their audience (if any) try their best to infer the original from the transcription. (Strictly speaking, every time we perform a harpsichord work on the piano we are playing a transcription of this type!) At the other extreme is Busoni's complete reworking of the same Chaconne, in which Busoni speaks through Bach, rather than Bach through Busoni. At both extremes and in between, exhibiting every degree of variation, are Liszt's innumerable arrangements, paraphrases, and fantasies. Some of these faithfully report the original composer's message; in others one hears above all the voice of Liszt; still others embody a clearly hybrid persona.

The particular type of transcription that interests us here is exemplified by the instrumental performance of the Mozart chorus, for the specific problems raised by instrumental versions of vocal originals elucidate some basic differences between vocal and instrumental music. How are such voice-to-instrument transcriptions to be heard?

Let us approach the problem in a roundabout way. Suppose that we are listening to a familiar song performed in such a way that we cannot make out the text. Perhaps it is vocalized rather than articulated, or perhaps it is translated into a strange language. Although we do not hear the words we know, we can still follow them mentally, rehearsing them as we hear the song. But now suppose that the song is an unfamiliar one, so that we cannot follow the words at all. The presence of the singer nevertheless forces us to recognize the existence of the vocal persona, even though this persona remains, under the circumstances, inarticulate for us. The persona may, in fact, actually *be* inarticulate; perhaps the song consists of nonsense syllables, or pure vocalization (like Debussy's "Sirènes"). No matter: in every case the singing voice invests its melodic line with human personality. We cannot help interpreting the vocalizer, not as the player of a wordless instrument, but as a protagonist who has deliberately chosen to remain inarticulate. We attribute to his song the connotations of words, no doubt on the tacit assumption that although his thoughts are not verbally expressed, they nevertheless could be, and at any point might be.

If we try, we can often listen to transcriptions in much the same way. If the song is a familiar one, its melody is presumably clear to us, and we can mentally follow the text along with it, thus recreating an imaginary vocal persona. We sometimes listen in this way to instrumentally realized cantus firmi, or to strictly instrumental compositions derived from vocal originals, as chorale-preludes are. If the song is not a familiar one, or if we do not remember its words, we can still imagine the melody as representing a protagonist – one who, like the vocalizer, has chosen to remain inarticulate. This is especially easy if the melody is assigned to a solo instrument that can preserve the cantabile character of the line. Indeed, the fact that we refer to lines in general as voices suggests that some such idea influences our perception of all melodies, including those of instrumental origin.

At the same time, the absence of the human voice crucially alters the content of the composition. Only our deliberate effort supplies the melody with words. Only our imagination turns the instrumental line into a singing voice that wishes to remain wordless. If we are willing to let the words go, if we can forget the singing voice, we listen in a different way, and what we hear is different. [. . .] When we listen to a transcription as a purely instrumental composition, all that is left of the vocal persona is its melody. Its leading role should, of course, still be distinguishable, but it will have lost its unique position, for any instrumental line may claim, at one time or another, status as a "voice." What is more, the originally vocal melody, once it is separated from voice and words, no longer belongs to the subconscious of a protagonist: he is not there! The line has become what I shall be calling, in the discussion of instrumental music, a *virtual agent.* It is now a component of the instrumental persona, a verbally unspecified subconscious that unites the agent with all the other instrumental parts. The song has become a tone poem, producing its effect through abstract musical means.

According to this view, the human voice occupies a special position among musical instruments. As human beings, we recognize the voice as belonging to one of us, and we accord it special attention. A violin or a clarinet, despite its singing powers, can be dominated, hidden, or superseded by other instruments. It is possible to treat the voice in this fashion, but the result is that it almost inevitably sounds abused. For when the human voice sings, it demands to be heard, and when it is heard it demands recognition. Contrast, for example, the baroque concerto with the aria which it resembles in design. The solo in a violin concerto, say, emerges from the orchestra, blends with the orchestra, disappears into the orchestra. Its priority is intermittent; its leadership is always subject to question. In an aria the voice is always clearly demarcated. One knows exactly when it enters and when it stops. When it sings, it is clearly supreme. The fact that only the human voice can adequately embody a protagonist or character is due to this natural supremacy, more than to its ability to verbalize. For, as we have seen, words are not necessary so long as the voice is there.

This point of view is beautifully supported by a composition that may seem an exception to some of the principles enunciated above: Milton Babbitt's *Philomel*. The dramatic situation requires the soprano to take shape from her electronic surroundings, gradually turning her vocalization into articulate language as the protagonist she portrays, transformed into a nightingale, discovers her new voice. This is a voice in the process of finding itself, but once it has succeeded, there is no question as to its supremacy. So far as I know, this is the unique example of a composition that seems to create its own protagonist, who in turn creates her own song. As such it appropriately symbolizes the relationship between the vocal persona and the musical persona that envelops and includes it – between the protagonist's voice and the composer's.

Note

1 David Cairns, trans., *The Memoirs of Hector Berlioz* (London: Gollancz, 1960), p. 479.

32

The Bell Song

Carolyn Abbate

Carolyn Abbate, *Unsung Voices: Opera and Musical Narrative in the Nineteenth Century* (Princeton, NJ: Princeton University Press, 1991), pp. 3–10.

In this item by Abbate on Delibes' Bell Song, the square brackets are the author's own. The terms *coloratura* and *roulade* both refer to florid ornamentation.

We begin with a scene that explores the power of narration, by showing us how a certain Hindu priestess comes to tell the "Tale of the Pariah's Daughter":

> *Nilakantha* (avec beaucoup de sentiment):
> Si ce maudit s'est introduit chez moi,
> S'il a bravé la mort pour arriver à toi,
> Pardonne-moi ce blasphème,
> C'est qu'il t'aime!
> Toi, ma Lakmé, toi, la fille des dieux.
> Il va triomphant par la ville,
> Nous allons retenir cette foule mobile.
> Et s'il te voit, Lakmé, je lirai dans ses yeux!
> Affermis bien ta voix! Sois souriante,
> Chante, Lakmé! Chante! La vengeance est là!
>
> (Les Hindous se rapprochent peu à peu.)
>
> Par les dieux inspirée,
> Cette enfant vous dira
> La légende sacrée
> De la fille du Paria . . .
>
> *Tous*: Ecoutons la légende, écoutons!
>
> *Lakmé*: Où va la jeune Indoue,
> Fille des Parias? (etc.)

[*Nilakantha* (with great emotion): If this villain has penetrated my domain, if he has defied death to come near you, forgive my blasphemy, but it is because he loves you, my Lakmé, you! You, the child of the gods! He's passing in triumph through the town, so let us gather this wandering crowd, and, if he sees you Lakmé, I shall read it in his eyes! Now steady your voice! Smile as you sing! Sing, Lakmé! Sing! Vengeance is near! (The crowd of Hindus gathers slowly around.) Inspired by the gods, this child will tell you the sacred legend of the pariah's daughter. *The Crowd*: Let's listen to the legend! Listen! *Lakmé*: Where does the young Hindu girl wander? This daughter of pariahs? (etc.)]

This is, of course, the setup for one of opera's most famous virtuoso numbers, the Bell Song from Delibes' *Lakmé*, which premiered – two months after Wagner died – in 1883. What happens in this scene will serve to underscore a series of distinctions critical to any interpretation of musical narration: plot and narrating, story and teller, utterance and enunciation.

Upon first being urged by Nilakantha to "steady your voice . . . sing" (the line is significant), Lakmé responds with a wash of wordless coloratura. This initial improvisatory vocalizing is what first fascinates the crowd, and, from their random wanderings (they are a "foule mobile"), strikes them into immobility as a closed circle of listeners. They hear a woman who transforms herself into a kind of musical instrument, a sonorous line without words and unsupported by any orchestral sound (Figure 32.1). Pure voice commands instant attention (both ours and that of the onstage audience), in a passage that is shockingly bare of other sound. In opera,

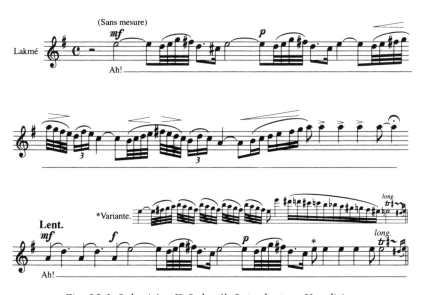

Fig. 32.1 *Lakmé* Act II: Lakmé's Introductory Vocalizing

we rarely hear the voice both unaccompanied and stripped of text – and when we do (in the vocal cadenzas typical of Italian arias, for instance), the sonority is disturbing, perhaps because such vocalizing so pointedly focuses our sense of the singing voice as one that can compel *without* benefit of words. Such moments enact in pure form familiar Western tropes on the suspicious power of music and its capacity to move us without rational speech. Beyond this, however, this moment of initial vocalization, with its strong phatic effect, prefigures the thrust of Lakmé's vocal performance as a whole.

In verse 1 of her song, Lakmé tells the tale of a poor girl who wanders in the woods, and in the course of her wandering encounters a stranger threatened by "fauves [qui] rugissent de joie" ["wild animals (who) roar with joy"]. She jumps in to save the stranger by charming the animals with a magic wand, decorated with a bell. In verse 2, the stranger, revealed as Vishnu, rewards her by transporting her to the heavens; the song ends with the narrator's address to the onstage audience, reminding them that "depuis ce jour au fond des bois, / Le voyageur entend parfois / Le bruit léger de la baguette / Où tinte la clochette / Des charmeurs" ["since that day, those who travel deep into the forest sometimes hear the gentle sound of the wand on which the enchanters' bell rings"].

Known now to most only as a coloratura showpiece (and one associated chiefly with such art-deco divas as Lily Pons), the Bell Song derives its name from the refrain that closes each of the two narrative verses, in which the soprano imitates, by vocalizing on open vowel sounds, the "magic bell" described in the story. (The coloratura passages in the refrain are similar to those initial improvisatory roulades that first pull the crowd.) Few are aware that the Bell Song is actually the "Légende de la fille du Paria," that it is a narrative, and that its fetishization of voice as pure sound is interwoven with the telling of a story. Nonetheless, the scene demonstrates the ways in which vocal performance will indeed overpower plot, for Gerald, the besotted British officer, is attracted not by the tale but by the voice that sings it. Gerald betrays himself involuntarily, and, acting equally against her will, Lakmé delivers an overtly seductive performance, and extracts one erotically fascinated listener from the crowd in which he hides. Implicit in all that has been said, of course, is the realization that the Bell Song is a scene of performance on two levels: a narrative performance, and a musical performance that the onstage audience can *hear as music*. The scene involves "phenomenal" performance, which might be loosely defined as a musical or vocal performance that declares itself openly, singing that is heard by its singer, the auditors on stage, and understood as "music that they (too) hear" by us, the theater audience.

A scene of seduction, Lakmé's performance nonetheless does not seduce by means of *plot*. This by no means implies that her "tale of the pariah's daughter" is irrelevant, for in the context of the opera as a whole it might well be read as an allegory of Lakmé's own fate – eventually, she sacrifices herself to save Gerald. Nilakantha's anger at Gerald's "blasphemous pollution" of the priestess is thus assuaged by *her* death, and when at the end of the opera Nilakantha cries "Elle porte là-haut nos voeux, / Elle est dans la splendeur des cieux!" ["She brings our prayers on high, she resides in the splendours of heaven"], he associates her with the transfigured maiden of her own tale. Gerald the foreigner and imperialist is at the same moment obliquely complimented by being, with Lakmé, inserted into the tale and equated with divine Vishnu (that the compliment is put in the mouth of an enraged native is one of the opera's covert means of luxuriating in its own Orientalist romance). In this allegorical role, the Bell Song represents a common operatic type, a song whose *reflexive* narrative text prefigures the plot of the opera in which it appears. Such songs generate complicated nested reflexive spheres [. . .] Within its immediate context, however, the tale that Lakmé tells *is* insignificant, for it is not the story that acts upon its listener. The act of telling it – the act of narrating – is the point.

The crowd can be understood as naive listeners, as eavesdroppers or an excluded audience, for the real force of the performance – the seduction – is not meant for them. They are content with the story of the pariah's daughter – they will, as they say, "listen to the *tale*," perhaps as a simpler reader might "read for the plot." Gerald, to the contrary, is envisaged by Nilakantha as listening not to plot but to voice and performance. By urging Lakmé to "steady her voice," by repeating his exhortation "chante, chante," he seems to realize that she must become much more than a story telling itself; she must be a sheer source of sound, to attract – fatally – the attention of that single listener. Gerald's experience of the song is deemed by the scene's stage-manager to be an experience of a musical voice-object. As if to confirm her own status as sonority rather than story, Lakmé produces music that might itself be regarded as *working against the story she narrates*, since the two musical verses, by remaining similar, by repeating, in some sense deny the progressive sequence of changing events that are recounted in Lakmé's words.

Gerald, the intended listener, is in fact never conscious of the tale (Lakmé's story of Vishnu and the pariah), because he is too far away to hear her words when Lakmé delivers her formal singing performance. When the song fails to flush his prey, Nilakantha urges Lakmé to sing again, to sing until the traitor is revealed. Lakmé, exhausted by formal performance, can no longer produce either the coherent narrative, or a whole verse of the song. She merely recapitulates textual fragments and bell sounds (Figure 32.2). The broken coloratura inverts the smooth virtuosity of Lakmé's improvisatory prelude (her "steadying" of the voice), and the bell-flourishes, repeated in upward sequence as Lakmé loses control of pitch, mark the end of the performance in the face of its success (Gerald has appeared at Lakmé's side). In this epilogue, both the sequential plot described by the words of the song, and the coherent sequence of musical

Fig. 32.2 After the Bell Song

Fig. 32.2 continued

events in the song, have dissolved into fragments as Lakmé becomes *explic-itly* a body emanating sonority. Finally, Gerald *hears*. The Bell Song's epilogue reinterprets the song, exposing plot as empty distraction, and affirming that a narrative performance can signify in ways that pass

Fig. 32.2 continued

beyond the tale told. Lakmé's singing has the same perlocutionary force as a command to Gerald to reveal himself, a force not connected to the structure or the content of her story.

Lakmé's performance [demonstrates] how we do well to examine narrative activities rather than the events that they describe, to examine forms of enunciation rather than forms taken by utterance. Put this way, the debate sounds merely institutional. The scene is far richer, of course, but it does enact certain oppositions and above all suggests the fascinations and complexities of *voice* in the musical work.

33

The Little Blueprint? An amplification of the meaning of 'libretto'

Gordon Kalton Williams

New for this volume.

This item by the librettist Gordon Kalton Williams was commissioned to complement other course materials relating to another *Words and Music* case study, Australian composer Andrew Schultz's cantata *Journey to Horseshoe Bend*. The piece is based on the anthropologist T. G. H. (Theo) Strehlow's novel of the same name, which describes the final journey of his father, Pastor Carl Strehlow, in 1922 – ostensibly from his remote missionary station among the Aranda people of Australia's Northern Territory to Adelaide for medical help, but in reality to his death. Njitiaka is their Aranda guide who explains the mythical significance of the landscape through which they travel.

A lyricist once couldn't help himself when he heard someone whistling a Tom Jones hit. 'I wrote the words', he skited. Annoyed at being interrupted, the whistler said, through clenched teeth, 'I wasn't . . . whistling . . . the words.' Does this sum up the problem for lyricists, and by extension librettists? Should we expect people to pay more attention to the words?

Actually, you'll get a much better sense of what makes a libretto if you see it as more than merely 'the words', or 'the words on the page'. In its largest sense a libretto is a suggestion to the composer of what s/he should achieve dramatically. That's not to say that a libretto can't possibly have its own reading pleasures. Many of the examples below are drawn from the libretto for Andrew Schultz's and my *Journey to Horseshoe Bend* which, to a greater-than-usual extent, betrays its origins in the book of the same name by T. G. H. Strehlow.[1] *Journey to Horseshoe Bend* (*JHB*) is not an opera, and it could be instructive to wonder why not. But a libretto, whether to an opera, oratorio or cantata, should only really be fully assessed alongside the music that it leads to.

When colleagues of mine derided the libretto of *La traviata* as 'terrible writing', I suspect they had mistakenly judged it as armchair reading or playscript. But were they reading it for the aurals and visuals suggested by the text, that is, testing to see if it contained what Verdi called 'scenic' words? Were they reading it to see what musical product Verdi could make of it?

I sense that much of the underestimation of libretti relates to an over-estimation of the importance of words in theatre. Being able to write good dialogue does not necessarily make a good playwright. This is to miss the other essential dimensions that make good theatre. It's probably best not to think of words as the basic unit in a libretto either. What's more impor-tant is something bigger – a physical action, a use of the space, a psycho-logical beat albeit all with musical resonance. You can, of course, suggest action and shape with any number of words. To produce something as refined as 20 pages of libretto requires precision and control as well as powers of suggestion.

Is Piave's libretto to *La traviata* so poor? It sets up strongly contrasting characters in strong situations reflected in different settings. It provides good opportunities for contrasting music, but guaranteeing a forward flow. This text may be sparse – and when you read it aloud you get through its transitions quicker than spoken dramatic development should let you – but the point is it is text waiting to be sung, action waiting to be set to music. When it is performed it is complete. Librettist and composer have contributed. They were both creators; they were each other's first audience.

It should be said that *Journey to Horseshoe Bend* was the result of a true collaboration. While Andrew and I didn't do each other's jobs, we dis-cussed the work for a good two years, shared ideas, felt comfortable making suggestions about either libretto or score and mostly found ways to incor-porate each other's suggestions, even if there were initial doubts. There was a vigorous to-and-fro.

Opera reformers have often started with the words. Wagner's theoretical text, *Oper und Drama*, demonstrated a relationship between words and music. Wagner is thought to have copped out when he came to write *Tristan und Isolde*, under the influence of the philosopher Schopenhauer, who had put music on a pedestal. We have in *Tristan* and Act III of *Siegfried* moments of pure sound, melismas on single syllables even, which the younger Wagner had derided. The music clearly comes first – or does it? After *Oper und Drama*, as Jack M. Stein pointed out years ago in *Richard Wagner and the Synthesis of the Arts*, Wagner wrote an essay called *Beethoven*, in which he lit on another opposite partner to music, what he called 'pantomime'.[2] It was music and *action* that he paired in *Die Meistersinger von Nürnberg*, the other work (besides *Tristan*) that he took time out to write before returning to the *Ring* and the dramatic high pressure of *Götterdämmerung*.

We have here a clue to what else the libretto is besides a 'little book'. It's a little springboard for musical action. The libretto is, in addition to words, and perhaps more importantly, the larger plot movements, sequence, scenes, mise-en-scène, characters, numbers, a suggestion of duration, proportion and pace. It might even hint at a compositional scheme. J. D. McClatchy *(1984, An American Tragedy)* tells of how he first presented a libretto, *A Question of Taste*, to William Schuman, who said 'they [the words] don't do anything for me'.[3] McClatchy tried to point out that 'the image in line 3 links up in line 6', but Schuman cut him off: 'I told you it [the libretto] didn't do anything for me.' McClatchy went back and introduced a new character to add a tenor voice, formulated more solos, duets and choruses, and thought less 'of the dramatic unfolding and more of the musical progression'.

Early on in the creation of *JHB* (at libretto stage) I developed a sense of musical numbers that Strehlow's work could be broken into. This partly determined the means of making the adaptation from T. G. H. Strehlow's 220-page novel. Bringing the chorale *Wachet auf* in as soon possible meant fast-forwarding through the first 22 pages of Strehlow's text. Indeed the first pages of Strehlow's book were rethought to provide musical opportunities – sunrise, chorale, travelling music. Andrew and I discussed the idea of the three significant stopping places in the novel (Henbury, Idracowra and Horseshoe Bend) being 'camps' or points of rest, defining three acts, or the parts of a broadly ternary form. Notwithstanding the fact that Andrew decided early on that the work would be through-composed (and this accounts greatly for the inexorability of the work's progress to Pastor Carl's death), I am convinced that thinking the libretto in terms of set numbers also helped crystallise the moments.

The first draft of the libretto for *JHB* is very like prose, a cut-and-paste from the novel to work out what more to cut. The cantata was initially conceived as a work for narrator, chorus and orchestra. To study the various drafts is to follow the course of a piece of writing towards the status of a libretto. Of course our *JHB* doesn't become a fully staged opera, but subsequent drafts took on more musico-dramatic aspects. At first there was no boy soprano Theo, and passages such as the third scene's night journey through the desert oaks were conveyed more prosaically:

Journey to Horseshoe Bend, scene 3 – 1st draft[4]

CHORUS

Friday, 25 October.

NARRATOR

'It was half past two next morning when Theo was wakened by the sudden blazing of the restoked campfire and the talking of Njitiaka and Lornie, who were rolling up their blankets (87).'
They broke camp 'and the van moved away from the cheery blaze of the campfire into –'

NARRATOR & CHORUS

– 'the moonlit sandhill silence (87).'
Processional (Brittania Sandhills) music: the 'sighing of casuarinas'. Sandhill music.

NARRATOR

'The resinous scent emanating from the bulging tufts of spinifex . . . was not as overwhelming in the cool night air as it had been in the heat of the previous evening; but it nevertheless pervaded the whole atmosphere with the unmistakable menace of its aroma. For here as elsewhere in the Centre this resinous fragrance drew attention to the deep loneliness and the dangerous waterlessness of the huge inland sandhill regions (87).'
'[The] continual sighing of the magnificent desert oaks in the soft night breeze indicated the extraordinary length to which their jointed needle-like leaves had grown (88).'
Theo thought of the *iliaka njemba*, the emu-like phantom that terrified Aranda children.
'The black forests of desert oaks, whose moon-silvered crests were shimmering so brightly, kept on exciting Theo's intense admiration (90);'
'Talpa, not taia,' said Njitiaka, correcting Theo's western Aranda word for 'moon' . . . He pointed out some of the prominent sites.

'NJITIAKA'[5]

Nakua potta kuka [ ], raka kngara [ ]

NARRATOR

'Gradually the dark eastern horizon became tinged with grey. The blurred and shapeless tree forms began to reveal their limbs with increasing clarity. The eastern sky became overspread by a reddish-yellow tinge, and finally the spinifex tips on the crests of the sand-dunes began to glow in the first rays of the rising sun . . . the sudden burst of warmth that accompanied its full revelation foretold that the day . . . would be, in local terms, a "real scorcher" (90).'

CHORALE

CHORUS

(*O Sacred Head sore wounded*) [1st verse]
Aka tjantjurrantjurrai, Ilkaartapartangai,
Ilakwala yirnintja, Arrampowumalai!
Alkaralkar' inthorra Untarrka nitjata;
Lyarta maamapapatha: 'Tha nganh' anparnama.[6]

NARRATOR

'About midday they reached the end of the Brittania Sandhills (97).'
'Njitiaka pointed out a dune which overtopped all other sandhill crests by
scores of feet –

And suddenly the sense of climax is interrupted, and we are still travelling . . .

It was only later that much of that information was transformed into a
duet between Njitiaka and Theo, raising the dramatic, and at the same
time, musical profile of the work. As the frequency of Theo and Njitiaka's
exchanges increased so action took over from narrative:

<u>*Journey to Horseshoe Bend,* scene 3 – final version</u>

T.G.H

It was half-past two next morning when I was wakened by the sudden
blazing up of the restoked campfire. Njitiaka rolled up the swags and unte-
thered the donkeys.

NJITIAKA

Keme-irreye tangkey ngkerne lhetyenele![7]

T.G.H.

And we moved away from the cheery blaze of the campfire into the moonlit
sandhill silence.

NJITIAKA

Unte irnterneme urnpe lhanhe? Lhanhe yurte-ipne urnpe. Unte irterlere-
tyeke kwatye kweke ware nemenhe nhanerle.

THEO

Spinifex tufts –
Kicked up by donkeys –
Have such an odour,
a certain smell?

Strange, lonely, dry;
Moonlight, sandhills, silence

NJITIAKA

Werlethenaye werinerle irrkepe ngketyeke ingkwarle mpareme. Ilpele thwerte-nirre ngkeleme.

THEO

Desert oaks,
Sighing,
Their long needles swishing,
Sighing, crying, calling . . .

NJITIAKA

(*pointing it out*) Pmere ngkweke lanhe, Kwatye pmere. Karte ngkwekeneke pmere.

THEO

Kwatye?

NJITIAKA

Ya, pmere ngkweke

THEO

Your home?

NJITIAKA

Leyeke pmere.

THEO

Taye parrtyeme
The moon is shining –

NJITIAKA

Terlpe!

THEO

What?

NJITIAKA

Terlpe parrtyeme?

THEO

Terlpe parrtyeme?
Showing our way

NJITIAKA

Unte arrtye irrtne ilmeletyeke? Lanhe renye 'terlpe' itye 'taye'. (*Dismissively*) Western Aranda!

THEO

Terlpe larnnga-larnnga . . .

NJITIAKA

Awa!

THEO

Shadows, moonlight, sandhills
Terlpe imerneme uwerneke.

You'll notice that in the first draft there was the suggestion of another chorale to be used in the musical texture. The repertoire of chorales was reduced as work proceeded. Andrew rightly sensed that too many chorales would create an excess of material to shape while having to stick to our brief for the duration of the work. But it is important to note that these decisions came out of discussions at the libretto-writing stage.

It has been said that music has a degree of persuasiveness that words can only aspire to. The completion of the chorale at the end of *JHB* is more moving than a mere spoken rendering would be. Music can even, handily sometimes, lead us up the wrong emotional path. So what do we miss if we don't know the words?

At the end of *Das Rheingold,* there is a shimmering and swelling in the music which finally blazes forth in a proud, even harsh, assertion of triumphal power. The Gods are finally crossing the rainbow bridge into their citadel Valhalla.

This is the most wonderful example of pure, unalloyed 'rubbing-the-loser's-nose-in-it' victory. An audience may even hate themselves for feeling excited, associating Wagner's music with Nuremberg Rallies and sheer unconscionable arrogance!

But the thing is: the 'Entry of the Gods into Valhalla' can only have this meaning *when you've paid no attention to the storyline;* when you've ignored the dramatic context. Because when you finally hear this passage in the theatre, or at least as part of the music drama, to use Wagner's term, you realise that the gods are entering a kingdom that has been doomed; that Wotan and the other gods are blind, as Loge says, 'to the end towards which they are heading'. He *says* it, but we even see them step over the dead body of Fasolt or freeze momentarily at the sound of the Rhinemaidens keening below. It is the most spectacular example of irony in the history of . . . well, what is it? Music or Drama? But one thing's for sure. You need the drama to 'get' this irony. The combination of both elements *together* creates an emotional nuance that libretto and music wouldn't be able to achieve on their own. And it's not just Loge's words that fulfil the whole condition of undermining. We have just watched two hours of Wotan tying himself in knots, back-pedalling and swindling. You can twig, even without selecting the subtitle option on your DVD. (If Loge had said, 'They are *not* heading to their doom', you would not have believed him. Any playwright knows that words cannot overpower accumulated action. Or as psychologist Steven Covey would say: 'You cannot talk yourself out of what you have behaved yourself into.')

True, we can be mightily swayed by music, but even misinterpreting depends on knowing what is conveyed by the sounds. Never having read the surtitles at the beginning of *Madama Butterfly*, we may overlook Pinkerton's bastardry (the fact that he is calculating the length of the marriage contract) because the opening of this opera is what romantic music sounds like to us; *we know from a thousand contexts*. Do we know enough about Inuit music to know what is moving in it? The opening bars of *Tristan* – what do they mean? Without the context – in this case 100 years of tonality – do we know that a minor sixth in nineteenth-century Romantic music denotes yearning?

Context is all important. In *JHB* I was able to convey the outcome of the story of the crow of Mbalka; how he was drowned by the rain women of Erea, in few enough words to allow the music to continue unimpeded, because the story bad been previously established. Context. And sequence!

Thinking any of this has much to do with the beauty of the words is a bit of a furphy. The words in fact should probably be as simple as possible. The score can pinpoint the exact shade of emotion; the libretto has an anchoring, orientating primacy. Be careful of being too flash.

I find John Adams and Alice Goodman's *Nixon in China* exceptionally, even movingly clear, so it may seem churlish to pounce on this next example. But I remember being impressed by certain lines in Act I, the chorus singing:

> The people are the heroes now
> The heroes pull the peasants' plow

I thought 'what a nice Shakespearian duality', and one that you could deduce easily sitting in the theatre. It was only when I read the libretto that I discovered that it was 'Behemoth' who was pulling the peasant's plough. It's nice poetry, but I couldn't help but feeling sorry for the poor bastard sitting in the theatre trying to light on 'behemoth' as the word being defined by that particular combination of vowels.

And on top of that in opera you've got the particular challenges to clarity posed by polyphony and melisma. Best to make sure the story's clear from your large structure, and set up strong, dramatic, character-driven situations that convey a larger message. You've got to make sure that the conflicts and crises of the plot have safely been established and resolved.

Of course, a successful libretto should provide the composer with musical opportunities which enhance the dramatic flow. It is an absolute master-stroke in the libretto of Verdi/Boito's *Otello* to begin with Shakespeare's second act and therefore give the composer and the drama a storm to start with.

Journey to Horseshoe Bend fast-forwards through the preparations and background to the journey to light on a chorale which arises, as if sponta-neously from the voices of the Ntaria women. The first pages draw from the novel to create a couple of musical situations – sunrise and chorale. It was a libretto-stage decision to leave out T. G. H. Strehlow's impressive ten-page description of the massacre history of Irbmangkara, even though it may be the most virtuosic piece of writing in the book. We had to get moving.

A libretto is a blueprint for musical action. If the job has been considered well enough, the composer can sit down and see the musical form inherent in the material. The libretto is good in so far that you can judge by the intelligence of its suggestion of actable music: momentum, weight, musical numbers (who sings what), purely musical segments, and, at the level of detail, what I call its 'play with specificity'.

JHB is a cantata. It is *meant* to be a concert work. This was the result of a number of decisions taken at the libretto stage. If *JHB* had been fully sung it would of course have been twice as long, but speech allowed us filmic pacing, a directness and spontaneity; to move quickly through concepts that don't normally make it into opera. We were aiming for a certain rich-ness and at the same time intelligibility. We rejected the idea of the narra-tion being sung in recitative (although recognising that the narrator fulfilled some of tbe function of an Evangelist in a Bach passion), partly to broaden the work's appeal, but also because we needed another speaking role to pair with Njitiaka. Nevertheless, it is worth testing this theory of libretto writing by examining the proximity of each cantata scene to com-pletely dramatised opera.

Scenes 3 and 4 are arguably the most fully dramatised. Strehlow's descriptions of conversations between Theo and Njitiaka as they travel at night through the sand-dune country are turned into duet. In scene 4 Carl's struggles with his faith, described in the third person by T. G. H. Strehlow in his novel, are turned into an aria with responding chorus. This aria is juxtaposed with a cinematic cutaway to Theo's ditty-like listing of sights around Idracowra station. I particularly love the melody that Andrew came up with when he arrived at what I considered the heart of the scene, and perhaps of the philosophy of the work:

> But God cannot be known
> Nor made to answer men.
> No use in us demanding
> The meaning of our pain.

Action and music? In *Journey* the ongoing movement of the music was complemented by verbal pointers to direction: '. . . 25 miles to the north-west rugged Rutjubma . . .'; '. . . already moving through the . . . saltbush flat which spread south . . .'; '. . . turned in a more easterly direction . . .' Njitiaka gives many of the directions. But these examples are taken from TGH, the narrator.

Journey to Horseshoe Bend stayed a cantata in some ways to preserve the flavour of Strehlow's original novel. But that meant particular problems. One of the big hazards for libretto writing is leaving too much 'on the page'. I say that having written a wordy libretto, and having early on tried to force Andrew into setting TGH's denser and slower-moving sentences. This example is from the third draft. The party have arrived at Horseshoe Bend.

Journey to Horseshoe Bend, scene 6 – 3rd draft

CHORUS (*continuing under*)
Horseshoe Bend is the eye of a flame
Horseshoe Bend is the eye of a fire

T.G.H.
Horseshoe Bend had been remarkable for its cruel heatwaves for as long as human memory went back.

NJITIAIKA
Atua Rubuntjaka janha ntoaka. Pota urbula arei. Itne uralalanga.

T.G.H.
(*Translating*) Everywhere the Rubuntja men vomited they left black pebbles whose heat essence is evoked to this day in freezing weather.

CHORUS (*continuing under*)
Horseshoe Bend is a fiery place
A land of burning cliffs

NJITIAKA
Nana pmara uraka. Nakua ngapa nama. Era ura taka, altjiraka.

CHORUS (*continuing under*)

Horseshoe Bend is a fiery place
A land of burning cliffs

NJITIAKA

Nana pmara uraka, Nakua ngapa nama. Era ura taka, altjiraka.

CHORUS

Of searing plains

T.G.H.

(*As if translating for Njitiaka*) The main totemic sites in the region were all associated in some way with fire or with the scorching heat of the summer sun. Worst was Mbalka, the home of a malicious crow who had flitted over the landscape at the dawn of time, lighting fires.

CHORUS

Fire
Exploding spinifex
Shrieking over sandhills
Shooting from branches screaming
Writhing from mulga, like pillars of
Fire,
Crackling torches of flame
(*Continuing*)

NJITIAKA

Erea tara rana rranthaka, rana lakarlalak . . .

T.G.H.

(*Translating*) At last, two rain ancestresses from Erea surprised the crow and drowned him. The lake of fire became a sea of water. Clouds of steam hissed up from sizzling tree stumps and charred stumps.

Listen to the music as it is now and you can hear that TGH's and Njitiaka's words would have impeded the flow. As a solution Andrew went ahead and composed music for this scene using only bits of the text. Only after the music had been freed in this way did I go back make sure that the characters told the same story in telegraphic form.

<u>*Journey to Horseshoe Bend*</u>, scene 6 – final version

NTARIA LADIES CHOIR (*very quietly*)

Kaartai, nurna-nha wurlathanai (*Father, hear our prayer*)

CHORUS

Horseshoe Bend is the eye of a flame
Horseshoe Bend is the eye of a fire

NJITIAKA

Urte Rubuntja ntwe-irrke nhakeke.

T.G.H.

The Rubuntja men vomited over there.

NJITIAKA

Perte urrpwerle raye . . .

T.G.H.

Yes, the black stones.

NJITIAKA

Itne metyepenhe . . .

T.G.H.

They're from fire?

CHORUS

Fire
Exploding spinifex
Shrieking over sandhils
Shooting from branches screaming
Writhing from mulga, like pillars of
Fire,
Crackling torches of flame

Horseshoe Bend is a fiery place
A land of burning cliffs

NJITIAKA

Nhanhe metyeke pmere.

T.G.H.

This is fire country.

NJITIAKA

Ngkape nhakele . . .

T.G.H.

That crow over there . . .

NJITIAKA

metye itekele, . . .

T.G.H.

He set all this country alight . . .

NJITIAKA

itekele ntgkerrnhe.

T.G.H

in the beginning.

CHORUS

Horseshoe Bend, etc. . . .

A libretto needs to be able to turn on a dime. While composing, the composer may ring up and say, 'I need eight syllables in the following rhythm.' The librettist knows s/he has to tie up three or four plot points in that space as well. There is so much more to appreciate if the libretto is examined hand in hand with the music.

I mentioned before the play with specificity. The relationship between text and music is far more fascinating than a side-by-side comparison would suggest.

Andrew often says that the music is the poetic element, and that's true. But well-placed words can enhance a poetic moment. 'The smell of rain-soaked earth fills the air . . .', sings Theo, as his final notes ring out.

I have myself tried to explain the relationship between music and text in terms of the text being the noun and the music the verb, but sometimes the text, acting as context, can be adverb. And sometimes the music is the noun. Andrew's chorale harmonies and counterpoint give reality to *JHB's* Lutheran setting. Is the libretto here the adjective? Can the music be the subtext revealing the *text's* true concerns? . . .

Journey to Horseshoe Bend ends with a storm. Music does storm beautifully. It can convey a storm without a word in sight. Think Beethoven, Rossini, Britten. Think *Otello.* But it's important for the audience in *JHB* to know that that storm *confirms Theo's decision to make his future in Central Australia by corroborating for him the reality of a storm that took place in the mythological era at the beginning of time.* That's the reason for the verbal exchanges between Njitiaka and TGH at the beginning of the third part (the arrival at Horseshoe Bend), and for this exchange towards the end:

> NJITIAKA: Kwatye ngkarle arpenhe petyeme
> TGH: More clouds?
> NJITIAKA: line renhe nyenhe inetyeke.
> TGH: Those rain-women get that crow always
> NJITIAKA: Ngampakala. Finish him.

Which brought all the elements to a point, *after* the score was completed – after Andrew had been set free to follow the course of the dramatically generated music.

A libretto may mask a great many decisions. It needs to be thin. But one decision taken at the libretto stage can say heaps. Strehlow spends many paragraphs describing Pastor Carl's character. We needed an authoritative voice. As a bass-baritone Carl had for me associations with a Wotan or a Boris, and in that one decision was all that we needed to say about that 'rockplate' clergyman who threw the murderous Constable Wurmbrand off the mission property and who stood in the path of a party of Kukatja avengers. I remember being fascinated by the changed significance that could be achieved merely by assigning words to different characters. Imagine the quite different cast of meaning if you assign the chorus's words: 'But God cannot be known . . .' to one of the other characters.

All this information can be encompassed by the libretto. And some of a libretto's achievement may literally be invisible, left to the composer or left out. It may only be realised on stage (another's job). But let's go back to the libretto as words, since that is the level on which the debate is usually waged.

The libretto is important. The words are significant. The librettist J. D. McClatchy's name was left off the CD cover for *Emmeline* (composer: Tobias Picker). I would have been ropable. And librettos and programs and texts can push composers in directions they might not have explored if left to their own devices. I think of the soundtrack to *Bullitt* and compare it with Lalo Schifrin's recording with the West German Radio Big Band.[8] To me the version made to showcase the music lacks the rhetorical pointedness of the soundtrack. It seems to lack the gestural definiteness, seems less urgent. Could it be that 'text' (the action) forestalls a converging on purely musical elements, a narrowing of meaning? And yet so often we read in annotations: 'The composer sensed rightly that the music was coherent in its own terms, and did not need the added literary explanation', or 'We may disregard the program. For the work stands as music.'

Charles Rosen speaks of music's 'emancipation from the word' in a *New York Review of Books* article on Richard Taruskin's *Oxford History of Music*; and of how that emancipation enabled sophisticated absolute structures.[9] True, but are they better or worse than texted musical works; there is a pleasure to be had from the way the words and music mesh and collide in Pitjantjatjara chant, for example. Perhaps annotators should accord the libretto and its relationship to the music the same subtlety of understanding that they plead for in relation to absolute music.

But to come back to the words, because I dispute (even discounting larger plot movements, sequence, scenes, mise-en-scène, characters, numbers, a suggestion of duration, proportion and pace) that the *words* are inferior or weaker carriers of meaning.

A colleague once cited *Some Enchanted Evening* to me as an example of the primacy of music: it's the music that we carry away from the performance. Now I guess we don't go out whistling the words, but even if you only know the first lines of hundreds of songs, the general sense and situation reinforce the message to be taken from the melody, harmony, pace and orchestration, and I doubt if music would be as meaningful if judged, as Stravinsky may have wished, 'powerless to express anything other than itself'. After all, what is *Some Enchanted Evening* <u>in</u> musical terms: tonic chord with a melodic turn on the fifth followed by a downward drop, the sharpened fourth in the turn undermining stability; that turn repeated followed by an upward lift to the leading note, but this time with the harmony shifting underneath to the dominant; the turn again, this time followed by a lift to the tonic, but with a sharpened fifth underneath preparing the way to a supertonic 6/5 harmony . . . Certainly the harmony creates an urging forward and there is a poignancy often found in Richard Rodgers' chordal progressions, one step beyond the harmonically obvious, but does that fully explain the emotional resonance? I still think you at least need to know that the song is about an enchanted evening where you may meet a stranger across a crowded room; what any of us would bring to that love at first sight; words and sentiments that *preclude* being set to a 'rumpty-tumpty' melody.

But don't take my word for it. Get an audience of Americans to stand with hands over their hearts and sing:

> To Anacreon in heav'n, where he sat in full glee,
> A few sons of Harmony sent a petition,
> That He their Inspirer and Patron would be;
> When this answer arrived from the Jolly Old Grecian:
> 'Voice, Fiddle, and Flute,
> no longer be mute,
> I'll lend you my Name and inspire you to boot,
> And besides, I'll instruct you, like me, to entwine
> The Myrtle of Venus with Bacchus's Vine'

and I bet not a single one of them would shed a tear, no matter how good the tune, at the original words of the drinking song that became - *The Star-Spangled Banner.*

Acknowledgements

I would like to thank Andrew Schultz, the Strehlow Research Centre, Katherine D. Stewart, Natalie Shea, Siobhan Lenilian and James Koehne.

Notes

1 Strehlow, T. G. H., *Journey to Horseshoe Bend* (Melbourne: Angus & Robertson, 1969).
2 Stein, Jack M., *Richard Wagner and the Synthesis of the Arts* (Westport, CT, 1973).
3 See Alenier, K., 'A poet's distraction: interview with J. D. McClatchy', *Scene4 Magazine*, Sept. 2005, http://www.archives.scene4.com/sep-2005/html/infocussep05.html.
4 Figures in parentheses after statements refer to page numbers in the novel, which were only removed late in the writing of the cantata.
5 In inverted commas because we had still not settled on having a separate character.
6 'Aka tjantjurrantjurrai' (O Sacred Head now Wounded) No. 75, p. 69, *Arrarnta Lyilhintja Lutheran Worlamparinyaka* (Arrarnta Lutheran Hymnal) Alice Springs: Finke River Mission Board, 1997). Used with the permission of Finke River Mission of the Lutheran Church of Australia and with gratitude to the Arrarnta Lutheran communities of Central Australia.
7 Now with Doug Abbott's Southern Arrernte corrections.
8 Schifrin, Lalo, *Bullitt*, ALEPH Records 018, 2000.
9 Rosen, Charles, 'From the troubadors to Frank Sinatra': review of Richard Tantskin's *Oxford History of Western Music*, *New York Review of Books*, 23 Feb. 2006.

34

Sondheim's technique

Stephen Sondheim and Trevor Herbert

'Sondheim's technique, Stephen Sondheim interviewed
by Trevor Herbert', *Contemporary Music Review*, 5 (1989),
pp. 204–11.

In this item Stephen Sondheim discusses facets of his compositional technique, referring particularly to *A Little Night Music* (1973) and *Sweeney Todd* (1979). Most of the square brackets are from the interview as originally published. This extract incorporates further editions made by Stephen Sondheim in June 2007.

TH: "Send in the clowns" was written when *A Little Night Music* was in rehearsal. What circumstances brought about its composition?

SS: I wrote a number of songs in rehearsal, about seven of them as a matter of fact, which is quite a lot for me in a five-week period, including "Weekend in the Country", which is an enormously complicated piece. I usually don't go into rehearsal with that many songs missing, [but I did that time] because I got to know the characters through the way the actors were playing them. The two main characters in *A Little Night Music* are a lawyer in his mid 40s and a woman with whom he had an affair a number of years earlier who comes back and they run into each other again. We decided that the woman had to be a woman of enormous charm, grace, style, etc., because the conflict is that the middle-aged lawyer has married a very young bride. So, if there's to be a triangle with a very young and beautiful bride then the woman has to be *at least* as attractive, in fact more so, than the young bride. And that isn't just a matter of the character writing, because Hugh Wheeler who wrote the libretto did make Desiree the woman of everybody's dreams – she's wise, she's witty, she's kind, she's compassionate, and the bride is a selfish, somewhat bitchy, certainly self-centred young woman. But that isn't enough to tilt the scales. Therefore, knowing that we were going to cast somebody beautiful, wise, witty, charming, [who] could play high comedy, we did not expect to get a singer, because [it] would be asking too much, to get all that in one package. So when I wrote the score, I very carefully avoided writing songs for Desiree so we would not be stuck in the casting department by saying "Gee, that woman is perfect but she can't sing", or, "that woman can sing but it's no contest for the beautiful young bride." So I . . . wrote one number for her in the first act, which was quite quick and the kind of number that can be sung by a non-singer, called "The Glamorous Life", and also backed her up with an ensemble of five and two other people who also sang in the number. . . . In rehearsal we realized when we cast Glynis Johns that Glynis had a really nice voice . . . a small voice but . . . a really musical one. She is very musical. However, she cannot sustain notes for very long because she's not a trained singer. Hal [Prince] said to me that in the love scene in the second act he thought we ought to give, not just because it was Glynis, but because [of] the character Desiree, to keep her alive musically since we had so many who could sing, that she should have a song. Well, [for] the love scene I had already started a song for Frederick, the man, who could sing, because we'd planned on the singer for the part, and I thought the scene was his scene and the impulse to sing must be his impulse. And in fact that's what we'd worked out, Hugh [Wheeler] and I. Hal said, let me redirect this scene and you come down to rehearsal and let me show you how that can be Desiree's scene. So I went down and indeed that's exactly what he'd done. Somehow even when you read it on the page, though the thrust of the scene seems to be Frederick's, it turns out to be Desiree's. And so I went home fired up with that kind of enthusiasm and wrote, very quickly for me, this song, which took about two nights to write . . . I was able to write it quickly partly because I not only knew the character and the kind of mood of the piece but also the character as played by Glynis Johns, who was suddenly very vivid. It's much easier to write for a character as played by somebody than just for a character because you start to think of colours that you might not have thought of before. So my problem was that I had to find a song of regret and even anger that was a ballad, because I wanted it to be a romantic moment, and something that could be reprised at the end of the play when the two of them did get together, although in this scene they go apart. [Also,] it had to be something [in] which she wouldn't have to sustain notes. So that meant I had to find a short-breathed melody, and came up with these things, because even if you're a heavy smoker you can sing this song.

Fig. 34.1 Example A

Even this phrase, which a regular singer would take in one breath,

Fig. 34.2 Example B

could be sung as Glynis did

Fig. 34.3 Example C

and the whole tune has this built-in *rubato*. I set it up right in the first bar, with that last beat of the first bar, [the anacrusis bar] a little *ritard* so that I would always have the excuse to do it later –

> Isn't it rich, [breathe, breathe] are we a pair [breathe, breathe] me here at last on the ground, [breathe] you in mid air.

And that doesn't sound like an affectation, to take that breath, because we've already set up a tune that stops and starts, and stops and starts, so that throughout this lady could always get her breath. And the result was she sang it exquisitely. It's the definitive thing, although Barbra Streisand has just made a recording of it that's also pretty spectacular.

TH: I've heard it sung by singers in a nineteenth-century opera style.

SS: The problem with that is that it's not a long-line melody. Renata Scotto sang it at a recital right after the show came out and I was all excited – a song sung by a major opera star – [but] it was wrong. I don't want to say it was dreadful, it was just the wrong voice for the wrong song. She made it into her own kind of piece, which it is not, because it is not that kind of line, it's a line built in chunks.

TH: Were you surprised at how popular the song was?

SS: Very. . . . It's the only big hit song I've ever had and I must tell you it did not become popular immediately after the show opened. It happened curiously enough in England. England is what made it popular. Judy Collins did a record and it became a best-seller in England. As a result of that, Frank Sinatra heard it and he made a record of it and that was a best-seller in the United States. And once he and she had sung it and they both had hit records then it entered the repertoire. But if Judy Collins had not made it a number one song in England, I don't think it ever would have been popular.

TH: What do you think gives the song its mass appeal?

SS: Generally popular songs come about from the right concatenation of circumstances, the right artist singing the right song at the right time. Louis Armstrong doing "Hello, Dolly". I don't think "Hello, Dolly" would have been a big hit if it hadn't been sung by Louis Armstrong in that arrangement at that given time. I mean it might have, but one associates the song with him and then as a result of that it becomes . . . widespread and everybody sings it and then it becomes a song on its own. The same thing is true here. I mean I've written songs in other shows that I . . . thought would have been big hits, you know, pretty ballads well written and grateful to the singer and that sort of thing. But this one is the one that became a hit.

TH: Do you expect singers to develop parts in your shows to the extent that they take liberties with the music . . . slight rhythmic changes and so on . . . or do you expect your music, as Stravinsky put it, to be executed rather than interpreted?

SS: I'm fairly much of a stickler for their sticking exactly to what I've written. However, during rehearsals, and working with individual singers sometimes you happen fortuitously, and sometimes unfortuitously, on notions of *rubato*. I just say I want the singers to feel that they can express the character. But primarily it's the job of the writer to express it. And when I put in a *rubato* or a pause there's usually a reason for it. If it isn't a specific physical reason like breathing or tuning or something like that, there may be a dramatic reason, for making a *ritard* or not making it. And when singers violate that it quite often distorts the intention. Now sometimes it helps, and sometimes I say that's a very good idea, let us mark that in the score, let us make a *ritard* on that bar, I hadn't thought of that, or, let us take that *ritard* out. But the more I write the more finicky I get. I used to, up until the last few years, just write a note that would sustain itself in the melodic line until the next note came in instead of being very careful about maybe taking an eighth rest or quarter rest after the note, just to help the singer phrase apart from anything else. Even though they might be able to sustain the note but because sometimes a singer will literally see on the page

Fig. 34.4 Example D

and a good singer will hold the "you" and what I hear in my head is

Fig. 34.5 Example E

and instead of writing half a note what I've written is a whole note because it goes to the next bar instead of writing a half note and a half rest. And that isn't the matter of giving the singer a chance to breathe, it's a matter of [wanting] to have just that much emphasis, I don't want it three-quarters and I don't want it one quarter, I want it two quarters.

[In the past] I just thought, well the singer will do that, [but now] I'm learning to put these rests in to help the singer know how to phrase. As I looked at this just now, "Send in the Clowns", I suddenly realized this [the second beat] is a dotted quarter –

Fig. 34.6 Example F

and I should have written that as a quarter and an eighth instead of a dotted quarter. But any good singer would be singing

Fig. 34.7 Example G

and I might not want that, and I think what I want is the phrases to be slightly separated because the dramatic context is "me here at last on the ground; you in mid air" as opposed to "me here at last on the ground you in mid air" – that's not what I meant – and it's tiny little details like that that often spell the difference between tone and no tone.

TH: Quite recently your musical, *Sweeney Todd,* was staged by the New York City Opera. There is a slight ambiguity in my mind about the difference between an opera and a musical in the hands of Stephen Sondheim. Do you have a view of what the distinction is?

SS: Yes, I've a very dogmatic view of it. I think an opera is something performed in an opera house in front of an opera audience by opera singers. I think the same piece performed in a Broadway house, in a West End house, by West End or Broadway singers, in front of a Broadway or West End audience is a show, meaning it's a musical. The approach is different, the audience's expectations are the major difference between operas and musicals. When an audience enters an opera house they are going for a specific kind of experience that's much more related to a rock concert than it is to a musical. They are going to hear performers, which is what rock concerts are about – to hear *that* performer – they don't care if it's their fifth *Tosca* as long as it's the lady that they want to hear sing *Tosca.* They're going primarily to hear a great instrumentalist and they do not go to be engulfed by the story or the experience. In fact they will quite often welcome, as in most classic operas, moments of respite and exploration of just an actor, just a singer, going on about a tiny subject and making it a relevant one for three minutes providing she is singing like a dream. That's why they go. So they don't care about understanding the lyrics, which is why I think it is just as well to have opera in foreign languages. Putting them in the native language is a mistake because then you understand about every tenth word and it upsets you because you're trying to get the rest of the sentence. But if it's in a foreign language you don't bother. Philip Glass did an opera a couple of years ago – he wrote it a number of years ago, called *Satyagraha* [1980], which is in Sanskrit, and when I read about this I thought what a pretentious foolish notion – Sanskrit. Well first of all I was knocked out by the opera and I'm not knocked out by very many operas, but secondly I realized what a brilliant choice he and his librettist had made, because Sanskrit is almost all open vowel sounds. And not only do you not care about understanding the words but it's perfect for the projection of the human voice. Everything is "ah", all the sounds, it's like Italian, the perfect language to sing opera in, because it allows everything to come out [of the throat] and not worry about [the lips].

TH: Opera often loses a lot in translation because of the timbre of language – Tchaikovsky done in English, or Janáček.

SS: Yes, Janáček spent his whole life trying to imitate his native tongue. But there's more to it than that. I think national musical characteristics come from the rhythm of the language of the countries. German music sounds like German speech. Italian music sounds like Italian speech. It should. And therefore to translate an opera seems to me at best a fool's errand . . . Obviously there are exceptions where operas might translate well, but I wouldn't [do it] – I have been asked to translate opera occasionally. I just think it's foolishness and simply . . . oil and water. The sound of the French language dictates that kind of rhythmless French music whereas the English language is heavily rhythmed language and you put that to French music and it just – something doesn't work, no matter how well it's written.

TH: One way of distinguishing between opera and musicals is that both are defined not by their content but by the institutions and the tradition of the institutions that are associated with them. It's also interesting that, in the late twentieth century, as some opera, and perhaps art music generally, has become more distant from audiences, a lot of the most eagerly awaited contemporary music is done on Broadway and the West End.

SS: Yes, and part of that alienation of the opera audience – everybody talks about, "oh, they don't write melody anymore" – it's not that, they don't write show-off parts for the singers. They forget that the major reason that an opera audience is there is not for the so-called epic theatre experience of Wagner, the Wagnerian vision. Most opera audiences go to hear the singers and if contemporary opera were written, no matter how dissonant, with parts where the opera singers would have numbers the way they do in Verdi and Puccini, the opera would probably work very well. Audiences want their singers to have numbers. And one of the few operas that doesn't have numbers that seems to work generally pretty well with audiences, though nowhere near as well as the old warhorses, is *Pelléas and Mélisande* which is actually one long song. But it never satisfies an audience the way Puccini and Verdi do, and not because it isn't pretty. It's because nobody gets a chance to just take the stage and do a number and have the house come down. Audiences want that release of applauding. And that's part of the theatre experience.

TH: I was going to ask you whether there was a distinction between the audience for an opera, at the Met for instance, and an audience in *Sweeney*

Todd or *Sunday in the Park with George* on Broadway; and from what you say they may be the same people who will come with a different expectation.

ss: That's right. You see *Sweeney Todd* is really an operetta, it requires operetta voices, that is to say the needs for the singers are slightly greater than the needs on Broadway but nowhere as great as the needs in grand opera. It's what I would call an operetta. A number of audiences who came to City Opera to see . . . [*Sweeney Todd*] are used to coming to see both opera and operetta there. Some of them [may] have never been to a Broadway musical because they think it just isn't substantial enough for them or whatever. To their surprise they enjoyed *Sweeney Todd* because they got both things at once: they got a story they didn't know, some music that had some melodic outline that they could recognize, whether they liked it or not – it wasn't all dissonant, it wasn't twelve-tone – and moments where the singers just show off . . . you know Tim Nolan singing the *Epiphany* is a man with an operatic baritone [voice], singing a large chunk of material – and the audience was allowed to applaud and cheer and felt like it at the end of it, because they saw a performer . . . That's the important part of the opera experience . . . seeing the performer. Now that's also of course true on Broadway – one wants to see the performer perform, but it's the *primary* reason for the opera experience. . . .

   [. . .]

I used to say quite proudly, "They don't know they're in an opera." By an opera I meant a sung piece. They don't hear the jagged melodies, because they're so interested in the story, because [Chris] Bond's story is so gripping that it doesn't matter what they're singing, and the audience often didn't know when they were speaking and when they were singing because they were the same.

They were so gripped by the story that you could actually take a poll, I think, and say, "Did she just sing that line or did she speak it?" and you'd get mixed reactions. . . .

35

Writing lyrics

Oscar Hammerstein

Oscar Hammerstein, *Lyrics* (New York: Simon & Schuster, 1949), pp. 3–15, 21–7.

This item comprises extracts from the introduction to Hammerstein's collection of lyrics. He refers mainly to his shows *Oklahoma* (1943), *South Pacific* (1949) and *Carousel* (1945).

Almost every layman I have ever met exhibits a real curiosity about songs and how they are written. It is a standing joke among authors and composers that when they meet people the first question asked of them is, "Which comes first, the words or the music?" Perhaps it is high time that one of us stopped laughing at the classic query and provided a sensible answer to it. There is nothing foolish about the question. A song is a wedding of two crafts, and it is a natural thing to wonder how they meet and live together. Feeling safe on the ground of an interest so frequently expressed, I will start these notes with this subject.

There is, as a matter of fact, no invariable or inevitable method for writing songs. Sometimes the words are written first, sometimes the music. Sometimes two or more collaborators lock themselves in a room and write words and music at the same time. The kind of songs, the individuals involved and the conditions under which they work dictate the process. Grand opera scores are almost always set to texts already written by the librettists. In the case of the most famous of all comic opera collaborations, it was the librettist, Gilbert, who wrote the words first. He would sometimes mail an entire act to Sullivan, who would then set music to his verses. On the other hand, the lyrics for most of the popular songs and musical comedies in our country today are written after the music. Up until my first collaboration with Richard Rodgers in 1943, I had always written this way. For twenty-five years, collaborating with Jerome Kern, Herbert Stothart, Sigmund Romberg, Rudolf Friml and Vincent Youmans, I set words to their music. It would seem to most people – and I am one of them – that writing the words first would be a more logical procedure, music being the more flexible and less specific of the two mediums. Why then did I write in this upside-down manner for so long a time? And why do most other writers in our country today continue to write in this way?

In the first decade of [the twentieth] century there were two factors which led songwriters into the custom of writing words to music. The best musical plays of that time were being created in Vienna. When they were imported, American librettists had to write translations and adaptations for melodies that had been set to another language. In those days we imported not only plays from Middle Europe. Many of the composers themselves came over here, settled down and became American citizens. They embraced our democratic philosophy, but they found it much more difficult to get used to our language. Lyric writers who submitted verses to be set were horrified by the abortive accents written to their words, and they soon found it less trying on their nerves to let the foreign musician have his say first and then write a lyric to fit his melody.

The second influence was not foreign at all. It was distinctly an American one – the broken rhythm. First came ragtime, then jazz. For the purpose of creating these eccentric deviations from orthodox meters, it was better to let the composer have his head. Concomitant with these new rhythms came what we called, in 1911, "the dance craze." Dancing, once confined to ballrooms and performed mainly by the young, became a new international sport indulged in by all people of all ages in all kinds of restaurants and at all meal times, lunch, tea, dinner and supper. The hit melodies of that time had to be good dance melodies. This being the most important consideration, it was better for the lyric writer to trail along after the composer and fit his words to a refrain written mainly to be danced to. Many lyrics of the period were about dancing. Irving Berlin wrote "Everybody's Doing It." (Doing what? The turkey trot!) People were also, in other songs, doing the bunny hug and the grizzly bear. Not satisfied with writing lyrics describing dances already established by leading teachers and famous dancing teams, lyric writers set to work creating dances, giving them names, and hoping that the public would follow them. (This tendency persisted and went into the twenties, when numbers like "Bambalina" and "The Varsity Drag" were urged upon the public by songwriters. It continued into the sound movies of the thirties. "The Carioca" and "The Continental" were names given by lyric writers to dances, and Fred Astaire and Ginger Rogers illustrated them for us. We have been told also what a treat it is to beat our feet on the Mississippi mud, and not long ago "The Jersey Bounce" was recommended to us as a constant exercise. Even as I write these notes we are being warned on the radio that if we don't do "The Hucklebuck" we will be out of luck.)

I have conducted no exhaustive investigation of this subject, but these developments, as I remember them, seem to have been the chief influences which established the American songwriter's habit of writing the music first and the words later. It is a strange habit, an illogical one, but not entirely without compensating virtues. Writing in this way, I have frequently fallen into the debt of my composers for words and ideas that might never have occurred to me had they not been suggested by music. If one has a feeling for music – and anyone who wants to write lyrics had better have this feeling – the repeated playing of a melody may create a mood or start a train of thought that results in an unusual lyric. Words written in this way are likely to conform to the spirit of the music. It is difficult to fit words into the rigid framework of a composer's meter, but this very confinement might also force an author into the concise eloquence which is the very essence of poetry. There is in all art a fine balance between the benefits of confinement and the benefits of freedom. An artist who is too fond of freedom is likely to be obscure in his expression. One who is too much a slave to form is likely to cripple his substance. Both extremes should be avoided, and no invariable laws or methods should be obeyed. In our collaboration Mr. Rodgers and I have no definite policy except one of complete flexibility. We write songs in whatever way seems best for the subject with which we are dealing, and the purposes of the song in the story which we are telling. Most often I write the words first, and yet in nearly all of our scores there are at least one or two songs in which he wrote the music first. When we first started to write together in 1943, we had no conversations on method. The first song we wrote was "Oh, What a Beautiful Mornin'!" and the words were written first. I would like to tell you how this happened, because it furnishes a typical illustration of composer-author collaboration in the structure of a musical play.

Attacking the job of turning Lynn Riggs' *Green Grow the Lilacs* into what eventually became *Oklahoma!*, the first serious problem that faced us involved a conflict of dramaturgy with showmanship. As we planned our version, the story we had to tell in the first part of the first act did not call for the use of a female ensemble. The traditions of musical comedy, however, demand that not too long after the rise of the curtain the audience should be treated to one of musical comedy's most attractive assets – the sight of pretty girls in pretty clothes moving about the stage, the sound of their vital young voices supporting the principals in their songs. Dick and I, for several days, sought ways and means of logically introducing a group of girls into the early action of the play. The boys were no problem.

Here was a farm in Oklahoma with ranches nearby. Farmers and cowboys belonged there, but girls in groups? No. Strawberry festivals? Quilting parties? Corny devices! After trying everything we could think of, and rejecting each other's ideas as fast as they were submitted, after passing through phases during which we would stare silently at each other unable to think of anything at all, we came finally to an extraordinary decision. We agreed to start our story in the real and natural way in which it seemed to want to be told! This decision meant that the first act would be half over before a female chorus would make its entrance. We realized that such a course was experimental, amounting almost to the breach of an implied contract with a musical comedy audience. I cannot say truthfully that we were worried by the risk. Once we had made the decision, everything seemed to work right and we had that inner confidence people feel when they have adopted the direct and honest approach to a problem.

Now, having met our difficulty by simply refusing to recognize its existence, we were ready to go ahead with the actual writing. We had agreed that we should start the play outside a farmhouse. The only character on the stage would be a middle-aged woman sitting at a butter churn. The voice of Curly, a cowboy, would be heard off-stage, singing. Searching for a subject for Curly to sing about, I recalled how deeply I had been impressed by Lynn Riggs' description at the start of his play.

> "It is a radiant summer morning several years ago, the kind of morning which, enveloping the shapes of earth – men, cattle in the meadow, blades of the young corn, streams – makes them seem to exist now for the first time, their images giving off a visible golden emanation that is partly true and partly a trick of imagination, focusing to keep alive a loveliness that may pass away."

On first reading these words, I had thought what a pity it was to waste them on stage directions. Only readers could enjoy them. An audience would never hear them. Yet, if they did, how quickly they would slip into the mood of the story. Remembering this reaction, I reread the description and determined to put it into song. "Oh, What a Beautiful Mornin'!" opens the play and creates an atmosphere of relaxation and peace and tenderness. It introduces the light-hearted young man who is the center of the story. My indebtedness to Mr. Riggs' description is obvious. The cattle and the corn and the golden haze on the meadow are all there. I added some observations of my own based on my experience with beautiful mornings, and I brought the words down to the more primitive poetic level of Curly's character. He is, after all, just a cowboy and not a playwright.

"The corn is as high as a elephant's eye" – I first wrote "cow pony's eye." Then I walked over to my neighbor's cornfield and found that although it was only the end of August, the corn had grown much higher than that. "Cow pony" was more indigenous to the western background, but I had reservations about it even before I gauged the height of the corn. It reads better than it sounds. Sing "cow pony" to yourself and try to imagine hearing it for the first time in a song. It would be hard for the ear to catch.

"All the cattle are standin' like statues." This picture had come into my brain several years before I wrote the song, and it had stayed there quietly waiting to be used. When I came to the second verse of "Oh, What a Beautiful Mornin'!" I remembered it. I remembered sitting on a porch in Pennsylvania one summer's day, watching a herd of cows standing on a hillside about half a mile away. It was very hot and there was no motion in the world. I suddenly found myself doing what I had never done before and have never done since. I was thinking up lines for a poem to describe what I saw. It was not to be used in a play, not to be set to music. I got this far with it:

> "The breeze steps aside
> To let the day pass.
> The cows on the hill
> Are as still as the grass."

I never wrote the lines on paper, nor did I ever do any work to polish them, nor did I extend the poem any further. Perhaps I was called to the phone, or perhaps I was infected with the laziness of an inactive landscape. But those cows on the hill "as still as the grass" were crystallized in my memory by the words I had quite idly and casually composed, and up they came several years later to inspire me when I needed them.

Inspire me? Do authors write from inspiration? This is another bromidic question asked so frequently that I think it deserves a brief parenthesis at this point in my discussion of songs.

Any professional author will scoff at the implication that he spends his time hoping and waiting for a magic spark to start him off. There are few accidents of this kind in writing. A sudden beam of moonlight, or a thrush you have just heard, or a girl you have just kissed, or a beautiful view through your study window is seldom the source of an urge to put words on paper. Such pleasant experiences are likely to obstruct and delay a writer's work.

The legend of inspiration is, however, not a completely silly one. If we broaden the base of the word and let it include the stored-up memories of the writer's emotional reactions, then inspiration figures very largely in what he puts down on paper. I suppose that every worth-while work is inspired by what has been seen or thought or felt by the writer at another time. Most bad fictional writing is the result of ignoring one's own experiences and contriving spurious emotions for spurious characters.

A term like "inspiration" annoys a professional author because it implies, in its common conception, that ideas and words are born in his brain as gifts from heaven and without effort. All who write know that writing is very, very hard work. Most of us do some work every day. Some get up early in the morning, as I do, and go straight to their studies as other men go to their business offices. Some writers prefer working at night and work very late, but all of us are trying to write something nearly all the time. Nobody waits to be inspired. Some days the work comes easier than other days, but you keep going because the chances of getting good ideas are more likely while you are trying to get them than when you are doing nothing at all.

To extend this already long "parenthesis" on inspiration, I submit another interesting illustration. About six years ago I attended the premiere of a musical play called *One Touch of Venus*, starring Mary Martin. In this play Mary portrayed the role of a kind of dream goddess, statuesque, romantic and very lovely indeed. In the last scene, however, she came on the stage transformed into the ideal desired by her lover. She wore a simple gingham dress. I turned to my wife and said, "There is a part she should play some day. She has been wonderful as 'Venus,' but here is the real Mary Martin, a little corn-fed girl from Texas." Today she is playing that part – a corn-fed girl from Arkansas named Nellie Forbush, invented by James Michener in his *Tales of the South Pacific*. When I started to write "I'm in Love With a Wonderful Guy," the picture of Mary in the gingham dress, entering in the last scene of *One Touch of Venus* six years ago, came into my mind and the first line of the refrain, "I'm as corny as Kansas in August," is a result of that memory. I could have said "as corny as Texas," where Mary came from, or I could have said "as corny as Arkansas," where the character Nellie Forbush came from but for the purposes of singing, "as corny as Kansas" is a much better line because of the two "k" sounds and the alliteration created thereby, and because Kansas is a state more naturally associated with corn than the other two. End of parenthesis!

If you can remember that far back, I was discussing why and how songs are put into musical plays. Let us take a case where the music was written first. The refrain of "People Will Say We're in Love" was a melody written by Richard Rodgers with the thought that it might serve well as a duet for the two lovers in *Oklahoma!* This procedure is the more usual approach to writing musical comedy scores. The composer dreams up some melodies which suggest certain treatments. One might seem to him to be the love duet of the piece, the other a good comedy song or a good tune to dance to. Almost all composers have a reservoir of melodies which come to them at different times and which they write down in what they call a sketch-book. When they start work on a new musical play, they play over these previously written melodies for their collaborator, and it is decided which ones can be used in this particular score. They then write additional melodies as required. Dick Rodgers, however, does not work in this way. He writes music only for a specific purpose. Ideas for tunes seldom come to him while he is walking down the street or riding in taxicabs, and he doesn't rush to his piano very often to write a tune just for the sake of writing a tune. I don't believe that either Dick or I would be very successful essentially as popular songwriters – writers of songs detached from plays. We can write words and music best when they are required by a situation or a characterization in a story.

The problem of a duet for the lovers in *Oklahoma!* seemed insurmountable. While it is obvious almost from the rise of the curtain that Curly and Laurey are in love with each other, there is also a violent antagonism between them, caused mainly by Laurey's youthful shyness, which she disguises by pretending not to care for Curly. This does not go down very well with him, and he fights back. Since this mood was to dominate their scenes down into the second act, it seemed impossible for us to write a song that said "I love you," and remain consistent with the attitude they had adopted toward each other. After talking this over for a long time, Dick and I hit upon the idea of having the lovers warn each other against any show of tenderness lest other people think they were in love. Of course, while they say all those things, they are obliquely confessing their mutual affection. Hence the title, "People Will Say We're in Love."

In all I have been saying, it will be noted that the composer and author work in very close collaboration during the planning of a song and the story that contains the song. This is an important point. It must be understood that the musician is just as much an author as the man who writes the words. He expresses the story in his medium just as the librettist expresses the story in his. Or, more accurately, they weld their two crafts and two kinds of talent into a single expression. This is the great secret of the well-integrated musical play. It is not so much a method as a state of mind, or rather a state for two minds, an attitude of unity. Musical plays, then, are not "books" written by an author with songs later inserted by a composer and a lyric writer. They are often written this way, but it is not a good way to write them and such plays seldom have a very long life. They are sure to lack form, and they cannot sustain a story interest when it is interrupted continually by songs that are of little value to the plot.

[. . .]

If one has fundamental things to say in a song, the rhyming becomes a question of deft balancing. A rhyme should be unassertive, never standing out too noticeably. It should, on the other hand, not be a rhyme heard in a hundred other popular songs of the time, so familiar that the listener can anticipate it before it is sung. There should not be too many rhymes. In fact, a rhyme should appear only where it is absolutely demanded to keep the pattern of the music. If a listener is made rhyme-conscious, his interest may be diverted from the story of the song. If, on the other hand, you keep him waiting for a rhyme, he is more likely to listen to the meaning of the words. A good illustration is "Ol' Man River." Consider the first part of the refrain:

> "Ol' Man River,
> Dat Ol' Man River,
> He mus' know sumpin'
> But don' say nuthin',
> He jes' keeps rollin',
> He keeps on rollin' along.
> He don' plant 'taters,
> He don' plant cotton,
> An' dem dat plants 'em
> Is soon forgotten."

"Cotton" and "forgotten" are the first two words that rhyme. Other words are repeated for the sake of musical continuity and design. The same idea could be set to this music with many more rhymes. "River," instead of being repeated in the second line, could have had a rhyme – "shiver," "quiver," etc. The next two lines could have rhymed with the first two, the "iver" sounds continuing, or they could have had two new words rhyming with each other. I do not believe that in this way I could have commanded the same attention and respect from a listener, nor would a singer be so likely to concentrate on the meaning of the words. There are, of course, compensations for lack of rhyme. I've already mentioned repetition. There is also the trick of matching up words. "He mus' know sumpin' but don' say nuthin'." "Sumpin'" and "nuthin'" do not rhyme, but the two words are related. "He don' plant 'taters, He don' plant cotton." These two lines also match and complement each other to make up for the lack of a rhyme. Here is a song sung by a character who is a rugged and untutored philosopher. It is a song of resignation with a protest implied. Brilliant and frequent rhyming would diminish its importance.

Take, as a contrast, the refrain of "I'm in Love With a Wonderful Guy" from *South Pacific*. You will find in it interior rhymes, undemanded rhymes and light-hearted similes. The emotion expressed in this song is so simple that it can afford to wear the decorations and embroidery of more ingenious rhyming. There is no subtle philosophy involved. A girl is in love and her heart is sailing. She is sentimental and exuberant and triumphant in the discovery. The job of the lyric is to capture her spirit. I think it does. I am very fond of this song.

After rhyming, I would place next in importance a study and appreciation of phonetics. Some words and groups of words that look beautiful in printed poetry are unavailable to one who is writing lyrics to be sung to music. There is an inexorable mathematics in music – so many measures in a refrain, so many beats in a measure, and they cannot be ignored. There is rhythm and tempo, and its continuity must be unbroken. The concessions with which a melody can favor words are limited. The larynxes of singers are limited. They must be given a chance to breathe after a certain number of words have been sung, and if they are building up to a high note at the finish, they must be given a good deep breath before they attack it. Both the lyric writer and the composer must worry about all these things. If a song is not singable, it is no song at all.

The job of the poet is to find the right word in the right place, the word with the exact meaning and the highest quality of beauty or power. The lyric writer must find this word too, but it must be also a word that is clear when sung and not too difficult for the singer to sing on that note which he hits when he sings it. Wherever there are vocal climaxes and high notes, singers are comfortable only with vowels of an open sound. A word like "sweet," for instance, would be a very bad word on which to sing a high note. The "e" sound closes the larynx and the singer cannot let go with his full voice. Furthermore, the "t" ending the word is a hard consonant which would cut the singer off and thwart his and the composer's desire to sustain the note. Now and then, when a lyric writer finds a word to which he is very attached, he tries to side-track these rules. He may say, "I don't care how many 's's' there are in this line, this is what I want to say and the singer will just have to slow up and sing very distinctly"; or he may say, "I don't care if that word does end with a hard consonant [like the 't' in 'sweet'], that is the only word I can use there and the singer will have to make the best of it." This kind of temperamental defiance is self-defeating because no word, however fine and lofty and exact its meaning may be, is a good word in a song if it is difficult to sing.

Dick Rodgers and I wrote a song, "What's the Use of Wond'rin'?" for *Carousel*. A great many people admired it and many of them have asked me why it was not more popular. Within the framework of the play it performed a dramatic service, but it was not sung a great deal on the radio, nor did it sell many copies or many phonograph records, and these factors are the modern measure of a song's popularity. I believe "What's the Use of Wond'rin'?" was severely handicapped because of the final word, "talk." The trouble with this word is the hard "k" sound at the end of it. The last two lines of the refrain are, "You're his girl and he's your feller, And all the rest is talk." This is exactly what I wanted the character to say. She is not a very well-educated girl, nor is she a subtle philosopher. Discussing the unpredictable, fascinating and sometimes brutal man with whom she is in love, she says in the song: What's the use of wond'rin' if the man you love is good or bad, or whether you like the way he wears his hat, or whether you ought to leave him or not, he's just the way he is and he can't be any different, and he has certain things given him by fate, and one of those things is you, and so whenever he wants you, you will go to him. After all, "you're his girl and he's your feller and all the rest is talk." I realized that I was defying convention in ending with the word "talk," but I had a perverse desire to try it anyway. Now, every once in a while you should try to break rules, to test them and see if, indeed, they are breakable. Sometimes you succeed and this is the way the most exciting things in the theater are done. Sometimes you fail. This time a good and sound rule slapped me down. I will not break it again. I believe that this song might have been very successful outside of the play had I finished it on an open vowel instead of a hard consonant. Suppose, for instance, the last line had been: "You're his girl and he's your feller – that's all you need to know." The singer could have hit the "o" vowel and held it as long as she wanted to, eventually pulling applause on it. (There is nothing wrong with pulling applause. No matter how much an audience enjoys a song, it likes to be cued into applause. It likes to be given a punctuation which says, "There, now it's over and we've given you our all, and now is exactly the right time for you to show your appreciation.")

One of the best examples of good singing endings in this book [of my lyrics] is the last line of "All the Things You Are": "When all the things you are, are mine." The singer opens his mouth wide to sing the word "are," and it is still open and he can give still more when he sings the second "are" right after it. It is true that the very last word ends in a consonant, but it is a soft consonant. Furthermore, the two notes that are hit by the repetition of the word "are" constitute the climax of the line, and the word "mine" becomes a sort of denouement.

All these last lines are good for singing: "Oh, what a beautiful day," "You'll never walk alone," "Once you have found her, never let her go," "Ol' Man River, he jes' keeps rollin' along," "Bali Ha'i, Bali Ha'i, Bali Ha'i." Try these out yourself, when you are taking your shower, and see how easily and effortlessly they roll out and up to the bathroom ceiling. In all cases you will find open vowels used and no hard consonants on high notes. The rule is not, of course, invariable and you will find freak endings, falsetto endings and dramatic endings, wherein the composer and the singer humor the line so that it can be sung without recourse to a conventional vocal climax. The last line, "The surrey with the fringe on the top" is a case in point. "Fringe" would seem an unpromising singing word, but somehow it sings very well. There is a softness to the "g" sound and although the vowel, a short "i," is a closed one, the singer usually takes it falsetto. In this case, it would be wrong for the composer to have written a dramatically vocal finish to a song so naïve and charming. The success of this unconventional musical and lyrical finish explains our temerity in breaking the rule in the case of "What's the Use of Wond'rin'?" but there we failed and with the other song we succeeded.

36

Afternoon Raag

Amit Chaudhuri

Amit Chaudhuri, *Afternoon Raag* (London: Minerva, 1993),
pp. 27–31, 47–9.

Amit Chaudhuri's autobiographical novel *Afternoon Raag* uses Indian
music extensively as metaphor, but nonetheless does not rely heavily
on technical terminology. Terms used here include *tanpura* (the name
of a plucked lute used to accompany vocal music), *shadja* and *nikhad*
(the first and seventh notes of the scale, respectively), *taan* (a kind of
rapid melodic figure), *sama* (the first beat of the rhythmic cycle) and
meend (a glide or portamento).

Sohanlal comes in the mornings. He is married to my music-teacher's
sister. Though he is quite short, he wears bright kurtas that come down
below his knees. He demands the tablas from Ponchoo, strutting around
the hall like a rooster in his early morning plumage. Then he tunes the
smaller tabla with a hammer, and the bigger one on the left he booms with
his fingertips. When he plays as my mother sings, his hands, which are old
now, produce a pitter-patter noise. After twenty minutes, he takes a break,
smoking a beedi on the veranda; and then, before he is finished, throws it
away and coughs a dramatic smoker's cough. He likes doing things;
returning, he takes out his handkerchief and dusts the harmonium, wiping
the smooth, rectangular top. It is a harmonium made in Calcutta by
Pakrashi, and he takes care to probe, his forefinger shrouded with the
handkerchief, each English letter of PAKRASHI carved largely on the
wood, blowing sensuously on the angular K and tracing the curves of the
P and the R till he is satisfied. Then he polishes the black and white keys,
and opens the cover; inside, the two rows of innumerable reeds lie bone-
white, each reed a delicate white splinter, with a pinhead on one end and
a flat metal strip on the belly. Sohanlal blows quietly upon them, as if they
were on fire; how silent music is as it rests in these reeds, white paper-thin
wands! He replaces the cover, because it is almost unpleasant to watch,

the inner nakedness of a harmonium. Eagerly, he moves about again, his spacious pyjamas billowing around him. As he prepares to sit, they open at the bottom like alligator-mouths that have swallowed up his legs. After an hour, he glances at his wristwatch and collects his money politely and hurries out of the front door. Then next morning he is reincarnated in his fantastic kurta and pyjamas as if from a magic lamp.

It was on an afternoon in August I bought my first tanpura. We were visiting Calcutta then, and my music-teacher, my guru, had come with us and was living in our house; he was going to sing at a 'conference'. He would practise in the mornings, and take time off to vanish to the Kali temple, returning with a tilak, a great vermilion stain on his forehead, telling my mother 'Didi, I went to see Ma Kali!' On some mornings we would sing raag Bhairav together, our two voices and styles mingling closely and floating over the other sounds of the house – pigeons, and the distracted noise of servants – his voice sometimes carrying my hesitant voice, and negotiating the pathways of the raag, as a boat carries a bewildered passenger. In the moments of simple imbibing, I would forget my voice was my own and become an echo of his style and artistry. The greater part of the unfolding of a raag consists of a slow, evasive introduction in which the notes are related to each other by curving glissandoes, or meends. The straight, angular notes of Western music, composed and then rendered, are like print upon a page; in contrast, the curving meends of the raag are like longhand writing drawn upon the air. Each singer has his own impermanent longhand with its own arching, idiosyncratic beauties, its own repetitive, serpentine letters. With the end of the recital, this longhand, which, in its unravelling, is a matter of constant erasures and rewritings, is erased completely, unlike the notes of Western music, which remain printed upon the page.

That afternoon, we took the car to Rashbehari Avenue. My guru was dressed as usual in a loose white kurta and pyjamas. It must have been six or seven years before his death, and he must have just turned forty. He was humming a complicated tune with tiny embellishments when he was not talking to me, and the oil he had put in his hair before he combed it smelled sweet. We walked to the shop, no bigger than a room, called Hemen and Co. Outside, the pavement was broken, its edges blue-grey with ash from charcoal stoves; mosquitoes hung in the air. Ascending the three steps, we saw unfinished tanpuras and sitars, long patient necks and the comical but gracefully distended round urns; some instruments hung upside down from the ceiling like bats; and a man was planing a piece of wood. My tanpura was ready with its four new strings; I remember the tentative shyness with which I touched it.

Later, we sat on the floor in my room, and my guru taught me to tune the instrument. The tanpura can be held vertically on the lap or next to the upraised knee as it is played, when it looks male and perpendicular, or laid horizontally on the ground before one, when, with the surrendering slope of its long neck and the stable fullness of its urn, its mixture of acqui-escence and poise, it looks feminine. The four strings provide only two notes as a background to the song; *sa*, or *shadja*, the first, the mother-note, from which all other notes come, with which one's relationship is perma-nent and unambiguous, and the second note, depending on the raag, the father-note, circumstantial but constructive. To tune the tanpura, you must turn the keys on its upper end, keys which are huge, ornate, and antique, like the doorknobs of a palace. On the nether end, upon the urn, there is a flat bridge on which the strings rest briefly, before they pass through small ivory-coloured beads that are used for the finer adjustments in tuning, and travel at last to a small plank of wood at the end, where, pierced through four open but infinitesimal eyes, they are knotted. While this painful business, this struggle, of tuning continues, four white threads are slipped beneath the strings as they lie on the bridge, and moved up and down till a point is discovered where each string loses its flat metallic note, and buzzes, a hum like that of the wandering drone, or electricity. This buzzing of the strings, this resonance, the musicians call *juwari*. That after-noon, my guru and I, like patient surgeons, tuned the tanpura till the room filled with notes *shadja* and *nikhad*.

When one remembers a scene from the past in which one is with a loved one who is now dead, it is not like a memory at all, but like a dream one is having before his death, a premonition. In this dream which precedes death, the person is tranquil and happy, and yet, without reason, you know he is to die. When we recall the dead, the past becomes a dream we are dreaming foretelling death, though in our waking moments we cannot properly interpret it or give it significance. My memory of the day I bought the tanpura with my guru is like such a dream.

In the afternoon, Mohan, my music-teacher's brother, and Sohanlal, his brother-in-law, ring the doorbell. Ponchoo then silently brings out the tablas and tuning-hammer from the cupboard, and the big tabla, shaped like half a globe, he balances between one arm and his chin maternally; the smaller one he clutches lightly but firmly by the strong cords of bark along its sides. Mohan and Sohanlal take a long time settling down, talking in their own language, the latter chattering very fast, while Mohan, a man of few words, sits carefully on the sofa. It is easy to see that Mohan is related to my music-teacher, that he is his brother, because their faces are similar, especially the colour of their skin, Mohan perhaps even a little darker than my music-teacher was. The timbre of Mohan's voice is also like my guru's, slightly husky, not loud or deep. Though he may not be aware of it, it is impossible for others not to see my guru come to life, in flashes, in Mohan's facial expressions, his turns of phrase, and his gestures. But Mohan is an unassuming man, while my guru, shorter and a little plump, was a showoff, doing astonishing feats with his voice and then chuckling gleefully at our admiration. Laughter is drawn out reluctantly from Mohan, who I think used to both hero-worship and self-effacingly humour his brother (he told me once he had turned to tabla-playing because there couldn't be two singers in a family, and that, when they were both learning the intricacies of vocal music from their father, he found his elder brother much too quick, much too clever to compete with), while my guru, especially when singing, would laugh happily after a difficult taan, and shake with mirth when he arrived at, after much deliberately drunken meandering, the sama, bringing a small, reluctant smile to his younger brother's lips. On tapes on which I recorded my guru singing in my house, complex melodic leaps and falls performed by him can be heard punctuated by brief chuckles.

When a singer performs, it is the job of the accompanists to support him dutifully and unobtrusively. A cyclical rhythm-pattern – say, of sixteen beats – is played at an unchanging tempo on the tabla, and the song and its syllables are set to this pattern, so that one privileged word in the poem will coincide ineluctably with the first of the sixteen beats in the cycle. This first beat is called the sama, and much drama, apprehension, and triumph surround it. For the singer is allowed to, even expected to, adventurously embark on rhythmic voyages of his own, only to arrive, with sudden, instinctive, and logical grace, once more at the sama, taking the audience, who are keeping time, unawares. Once this is achieved, the logic seems at first a flash of genius, and then cunningly pre-meditated. While the pretence is kept up, and the singer's rhythm appears to have lost itself, the tabla-player, with emotionless sobriety, maintains the stern tempo and cycle, until the singer, like an irresponsible but prodigious child, decides to dance in perfect steps back into it. Similarly, when a singer is executing his difficult melodic patterns, the harmonium-player must reproduce the notes without distracting him. The tabla and harmonium players behave like palanquin-bearers carrying a precious burden, or like solemn but indulgent guardians who walk a little distance behind a precocious child as it does astonishing things, seeing, with a corner of their eye, that it does not get hurt, or like deferential ministers clearing a path for their picturesque prince, or like anonymous and selfless spouses who give of themselves for the sake of a husband. Mohan, who plays the tabla with clarity and restraint, created the ground on which my guru constructed his music, and Sohanlal, attentively playing the harmonium, filled in the background. In the care of these two custodians, my guru sang and shone with his true worth.

37

The Vinteuil Sonata

Marcel Proust

Marcel Proust, *In Search of Lost Time. Volume 1: Swann's Way*,
trans. C. K. Scott Moncrieff and Terence Kilmartin, revised by
D. J. Enright (London: Vintage, 2002), pp. 245–63.

Swann's Way forms the first volume of Proust's eight-volume master-piece, *In Search of Lost Time*. Music and painting both play important roles in the descriptions of the relationship between Charles Swann and Odette. Proust's descriptions of Swann's changing experiences of music, particularly of the fictional Vinteuil Sonata – which becomes a symbol of his love for Odette – are fascinating both for their evocations of the French bourgeois salon (much of the action takes place in those of the Verdurins and the Saint-Euvertes), and for the author's insights into musical experience. Pieter de Hooch (1629–84) is a real painter; Biche a fictional one.

Mme Verdurin was seated on a high Swedish chair of waxed pinewood, which a violinist from that country had given her, and which she kept in her drawing-room although in appearance it suggested a work-stand and clashed with the really good antique furniture which she had besides; but she made a point of keeping on view the presents which her "faithful" were in the habit of making her from time to time, so that the donors might have the pleasure of seeing them there when they came to the house. She tried to persuade them to confine their tributes to flowers and sweets, which had at least the merit of mortality; but she never succeeded, and the house was gradually filled with a collection of foot-warmers, cushions, clocks, screens, barometers and vases, a constant repetition and a boundless incongruity of useless but indestructible objects.

From this lofty perch she would take a spirited part in the conversation of the "faithful," and would revel in all their "drollery"; but, since the accident to her jaw, she had abandoned the effort involved in whole-hearted laughter, and had substituted a kind of symbolical dumb-show which signified, without endangering or fatiguing her in any way, that she was "splitting her sides." At the least witticism aimed by a member of the circle against a bore or against a former member who was now relegated to the limbo of bores – and to the utter despair of M. Verdurin, who had always made out that he was just as affable as his wife, but who, since his laughter was the "real thing," was out of breath in a moment and so was overtaken and vanquished by her device of a feigned but continuous hilarity – she would utter a shrill cry, shut tight her little bird-like eyes, which were beginning to be clouded over by a cataract, and quickly, as though she had only just time to avoid some indecent sight or to parry a mortal blow, burying her face in her hands, which completely engulfed it and hid it from view; would appear to be struggling to suppress, to annihilate, a laugh which, had she succumbed to it, must inevitably have left her inanimate. So, stupefied with the gaiety of the "faithful," drunk with goodfellowship, scandal and asseveration, Mme Verdurin, perched on her high seat like a cage-bird whose biscuit has been steeped in mulled wine, would sit aloft and sob with affability.

Meanwhile M. Verdurin, after first asking Swann's permission to light his pipe ("No ceremony here, you understand; we're all pals!"), went and asked the young musician to sit down at the piano.

"Leave him alone; don't bother him; he hasn't come here to be tormented," cried Mme Verdurin. "I won't have him tormented."

"But why on earth should it bother him?" rejoined M. Verdurin. "I'm sure M. Swann has never heard the sonata in F sharp which we discovered. He's going to play us the pianoforte arrangement."

"No, no, no, not my sonata!" she screamed, "I don't want to be made to cry until I get a cold in the head, and neuralgia all down my face, like last time. Thanks very much, I don't intend to repeat that performance. You're all so very kind and considerate, it's easy to see that none of you will have to stay in bed for a week."

This little scene, which was re-enacted as often as the young pianist sat down to play, never failed to delight her friends as much as if they were witnessing it for the first time, as a proof of the seductive originality of the "Mistress" and of the acute sensitiveness of her musical ear. Those nearest to her would attract the attention of the rest, who were smoking or playing cards at the other end of the room, by their cries of "Hear, hear!" which, as in Parliamentary debates, showed that something worth listening to was being said. And next day they would commiserate with those who had been prevented from coming that evening, assuring them that the scene had been even more amusing than usual.

"Well, all right, then," said M. Verdurin, "he can play just the andante."

"Just the andante! That really is a bit rich!" cried his wife. "As if it weren't precisely the andante that breaks every bone in my body. The Master is really too priceless! Just as though, in the Ninth, he said 'we'll just hear the finale,' or 'just the overture' of the *Mastersingers*."

The doctor, however, urged Mme Verdurin to let the pianist play, not because he supposed her to be feigning when she spoke of the distressing effects that music always had upon her – for he recognised certain neur-asthenic symptoms therein – but from the habit, common to many doctors, of at once relaxing the strict letter of a prescription as soon as it jeopardises something they regard as more important, such as the success of a social gathering at which they are present, and of which the patient whom they urge for once to forget his dyspepsia or his flu is one of the essential ingredients.

"You won't be ill this time, you'll find," he told her, seeking at the same time to influence her with a hypnotic stare. "And if you are ill, we'll look after you."

"Will you really?" Mme Verdurin spoke as though, with so great a favour in store for her, there was nothing for it but to capitulate. Perhaps, too, by dint of saying that she was going to be ill, she had worked herself into a state in which she occasionally forgot that it was all a fabrication and adopted the attitude of a genuine invalid. And it may often be remarked that invalids, weary of having to make the infrequency of their attacks depend on their own prudence, like to persuade themselves that they can do everything that they enjoy, and that does them harm, with impunity, provided that they place themselves in the hands of a higher authority who, without putting them to the least inconvenience, can and will, by uttering a word or by administering a pill, set them once again on their feet.

Odette had gone to sit on a tapestry-covered settee near the piano, saying to Mme Verdurin, "I have my own little corner, haven't I?"

And Mme Verdurin, seeing Swann by himself on a chair, made him get up: "You're not at all comfortable there. Go along and sit by Odette. You can make room for M. Swann there, can't you, Odette?"

"What charming Beauvais!" said Swann politely, stopping to admire the settee before he sat down on it.

"Ah! I'm glad you appreciate my settee," replied Mme Verdurin, "and I warn you that if you expect ever to see another like it you may as well abandon the idea at once. They've never made anything else like it. And these little chairs, too, are perfect marvels. You can look at them in a moment. The emblems in each of the bronze mouldings correspond to the subject of the tapestry on the chair; you know, you'll have a great deal to enjoy if you want to look at them – I can promise you a delightful time, I assure you. Just look at the little friezes round the edges; here, look, the little vine on a red background in this one, the Bear and the Grapes. Isn't it well drawn? What do you say? I think they knew a thing or two about drawing! Doesn't it make your mouth water, that vine? My husband makes out that I'm not fond of fruit, because I eat less of them than he does. But not a bit of it, I'm greedier than any of you, but I have no need to fill my mouth with them when I can feed on them with my eyes. What are you all laughing at now, pray? Ask the doctor, he'll tell you that those grapes act on me like a regular purge. Some people go to Fontainebleau for cures; I take my own little Beauvais cure here. But, M. Swann, you mustn't run away without feeling the little bronze mouldings on the backs. Isn't it an exquisite patina? No, no, you must feel them properly, with your whole hand!"

If Mme Verdurin is going to start fingering her bronzes," said the painter, "we shan't get any music tonight."

"Be quiet, you wretch! And yet we poor women," she went on, turning towards Swann, "are forbidden pleasures far less voluptuous than this. There is no flesh in the world to compare with it. None. When M. Verdurin did me the honour of being madly jealous . . . Come, you might at least be polite – don't say that you've never been jealous!"

"But, my dear, I've said absolutely nothing. Look here, Doctor, I call you as a witness. Did I utter a word?"

Swann had begun, out of politeness, to finger the bronzes, and did not like to stop.

"Come along; you can caress them later. Now it's you who are going to be caressed, caressed aurally. You'll like that, I think. Here's the young gentleman who will take charge of that."

After the pianist had played, Swann was even more affable towards him than towards any of the other guests, for the following reason:

The year before, at an evening party, he had heard a piece of music played on the piano and violin. At first he had appreciated only the material quality of the sounds which those instruments secreted. And it had been a source of keen pleasure when, below the delicate line of the violin-part, slender but robust, compact and commanding, he had suddenly become aware of the mass of the piano-part beginning to emerge in a sort of liquid rippling of sound, multiform but indivisible, smooth yet restless, like the deep blue tumult of the sea, silvered and charmed into a minor key by the moon-light. But then at a certain moment, without being able to distinguish any clear outline, or to give a name to what was pleasing him, suddenly enraptured, he had tried to grasp the phrase or harmony – he did not know which – that had just been played and that had opened and expanded his soul, as the fragrance of certain roses, wafted upon the moist air of evening, has the power of dilating one's nostrils. Perhaps it was owing to his ignorance of music that he had received so confused an impression, one of those that are none the less the only purely musical impressions, limited in their extent, entirely original, and irreducible to any other kind. An impression of this order, vanishing in an instant, is, so to speak, *sine materia.* Doubtless the notes which we hear at such moments tend, according to their pitch and volume, to spread out before our eyes over surfaces of varying dimensions, to trace arabesques, to give us the sensation of breadth or tenuity, stability or caprice. But the notes them-selves have vanished before these sensations have developed sufficiently to escape submersion under those which the succeeding or even simultane-ous notes have already begun to awaken in us. And this impression would continue to envelop in its liquidity, its ceaseless overlapping, the motifs which from time to time emerge, barely discernible, to plunge again and disappear and drown, recognised only by the particular kind of pleasure which they instil, impossible to describe, to recollect, to name, ineffable – did not our memory, like a labourer who toils at the laying down of firm foundations beneath the tumult of the waves, by fashioning for us facsimi-les of those fugitive phrases, enable us to compare and to contrast them with those that follow. And so, scarcely had the exquisite sensation which Swann had experienced died away, before his memory had furnished him with an immediate transcript, sketchy, it is true, and provisional, which he had been able to glance at while the piece continued, so that, when the same impression suddenly returned, it was no longer impossible to grasp. He could picture to himself its extent, its symmetrical arrangement, its notation, its expressive value; he had before him something that was no longer pure music, but rather design, architecture, thought, and which allowed the actual music to be recalled. This time he had distinguished quite clearly a phrase which emerged for a few moments above the waves of sound. It had at once suggested to him a world of inexpressible delights, of whose existence, before hearing it, he had never dreamed, into which he felt that nothing else could initiate him; and he had been filled with love for it, as with a new and strange desire.

With a slow and rhythmical movement it led him first this way, then that, towards a state of happiness that was noble, unintelligible, and yet precise. And then suddenly, having reached a certain point from which he was preparing to follow it, after a momentary pause, abruptly it changed direction, and in a fresh movement, more rapid, fragile, melancholy, inces-sant, sweet, it bore him off with it towards new vistas. Then it vanished.

He hoped, with a passionate longing, that he might find it again, a third time. And reappear it did, though without speaking to him more clearly, bringing him, indeed, a pleasure less profound. But when he returned home he felt the need of it: he was like a man into whose life a woman he has seen for a moment passing by has brought the image of a new beauty which deepens his own sensibility, although he does not even know her name or whether he will ever see her again.

Indeed this passion for a phrase of music seemed, for a time, to open up before Swann the possibility of a sort of rejuvenation. He had so long ceased to direct his life towards any ideal goal, confining himself to the pursuit of ephemeral satisfactions, that he had come to believe, without ever admitting it to himself in so many words, that he would remain in that condition for the rest of his days. More than this, since his mind no longer entertained any lofty ideas, he had ceased to believe in (although he could not have expressly denied) their reality. Thus he had grown into the habit of taking refuge in trivial considerations, which enabled him to disregard matters of fundamental importance. Just as he never stopped to ask himself whether he would not have done better by not going into society, but on the other hand knew for certain that if he had accepted an invitation he must put in an appearance, and that afterwards, if he did not actually call, he must at least leave cards upon his hostess, so in his conversation he took care never to express with any warmth a personal opinion about anything, but instead would supply facts and details which were valid enough in themselves and excused him from showing his real capacities. He would be extremely precise about the recipe for a dish, the dates of a painter's birth and death, and the titles of his works. Sometimes, in spite of himself, he would let himself go so far as to express an opinion on a work of art, or on someone's interpretation of life, but then he would cloak his words in a tone of irony, as though he did not altogether associate himself with what he was saying. But now, like a confirmed invalid in whom, all of a sudden, a change of air and surroundings, or a new course of treatment, or sometimes an organic change in himself, spontaneous and unaccountable, seems to have brought about such an improvement in his health that he begins to envisage the possibility, hitherto beyond all hope, of starting to lead belatedly a wholly different life, Swann found in himself, in the memory of the phrase that he had heard, in certain other sonatas which he had made people play to him to see whether he might not perhaps discover his phrase therein, the presence of one of those invisible realities in which he had ceased to believe and to which, as though the music had had upon the moral barrenness from which he was suffering a sort of re-creative influence, he was conscious once again of the desire and almost the strength to consecrate his life. But, never having managed to find out whose work it was that he had heard played that evening, he had been unable to procure a copy and had finally forgotten the quest. He had indeed, in the course of that week, encountered several of the people who had been at the party with him, and had questioned them; but most of them had either arrived after or left before the piece was played; some had indeed been there at the time but had gone into another room to talk, and those who had stayed to listen had no clearer impression than the rest. As for his hosts, they knew that it was a recent work which the musicians whom they had engaged for the evening had asked to be allowed to play; but, as these last had gone away on tour, Swann could learn nothing further. He had, of course, a number of musical friends, but, vividly as he could recall the exquisite and inexpressible pleasure which the little phrase had given him, and could see in his mind's eye the forms that it had traced, he was quite incapable of humming it to them. And so, at last, he ceased to think of it.

But that night, at Mme Verdurin's, scarcely had the young pianist begun to play than suddenly, after a high note sustained through two whole bars, Swann sensed its approach, stealing forth from beneath that long-drawn sonority, stretched like a curtain of sound to veil the mystery of its incubation, and recognised, secret, murmuring, detached, the airy and perfumed phrase that he had loved. And it was so peculiarly itself, it had so individual, so irreplaceable a charm, that Swann felt as though he had met, in a friend's drawing-room, a woman whom he had seen and admired in the street and had despaired of ever seeing again. Finally the phrase receded, diligently guiding its successors through the ramifications of its fragrance, leaving on Swann's features the reflection of its smile. But now, at last, he could ask the name of his fair unknown (and was told that it was the andante of Vinteuil's sonata for piano and violin); he held it safe, could have it again to himself, at home, as often as he wished, could study its language and acquire its secret.

And so, when the pianist had finished, Swann crossed the room and thanked him with a vivacity which delighted Mme Verdurin.

"Isn't he a charmer?" she asked Swann, "doesn't he just understand his sonata, the little wretch? You never dreamed, did you, that a piano could be made to express all that? Upon my word, you'd think it was everything but the piano! I'm caught out every time I hear it; I think I'm listening to an orchestra. Though it's better, really, than an orchestra, more complete."

The young pianist bowed as he answered, smiling and underlining each of his words as though he were making an epigram: "You are most generous to me."

And while Mme Verdurin was saying to her husband, "Run and fetch him a glass of orangeade; he's earned it," Swann began to tell Odette how he had fallen in love with that little phrase. When their hostess, who was some way off, called out, "Well! It looks to me as though someone was saying nice things to you, Odette!" she replied, "Yes, very nice," and he found her simplicity delightful. Then he asked for information about this Vinteuil: what else he had done, at what period in his life he had composed the sonata, and what meaning the little phrase could have had for him – that was what Swann wanted most to know.

But none of these people who professed to admire this musician (when Swann had said that the sonata was really beautiful Mme Verdurin had exclaimed, "Of course it's beautiful! But you don't dare to confess that you don't know Vinteuil's sonata; you have no right not to know it!" – and the painter had added, "Ah, yes, it's a very fine bit of work, isn't it? Not, of course, if you want something 'obvious,' something 'popular,' but, I mean to say, it makes a very great impression on us artists"), none of them seemed ever to have asked himself these questions, for none of them was able to answer them.

Even to one or two particular remarks made by Swann about his favourite phrase: "D'you know, that's a funny thing; I had never noticed it. I may as well tell you that I don't much care about peering at things through a microscope, and pricking myself on pin-points of difference. No, we don't waste time splitting hairs in this house," Mme Verdurin replied, while Dr Cottard gazed at her with open-mouthed admiration and studious zeal as she skipped lightly from one stepping-stone to another of her stock of ready-made phrases. Both he, however, and Mme Cottard, with a kind of common sense which is shared by many people of humble origin, were careful not to express an opinion, or to pretend to admire a piece of music which they confessed to each other, once they were back at home, that they no more understood than they could understand the art of "Master" Biche. Inasmuch as the public cannot recognise the charm, the beauty, even the out-lines of nature save in the stereotyped impressions of an art which they have gradually assimilated, while an original artist starts by rejecting those stereotypes, so M. and Mme Cottard, typical, in this respect, of the public, were incapable of finding, either in Vinteuil's sonata or in Biche's portraits, what constituted for them harmony in music or beauty in painting. It appeared to them, when the pianist played his sonata, as though he were striking at random from the piano a medley of notes which bore no relation to the musical forms to which they themselves were accustomed, and that the painter simply flung the colours at random on his canvases. When, in one of these, they were able to distinguish a human form, they always found it coarsened and vulgarised (that is to say lacking in the elegance of the school of painting through whose spectacles they were in the habit of seeing even the real, living people who passed them in the street) and devoid of truth, as though M. Biche had not known how the human shoulder was constructed, or that a woman's hair was not ordinarily purple.

However, when the "faithful" were scattered out of earshot, the doctor felt that the opportunity was too good to be missed, and so (while Mme Verdurin was adding a final word of commendation of Vinteuil's sonata), like a would-be swimmer who jumps into the water so as to learn, but chooses a moment when there are not too many people looking on: "Yes, indeed; he's what they call a musician *di primo cartello*!" he exclaimed with sudden determination.

Swann discovered no more than that the recent appearance of Vinteuil's sonata had caused a great stir among the most advanced school of musicians, but that it was still unknown to the general public.

"I know someone called Vinteuil," said Swann, thinking of the old piano-teacher at Combray who had taught my grandmother's sisters.

"Perhaps he's the man," cried Mme Verdurin.

"Oh, no, if you'd ever set eyes on him you wouldn't entertain the idea."

"Then to entertain the idea is to settle it?" the doctor suggested.

"But it may well be some relation," Swann went on. "That would be bad enough; but, after all, there's no reason why a genius shouldn't have a cousin who's a silly old fool. And if that should be so, I swear there's no known or unknown form of torture I wouldn't undergo to get the old fool to introduce me to the man who composed the sonata; starting with the torture of the old fool's company, which would be ghastly."

The painter understood that Vinteuil was seriously ill at the moment, and that Dr Potain despaired of his life.

"What!" cried Mme Verdurin, "Do people still call in Potain?"

"Ah! Mme Verdurin," Cottard simpered, "you forget that you are speaking of one of my colleagues – I should say one of my masters."

The painter had heard it said that Vinteuil was threatened with the loss of his reason. And he insisted that signs of this could be detected in certain passages in the sonata. This remark did not strike Swann as ridiculous; but it disturbed him, for, since a work of pure music contains none of the logical sequences whose deformation, in spoken or written language, is a proof of insanity, so insanity diagnosed in a sonata seemed to him as mysterious a thing as the insanity of a dog or a horse, although instances may be observed of these.

"Don't speak to me about your masters; you know ten times as much as he does!" Mme Verdurin answered Dr Cottard, in the tone of a woman who has the courage of her convictions and is quite ready to stand up to anyone who disagrees with her. "At least you don't kill your patients!"

"But, Madame, he is in the Academy," replied the doctor with heavy irony. "If a patient prefers to die at the hands of one of the princes of science . . . It's much smarter to be able to say, 'Yes, I have Potain.' "

"Oh, indeed! Smarter, is it?" said Mme Verdurin. "So there are fashions, nowadays, in illness, are there? I didn't know that . . . Oh, you do make me laugh!" she screamed suddenly, burying her face in her hands. "And here was I, poor thing, talking quite seriously and never realising that you were pulling my leg."

As for M. Verdurin, finding it rather a strain to raise a laugh for so little, he was content with puffing out a cloud of smoke from his pipe, reflecting sadly that he could no longer catch up with his wife in the field of amiability.

"D'you know, we like your friend very much," said Mme Verdurin when Odette was bidding her good night. "He's so unaffected, quite charming. If they're all like that, the friends you want to introduce to us, by all means bring them."

M. Verdurin remarked that Swann had failed, all the same, to appreciate the pianist's aunt.

"I dare say he felt a little out of his depth, poor man," suggested Mme Verdurin. "You can't expect him to have caught the tone of the house already, like Cottard, who has been one of our little clan now for years. The first time doesn't count; it's just for breaking the ice. Odette, it's agreed that he's to join us tomorrow at the Châtelet. Perhaps you might call for him?"

"No, he doesn't want that."

"Oh, very well; just as you like. Provided he doesn't fail us at the last moment."

[. . .]

Swann told himself that if he could make Odette feel (by consenting to meet her only after dinner) that there were other pleasures which he preferred to that of her company, then the desire that she felt for his would be all the longer in reaching the point of satiety. Besides, as he infinitely preferred to Odette's style of beauty that of a young seamstress, as fresh and plump as a rose, with whom he was smitten, he preferred to spend the first part of the evening with her, knowing that he was sure to see Odette later on. It was for the same reason that he never allowed Odette to call for him at his house, to take him on to the Verdurins'. The little seamstress would wait for him at a street corner which Rémi, his coachman, knew; she would jump in beside him, and remain in his arms until the carriage drew up at the Verdurins'. He would enter the drawing-room; and there, while Mme Verdurin, pointing to the roses which he had sent her that morning, said: "I'm furious with you," and sent him to the place kept for him beside Odette, the pianist would play to them – for their two selves – the little phrase by Vinteuil which was, so to speak, the national anthem of their love. He would begin with the sustained tremolos of the violin part which for several bars were heard alone, filling the whole foreground; until suddenly they seemed to draw aside, and – as in those interiors by Pieter de Hooch which are deepened by the narrow frame of a half-opened door, in the far distance, of a different colour, velvety with the radiance of some intervening light – the little phrase appeared, dancing, pastoral, interpolated, episodic, belonging to another world. It rippled past, simple and immortal, scattering on every side the bounties of its grace, with the same ineffable smile; but Swann thought that he could now discern in it some disenchantment. It seemed to be aware how vain, how hollow was the happiness to which it showed the way. In its airy grace there was the sense of something over and done with, like the mood of philosophic detachment which follows an outburst of vain regret. But all this mattered little to him; he contemplated the little phrase less in its own light – in what it might express to a musician who knew nothing of the existence of him and Odette when he had composed it, and to all those who would hear it in centuries to come – than as a pledge, a token of his love, which made even the Verdurins and their young pianist think of Odette at the same time as himself – which bound her to him by a lasting tie; so much so that (whimsically entreated by Odette) he had abandoned the idea of getting some professional to play over to him the whole sonata, of which he still knew no more than this one passage. "Why do you want the rest?" she had asked him. "Our little bit; that's all we need." Indeed, agonised by the reflection, as it floated by, so near and yet so infinitely remote, that while it was addressed to them it did not know them, he almost regretted that it had a meaning of its own, an intrinsic and unalterable beauty, extraneous to themselves, just as in the jewels given to us, or even in the letters written to us by a woman we love, we find fault with the water of the stone, or with the words of the message, because they are not fashioned exclusively from the essence of a transient liaison and a particular person.

Often it would happen that he had stayed so long with the young seamstress before going to the Verdurins' that, as soon as the little phrase had been rendered by the pianist, Swann realised that it was almost time for Odette to go home. He used to take her back as far as the door of her little house in the Rue La Pérouse, behind the Arc de Triomphe. And it was perhaps on this account, and so as not to demand the monopoly of her favours, that he sacrificed the pleasure (not so essential to his well-being) of seeing her earlier in the evening, of arriving with her at the Verdurins', to the exercise of this other privilege which she accorded him of their leaving together, a privilege he valued all the more because it gave him the feeling that no one else would see her, no one would thrust himself between them, no one could prevent him from remaining with her in spirit, after he had left her for the night.

Index

Note: figures in *italics* refer to illustrations